Early Childhood Education and Care:
Policy and practice

Early Childhood Education and Care:
Policy and practice

Edited by
Margaret M Clark
Tim Waller

SAGE Publications
Los Angeles • London • New Delhi • Singapore

SAGE Publications Ltd
1 Oliver's Yard
55 City Road
London EC1Y 1SP

SAGE Publications Inc.
2455 Teller Road
Thousand Oaks, California 91320

SAGE Publications India Pvt Ltd
B 1/I 1 Mohan Cooperative Industrial Area
Mathura Road, New Delhi 110 044
India

SAGE Publications Asia-Pacific Pte Ltd
33 Pekin Street #02-01
Far East Square
Singapore 048763

British Library Cataloguing in Publication data

A catalogue record for this book is available
from the British Library

ISBN 978-1-4129-3571-5
ISBN 978-1-4129-3572-2 (pbk)

Library of Congress Control Number: 2006939577

Typeset by C&M Digitals (P) Ltd., Chennai, India
Printed in Great Britain by Athenaeum Press Ltd, Gateshead
Printed on paper from sustainable resources

CONTENTS

LIST OF FIGURES AND TABLES

FIGURES

TABLES

ACKNOWLEDGEMENTS

We are grateful to the authors of Chapters 2–6 who have so enthusiastically co-operated in the writing of this book. Their chapters have been drafted and re-drafted with good grace to meet our guidelines. This has enabled us, while retaining some originality in the presentation, to give uniformity of layout for the benefit of our student readers.

Thanks to Colette Murray, Early Years Co-ordinator, Pavey Point for preparing Owney's story and Karen Argent of Manchester Metropolitan University, who worked on a Trailblazer local SureStart Programme in Birmingham, for preparing Suraya's story.

The ten case studies, though not based on specific children, are written to represent possible experiences that real children born in 2000 might have encountered during their first six years of life. We are grateful to B. Cohen, P. Moss, P. Petrie and J. Wallace, the authors of *A New Deal for Children? Re-forming education and care in England, Scotland and Sweden* (2004, Policy Press), whose book stimulated us to bring the chapters alive with case studies.

Thanks to Early Years colleagues at Newman College of Higher Education, Birmingham, for commenting on draft chapters taking the perspective of potential student readers – in particular Julie Boardman, Helen Davies and Allison Tatton.

It has been a pleasure to work with Helen Fairlie, our Commissioning Editor at Sage, who has been helpful and supportive throughout.

Margaret M Clark and Tim Waller, 2007

ABOUT THE AUTHORS

Margaret M Clark has both a PhD and a DLitt, the latter for published work, and is a Fellow of both the British Psychological Society and the Scottish Council for Research in Education. Currently she is Visiting Professor at Newman College of Higher Education, Birmingham and Emeritus Professor of Education, University of Birmingham. She has an international reputation for research in early education and literacy, and has been awarded on OBE in the 2007 New Year's Honours for services to Early Years education. Her publications include *Children Under Five: Educational research and evidence* (1988, Gordon and Breach), *Education in Scotland: Policy and practice from pre-school to secondary*, edited with Pamela Munn (1997, Routledge) and *Understanding Research in Early Education: The relevance for the future of lessons from the past* (2005, Routledge). She is also Book Reviews Editor for the *Journal of Early Childhood Research*.

Tim Waller is Director of Taught Programmes in the Department of Childhood Studies at Swansea University. He was formerly Early Years Research Group Leader at the University of Northampton. Previously he taught in nursery, infant and primary schools in London and has also taught in the USA. His research interests include ICT and social justice, outdoor learning and equality. He has been investigating the use of computers by young children and he completed his doctoral thesis on scaffolding young children's learning and ICT. Over the past three years he has been co-ordinating a research project designed to investigate the promotion of children's well being and learning through outdoor play. Tim has recently edited a book entitled *An Introduction to Early Childhood: A multi-disciplinary approach* (2005, Sage).

CONTRIBUTORS

Eileen Carmichael is Development Officer, Early Years with Learning and Teaching Scotland where she is responsible for the development of Early Years Online, www.ltscotland.org.uk/earlyyears and for the *Early Years' Matters* newsletter among other LTS Early Years initiatives. Eileen has taught in primary, further and higher education and was a nursery school headteacher for twenty five years. She has been seconded to a number of staff support posts, including as National Development Officer in Scotland at the time of the pre-school education initiative and the development of *A Curriculum Framework for Children 3–5*.

Philomena Donnelly PhD taught for many years in primary schools before taking up her present position as Lecturer in Early Childhood Education in St Patrick's College, Dublin City University. She was one of the principal research directors for an EU-funded research project on *Diversity in Early Years Education North and South: Implications for teacher education*. She is presently researching the experience of recent immigrant families starting school in Ireland. She has published articles in a number of educational journals and chapters in books. Her PhD thesis is on an ancient proto-philosophy and young children's philosophical thinking.

Juliet Hancock has a BA Honours degree and a postgraduate certificate in education, specialising in working with children from three to eight years of age. She has taught at nursery, primary, secondary and further education level and has worked in the statutory and voluntary sectors within Scotland, holding several posts at national level. Juliet until recently worked for Learning and Teaching Scotland as Early Years Development Officer for *Emerging Trends*, responsible as chief author for taking forward Scotland's recently published national guidance on children from birth to three years old, as well as an occasional paper (published in May 2005) on pedagogy. Juliet is President of the Scottish Childminding Association and external examiner for the BA in Early Childhood at Moray House, University of Edinburgh. In January 2006 Juliet took up a post with Stirling Council as Children's Services Early Childhood Link Officer.

Gill McGillivray is Senior Lecturer in Early Years Studies at Newman College of Higher Education in Birmingham. She has a BSc (Hons) in Human Psychology and an MA in Early Childhood Studies from the University of Sheffield. Gill's previous posts have included teaching in Birmingham and working in further education within Early Years care and education and Psychology. Her current research interests are the assessment of children in Early Years care and education, workforce reform and professional identity within the Early Years workforce. She has led a small-scale research project at Newman College into the Early Years Foundation Degree, of which she was course co-ordinator.

Sally Thomas has an MA in Early Years Education for which she undertook research on The Foundation Phase: perceptions, attitudes and expectations. She is currently Senior Lecturer in Early Years Education in the Faculty of Education and Training, Trinity College, Carmarthen. Sally has extensive experience as a nursery teacher in ILEA, as an advisory teacher with responsibility for multicultural education and Early Years education, and as a nursery teacher with responsibility for home school liaison. She is a member of the Early Years and Childcare Advisory Group, Children in Wales.

Siân Wyn Siencyn is Head of the School of Early Years Education at Trinity College, Carmarthen which she established in 2000. She has a BA in English and an MA in Education and Language from the University of Wales, Aberystwyth. She has worked in and with both the voluntary and statutory sectors in Wales. Her research interest has been, for over thirty years, Welsh as a second language in Early Years settings, the area of her doctoral studies. She is now heading a national project in this field for the Welsh Assembly. She has also been a member of the Minister of Education's Early Years advisory group in Wales.

Glenda Walsh BEd (hons), PhD, ALCM, Member HEA, is a Principal Lecturer in Early Childhood Education at Stranmillis University College, Belfast where she teaches on a range of Early Years programmes. She is course director of the Post Graduate Certificate in Early Years and Psychology and co-ordinator of the MEd in Early Years Education. Her research interests fall particularly into the field of quality issues and the Early Years curriculum. She is currently involved in the longitudinal evaluation of the Early Years enriched curriculum project with the School of Psychology at Queen's University, Belfast, an evaluation that is guiding the course of the Foundation Stage of the revised Northern Ireland curriculum. She has also led a project on activating thinking skills through play in the early years. Her doctoral thesis concentrated on the play versus formal education debate in Northern Ireland and Denmark. The observation instrument she devised is now being used as the main assessment instrument in the Early Years enriched curriculum evaluation project.

GUIDELINES FOR PRACTICAL WORK
BASED ON THE CASE STUDIES

You may make photocopies of these guidelines and the case studies.

Chapters 2–6, on England, Northern Ireland, the Republic of Ireland, Scotland and Wales, will give you an opportunity to compare and contrast policy and practice in early childhood education and care across the United Kingdom and in the Republic of Ireland. Each chapter is introduced and brought alive by the stories of two children born in 2000 and living in that country for the first six years of their lives. In the final section of each chapter a further child is introduced, born in 2006, whose early experience might be influenced by the developing policies described elsewhere in the chapter.

The ten case studies are a valuable resource from which to consider the factors that influence the early experiences of young children in the twenty-first century. The case studies, though not based on specific children, are included to represent possible experiences that real children born in 2000 might have encountered during their first six years of life. We are grateful to B. Cohen, P. Moss, P. Petrie and J. Wallace, the authors of *A New Deal for Children? Re-forming education and care in England, Scotland and Sweden* (2004, Policy Press), whose book stimulated us to bring the chapters alive with case studies.

> In order to undertake the practical work it is important that you have your own copy of the children's stories. For that reason you are given permission to make photocopies of the case studies.

The experiences encountered by these young children would be influenced by family circumstances, by services from which the family could benefit, depending on where they lived, and the curricular guidelines under which the pre-school and early primary school curriculum operated.

Make a summary of the family background and early experiences of each child in such a way that you can compare them. Alternatively, each student in a class might like to choose two children and prepare their summaries as a basis for discussion. Below are some suggestions of key features to include:

Family background

- Name and month of birth of target child
- Number, sex and age of siblings relative to the target child
- Details of parent(s) and their social and educational background
- Mother's and father's employment during first six years and whether full- or part-time
- Language(s) spoken in the home and in the community
- Place(s) of residence (whether urban or rural)
- Any grandparents or other extended family locally
- Changes of residence during first six years
- Any traumatic events during first six years
    Became one instead of two parent family
    Illness of close relative (or death).

Experiences of the child during the first six years

(note the age of the child when in each placement and duration of placement)

- Cared for by one or other parent at home
- With extended family, regularly or occasionally
- With childminder(s) occasionally or regularly
- In pre-school setting
    With mother
    Without mother
- List settings
- Other professionals involved with the family
    In the home
    Elsewhere
- List the services from which the child/family benefited.

Pre-school curricular experiences

Note the type of curriculum, and at what age the child experienced it.

Primary schooling

Please note that all the case study children were born in 2000. However, their month of birth may have influenced the exact age at which they entered primary school.

- The exact age at which the child entered primary school
- If given, the size of school and class and age range in the class
- Number of adults, for example teaching assistant in addition to teacher
- Any information on the teacher's background and training
- Curriculum experienced by the child up to six years of age
- The curriculum likely to be experienced by the child up to eight years of age (you may need to consult the relevant chapter for that information)
- In addition to attending primary school, what if any other care/provision did the child attend (for example, out of school care, a childminder, grandparents)?

Transitions

Finally, make a list of all the types of provision the child had attended by the age of six. Also note in how many instances, and at what ages, the child was attending more than one provision concurrently.

Note that although some of the children did move from one part of the country to another, none of them moved to a different part of the United Kingdom, or to or from the Republic of Ireland in their first six years. These are further moves that might be experienced by young children and their families. As you will appreciate after studying the following chapters this will mean even more adjustments for the families. How different might the early experiences of these children have been had they moved to one of the other countries, or elsewhere in Europe, and how might that have influenced their early education and care?

These guidelines should also enable you to prepare your own case studies of children with whom you work, or those of family and friends.

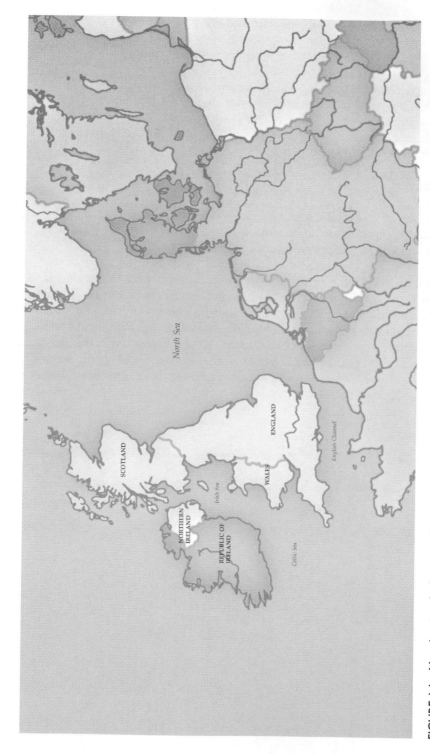

FIGURE 1.1 Map showing the location of the countries making up the United Kingdom and the Republic of Ireland

INTRODUCTION

Margaret M Clark and Tim Waller

We hope this book will help you to understand the similarities and differences between the developments in early childhood education and care across the United Kingdom (England, Northern Ireland, Scotland and Wales) and the Republic of Ireland. As far as we are aware there is no current publication that distinguishes the developments across these five countries. Indeed many publications are misleading in that they refer to the United Kingdom, then discuss only developments specific to England.

The impetus for this book was our awareness that:

- Many of those involved in framing government policy, and its implementation, may not consider the broader picture.
- Not all students are made aware of just how different developments are in those parts of the UK other than where they are studying or working.

Bearing these points in mind, this book is planned to meet the needs of a wide readership in the UK and overseas.

THE AIMS OF THE BOOK

The following are important features of this book:

- It is planned as a textbook for students of Early Childhood and Early Years education and care (interpreting the term 'student' widely).
- It should be of interest to practitioners working with children in the age range birth to eight years of age.
- It should help readers to appreciate the differences in policy and practice across the United Kingdom and the Republic of Ireland.
- The reality for young children and their families of current provision is brought alive by case studies of children born in 2000.

- Developments in early education and care across the United Kingdom and the Republic of Ireland are compared with those in other countries.
- Key issues and discussion points are highlighted throughout the book.

THE UNITED KINGDOM AND THE REPUBLIC OF IRELAND

You will see from the map of the United Kingdom and the Republic of Ireland (Figure 1.1) that the British Isles – as, a geographical and not a political area – lies off the west coast of the mainland of Europe. The United Kingdom consists of England, Northern Ireland, Scotland and Wales. Northern Ireland covers about 20 per cent of the north east of the island of Ireland: the remaining 80 per cent forms the Republic of Ireland, an independent democracy. The terminology used to describe the area that might geographically be referred to as the British Isles is confusing; this you will discover if you try to access any statistics on the web! Furthermore both the terminology and the relative autonomy of the various parts have changed over time. The problem is also exacerbated by a tendency for publications, even statistical analyses, to use the terms 'United Kingdom' or 'Britain' for information that does not apply to the whole of the UK.

The majority of the UK's population lives in England, with only about 16 per cent in the remaining three countries (see Table 1.1). However, if you look at the map you will see that the areas covered by the remaining three countries are extensive; in Scotland and Wales in particular there are many rural communities, and Scotland also encompasses island communities. The population of the Republic of Ireland in 2006 was about 4.2 million, an increase of 318,000 since the previous census in 2002.

The most comprehensive source of background information on the many aspects of life relevant to education and care – including population trends and distribution, family make-up and minority ethnic groups – is the census that takes place every ten years in the United Kingdom, with the most recent in 2001. However the data for England and Wales, Scotland and Northern Ireland are reported separately, with some questions differing and the results also processed separately (see www.statistics.gov.uk).

TABLE 1.1 The United Kingdom population in 2004

Country	Population	Percentage of UK population
England	50,093,100	83.7%
Scotland	5,078,400	8.5%
Wales	2,953,500	4.9%
Northern Ireland	1,710,300	2.9%

The above information for the United Kingdom is taken from mid-2004 (see www.statistics.gov.uk).

Over the intervening years further analyses have taken place using the census data, some with important implications for the education and care of young children. These can be accessed on the web in a user-friendly format which is helpful for school projects and for researchers. In two articles (Clark, 2003; 2004) the implications of the 2001 census for education in Scotland, England and Wales are discussed. The information for these articles was taken from the analyses as these were appearing on the web. As the census takes place every ten years it is possible to study whether the population is growing; if it is an ageing population; the ethnic distribution; the urban/rural distribution; whether there is a drift away from the cities – all relevant to expenditure on education and care.

It should be remembered that major changes may take place over the ten-year period, and concern has been expressed at possible unreliability in recent census returns. It is necessary to consult different sources for statistical information on the Republic of Ireland as the census there is taken on a different date; the last census in the Republic of Ireland was in 2006, and so by 2007 detailed analyses should begin to appear (see www.cso.ie).

There has been a number of changes in population since the census of 2001 as a consequence of inward migration (particularly in England). By the time of the last census in 2001 the population of the UK had risen to 59 million. It is predicted that the population of the United Kingdom will further rise by 7 million by 2031, with different trends in the four countries and the majority of the rise in England.

The case studies will help you to appreciate how the provision for young children and their families varied between countries, and differed when some moved from one part of a country to another.

Imagine you are the parent of young children. How might you find out what provision is available in your area, and how suitable it might be for your family's needs? One source of such information would be the web. It is worth attempting this task as it is a problem faced by many parents.

What aspects of population trends are important for those planning early education and care for young children? For example, why are the following important in ensuring that provision meets need – the predicted age distribution, the urban/rural pattern, minority ethnic population trends and their distribution across the countries?

A BRIEF OUTLINE OF DEVELOPMENTS TOWARDS DEVOLUTION IN THE UNITED KINGDOM AND THE REPUBLIC OF IRELAND

1922   the setting up of the Irish Free State meant that Ireland, apart from Northern Ireland, was no longer ruled by Britain.

1937 the written constitution of Ireland was adopted that defines Ireland as a sovereign, independent and democratic state.

1948 the Irish Republic was declared with its parliament based in Dublin. As you will see from the map (Figure 1.1) this applies only to part of the island of Ireland (see Chapter 4 for further details).

The United Kingdom refers to England, Northern Ireland, Scotland and Wales. However, powers over a number of aspects of life including education and care have progressively been developed as follows:

1998 the Northern Ireland Assembly was set up to govern Northern Ireland, based in Belfast. During the intervening years direct rule was reintroduced (see Chapter 3).

1999 the Scottish Executive was established, answerable to a re-established Scottish parliament based in Edinburgh (see Chapter 5).

1999 the National Assembly was created in Wales, based in Cardiff and with executive powers including those for education. Further developments are currently under way (see Chapter 6).

It should be noted that the Channel Islands (between the south coast of England and France) with a population of about 150,000 consists of two separate dependencies, Jersey and Guernsey. The Isle of Man (in the Irish Sea and almost equidistant from England, Ireland, Scotland and Wales) with a population of about 76,000 is a UK dependency. Early education and care in these communities are not covered in this publication.

With devolved government developing in the United Kingdom, and Northern Ireland, Scotland and Wales gaining greater power over their own destinies, the policies for early education and care for children from birth to eight years of age are likely to diverge further. The differences and continuing similarities in policy and practice should become clearer to you after reading the following chapters.

In Chapter 7 we will help you to relate developments in the five countries to each other and to developments elsewhere.

OECD REPORTS ON DEVELOPMENTS IN EARLY CHILDHOOD EDUCATION AND CARE

In 1996 the Organisation for Economic Co-operation and Development (OECD) initiated a review of early childhood education and care. This review over the period 1998–2004 involved 20 countries, with expert teams evaluating each country's policy for children from birth to compulsory school age. The report covering the first 12 countries was published as *Starting Strong* (OECD, 2001). The second report, *Starting Strong II*, was published in 2006 and covers all 20 countries, also assessing progress in the original 12 countries. The countries involved provide a diverse range of social, economic and political contexts and also approaches to policy. The reports for each of the participating countries are to be found in the appendices to *Starting Strong* (OECD, 2001) and *Starting Strong II* (OECD, 2006). There are 'Background Reports' for each country, which precede and inform the 'Country Notes'. There are also brief résumés for each country under the following headings:

- developments
- country context
- provision
- staffing and training
- policy issues.

You can access the summary and the detailed reports on the OECD website (see www.oecd.org/edu/earlychildhood). This is a useful source for you to compare developments in these 20 countries.

Among the original 12 countries were the Republic of Ireland (referred to as Ireland in the publications) and, as it appears on the list, the United Kingdom. When you look more closely you will find that much of the information given is either specific to England, or it is difficult to determine whether or not it applies to all four countries of the UK. The detailed *Background Note* Bertram and Pascal, (2000), for example, is misleading as its title is 'Early Childhood Education and Care Policy in the United Kingdom'. While in places it is possible for someone knowledgeable about differences in the constituent parts of the UK to appreciate what does and does not apply as a whole, this would not be clear to the general reader. Furthermore, the reference list cites no official sources other than those that apply to England. In the brief 'Country Notes' in the appendix to *Starting Strong* (OECD, 2001) the heading is 'United Kingdom (England)' and in *Starting Strong II* (OECD, 2006) the heading reads 'United Kingdom', but underneath in brackets states 'most of the following profile applies to England only'.

These recent publications reinforced our conviction that a book such as the present one is timely in which the differences between policy and practice in the various countries that make up the United Kingdom are clearly identified. This is not possible from either of the two OECD reports mentioned above. *Starting Strong* (2001) could have left readers assuming there is a general policy for early education and care in the UK, or that only minor differences existed. In their introduction to the *Background Report for the United Kingdom*, Bertram and Pascal report that:

> The component elements of the United Kingdom – England, Northern Ireland, Wales and Scotland – are each developing slightly different systems of ECEC, a process that will gain greater impetus from the recent measures devolving greater political autonomy. In this document, the authors have focused primarily on the English system and have attempted to show where and how there are differences in the other countries and province which make up the UK, including evidence on Scotland, Wales and Northern Ireland where appropriate. (Bertram and Pascal, 2000: 6 – also available on the OECD website under the authors' names)

Readers of that report could be forgiven for believing that the differences were minor and that the government institutions controlling the developments were the same. This is not so, and indeed as far as Scotland is concerned the Secretary of State for Education, the DfES and Ofsted have never had powers in that country; there have been no 'Key Stages', nor has *the* National Curriculum ever applied there. Different education acts existed even before a Scottish parliament was re-established in 1999 (see Chapter 5).

Elsewhere, while policy for education in Wales may have mirrored that of England's in many respects until the Government of Wales Act in 1999 and the establishment of the Welsh Assembly, since then policies still current in England have increasingly been rejected (see Chapter 6). The situation in Northern Ireland has been complex over the many years of what has been referred to as 'The Troubles', with tragic effects on the lives not only of adults but also of children and their families. In recent years policy differences in Northern Ireland have also been on the increase since the Belfast Agreement of 1998, although as we write the Northern Ireland Assembly is currently suspended (see Chapter 3).

You will find information on the Republic of Ireland in both *Starting Strong* reports; in the 2006 report there is both an appraisal of developments in the Republic of Ireland, and an assessment of the extent to which recommendations made in the earlier report in 2001 have been implemented, (readers are alerted to these points in Chapter 4).

John Bennett, programme manager for the OECD's early childhood reviews, has stressed the importance of not leaving early childhood provision at the mercy of the market; that a strong infrastructure provided by government is required. In addition he identifies a need to strengthen parental leave policies and full-time home care for children in their first year. This he argues is needed to produce a life-work balance and reconcile family responsibilities with employment. He also expresses concern that the conceptual divide between education and care that still remains in many countries has negative consequences for children, inducing an over-emphasis on the cognitive development of children in education to the detriment of care and social attachment (Bennett, 2003: 44).

> Consult the OECD website (available at www.oecd.org/edu/earlychildhood) and assess the extent to which the 20 countries involved in the review differ with regard to the issues identified by Bennett (2003), namely government infrastructure versus market forces, parental leave to enable life-work balance, full-time home care for children in their first year and the emphasis on cognitive development in the curricular guidelines.

CONCEPTS OF CHILDHOOD

As in the five Nordic countries (Denmark, Finland, Iceland, Norway and Sweden), the differences between the developments in the five UK countries and the Republic of Ireland, as considered in this book, are no doubt underpinned by common assumptions about childhood not made explicit in the policy documents (see *Nordic Childhoods and Early Education*: Einarsdottir and Wagner, 2006). However, as in the Nordic countries there are real differences in some aspects of provision for education and care across the constituent parts of the UK and also the Republic of Ireland.

We should remember that what we do to and for young children is not 'natural', but to quote Spodek 'rather a cultural invention that was created over a period of time' … We value childhood, but one is not sure that we appreciate the nature of childhood itself … too often we value childhood as preparation for later life rather than as a stage of life in its own right'. Spodek, as an American writing the preface to *Nordic Childhoods and Early Education* (Einarsdottir and Wagner, 2006), stresses that any study of the policies and practices in other countries not only enables us to learn about their approaches, but also should help us to gain a greater understanding of the cultural assumptions that underpin our own practices.

Einarsdottir and Wagner in Chapter 1 of their book stress that Nordic people generally view childhood as important in its own right, not simply as a platform from which to become an adult. Furthermore they begin formal schooling later than children in many other parts of the world, so Nordic children have both the time and freedom during their early childhood years to play and explore the world around them, unencumbered by excessive supervision and control by adults.

Some of the contributors to *Nordic Childhoods and Early Education* express the fear that more formal and academic curricula are beginning to spread from other countries into the Nordic countries. The Nordic region includes five countries (Denmark, Finland, Iceland, Norway and Sweden), each with their own language, and while all are distinct in important ways (which is possibly more apparent to themselves than to outsiders), they each share deeply cherished views of childhood and children as reflected in their social welfare and educational policies. Children's right to free play has been a core value in Nordic early childhood education as has the almost universal right of access to preschool, which is not the case in some countries where targeted provision is the norm. The authors comment that a recent United Nation's report claims that the Scandinavian societies are the world's most equal, especially economically and between genders.

In the Nordic countries the following characteristics would be stressed:

- An holistic approach to caring, upbringing and learning.
- A resistance to sequential discipline-based learning, cognitive skills and school readiness.
- A disapproval of testing and assessments that rank young children.
- The primacy of play, (From an oral presentation by Thomas Moser at the EECERA 16th Conference in Reykjavik 2006).

Moser stresses the fear common amongst Early Years practitioners in the Nordic countries that the pedagogical curricula currently being introduced might change the focus from social learning and play – with children as the active creators of their culture and as actors of their own development and learning (child-based not teacher-based) – to an emphasis where school readiness, teacher-directed learning and testing become the norm.

You will find that in the Nordic countries early childhood, and the views of children themselves, have been paramount in policy decisions. Thus there is a tendency for childcare to be provided as a universal right. There has also been respect for the rights of women and for gender equality for many years: these perceptions influence the provision of childcare, and indeed mean that maternity and paternity leave have each been regarded as a right. In contrast you will also find that in the UK and the Republic of Ireland, as in some other countries, (at least so far) early education and care have tended to be 'targeted'; aimed to provide for the most disadvantaged, to eliminate poverty and enable lone parents to work or to study.

> Four of the five Nordic countries took part in both OECD reviews *Starting Strong* (2001) and *Starting Strong II* (2006) (Denmark, Finland, Norway and Sweden), so you can find further information on the recent developments in these four countries on the OECD website (www.oecd.org/edu/earlychildhood).

Further information on these issues is to be found in the comparison of developments in early education and care in England, Scotland and Sweden, based on research between 2000 and 2002. In *A New Deal for Children? Re-forming education and care in England, Scotland and Sweden* (2004) Cohen et al. report on a research project undertaken across these three countries. They consider how the national government in each has been changing the relationship between three types of children's services:

- Early childhood education and care (all the services for children below compulsory school age).
- Schools (for children of school age and beyond).
- School-age childcare.

The research reveals large differences between the position with regard to early education and care in England and Scotland and that of Sweden at the time of the study, as well as a growing divergence between developments in England and Scotland. They stress that in England and Scotland, the reform process inherited a particular economic and political context very different from that in Sweden; high levels of poverty in families with children and fast-growing employment but with specific groups lagging behind, especially women with low educational attainment and lone mothers. In England, they claim, the rhetoric may be of universality yet so far the evidence has shown targeted provision.

Sweden's high level of childcare, before and outside of school provision, dates from much earlier than in the British Isles, appearing in the 1970s to meet the needs of working parents and to promote gender equality by enabling women to enter the workforce. However, provision in Sweden should not be seen only in terms of promoting gender equality. As noted earlier, with reference to Einarsdottir and Wagner's *Nordic Childhoods and Early Education* (2006), Sweden places a high value on childhood in its own right. In that book important issues are raised about current developments within provision for children and how these may affect the childhoods lived by such children. It also stresses that we are passing through a period when childhood is being increasingly institutionalised and brought into the public sphere, and at a much earlier age. Early childhood education and care provision is increasingly being demanded and used. This may be to free parents to enter the workforce, or to begin the process of education at an earlier age.

A very different perspective from that in the Nordic countries is to be found in a recent publication by Zigler et al., *A Vision for Universal Preschool Education* (2006), where the aims of such education in the USA are set out as a summary and recommendations. The authors stress that research has demonstrated the positive effects of high-quality pre-school programmes. Benefits are listed as including:

- Improved school readiness.
- Reduced grade retention.
- Reduced need for costly remedial and special education services.
- Improved educational test scores. (Zigler et al., 2006: 262)

> The United States also took part in the OECD review (2001, 2006) so further information for comparison is available on the OECD website (www.oecd.org/edu/earlychildhood).

Concern has been expressed recently in the UK in a speech by the chairman of the Education and Skills Select Committee of the House of Commons. Barrie Sheerman claimed that 'children should not start formal schooling until the age of seven'. He suggested that young children are being robbed of their childhood and he contrasted the type of developments in England in particular with those in other European countries that afford a high standard of care for under-sevens without putting them in formal education. This issue, which has so far received scant attention in any policy documents in the UK, was reported under the headline 'Early schooling robs kids of childhood' in a weekly online publication available to subscribers to the *Education Journal* (see *Education*, 232, 4 August 2006).

> It is important that as you consider the differences in developments across the UK you give thought to some of the commonly held beliefs about childhood and the role of the state in influencing these.

Waller (2005) also gives an overview of current international literature and research that underpin the study of early childhood. Chapter 5 in *An*

Introduction to Early Childhood provides a contemporary account of the young child, identifying the following five key tenets of modern theory:

- There are multiple and diverse childhoods.
- There are multiple perspectives of childhood.
- Children are involved in co-constructing their own childhood.
- Children's participation in family, community and culture makes a particular contribution to their life.
- We are still learning about childhood. (Waller, 2005: 77)

A complex model of childhood is further articulated, which is fundamentally different from a narrow 'developmental' approach. This model acknowledges that there are multiple and diverse childhoods. There are local variations and global forms, depending on class, 'race', gender, geography and time. This model also acknowledges that whilst there are multiple perspectives of childhood, it would be wrong to ignore or disregard developmental insights. Views of childhood have changed and are still changing. Waller argues that:

> a critical difference between contemporary and traditional views of childhood is that the former recognises the differing contexts of children's lives, children's agency and the significance of children's involvement in co-constructing their own childhood through participation in family, community and culture. (Waller, 2005: 95)

> Do you view childhood as a stage in its own right, or mainly as a preparation for adulthood? What are the implications for young children and their families of the expansion of early education and care and the encouraging of mothers of young children to return to work? How important would the type of curriculum advocated be? Do you think there is truth in the statement that 'Early schooling robs kids of childhood'?

DEVELOPMENTS IN EARLY EDUCATION AND CARE

Child-rearing practices and labour patterns had led many governments by the late 1980s to invest in, or greatly expand, early childhood services. Previous policy initiatives in early education were often curtailed because of economic vicissitudes, or a feeling still held by many of those in power that a mother's place was in the home, at least while her children were young (see Chapter 4 on the Republic of Ireland). This new priority, in some instances aimed to eradicate poverty, was both to enable women to participate in the workforce and to allow women with young children equality of opportunity with regard to work. Recent research has also emphasised the value of positive early childhood experiences in promoting the cognitive and social experiences of children and their long-term success at school.

Major changes have been taking place in the early education and care of young children and the following represent important issues in many countries:

- An increase in the quantity of provision.
- The relationship between care and education.
- The quality of provision.
- The appropriate curriculum for young children.
- The training of Early Years professionals.

Not only is there an increase in funding for Early Years services in many countries, but there is also a change in the way such services are delivered.

The early education and care of young children under five years of age, and out-of-hours care for children in schools, currently have a high profile with all political parties in the United Kingdom, in part driven by a desire to encourage more mothers of young children to enter the workforce, or to train to do so. It has yet to be seen whether such rhetoric will be transferred into practice.

Concerns have been expressed by Sylva and Pugh in an article entitled 'Transforming the Early Years in England', where they consider whether the government's promises can indeed be delivered. Though the focus in the article is on England, many of their comments are generally applicable to any government-led initiative (Sylva and Pugh, 2005). Such concerns are worth bringing to your attention before you turn to the following chapters.

- To what extent is the expansion focussed on the needs of children for high quality early education, or is it mainly driven by a wish to enable as many parents as possible to return to work?
- Will there be high quality early education led by well-trained staff, or edu-care provided by a poorly-trained and low-paid workforce?
- How successfully can professionals be integrated into teams when they have different professional cultures, training, salaries and conditions of service?
- Is there a danger that further expansion of the non-statutory sectors may compromise quality?
- Might a government as an election comes closer curtail expansion, or sacrifice quality and put quantity higher up the political agenda? (adapted from Sylva and Pugh, 2005: 24)

As Sylva and Pugh claim, the vision is an excellent one but tensions remain; can we travel this far so fast (p. 22)?

The OECD review team for the UK stressed that provision for early childhood education and care had started from a very low base compared with many other countries (*Starting Strong*, 2001: 180). A number of issues for policy attention was identified in 2001:

- Co-ordination issues.
- Progress requires continued funding.
- Staff recruitment, training and status must be addressed.

- Creation of a quality assurance and inspection regime that will respect diversity.
- A need to increase work-family supports. (adapted from *Starting Strong*, 2001: 180–1)

However, if the emphasis is on structural change, this may hide the need for cultural change as different workforces with different ways of working come together. There are other policy issues that have scarcely found their way on to the agenda. The government may have failed to recognise the enormity of the transition required to implement such changes.

As you read the following chapters it would be helpful for you to check the extent to which the developments described do reflect the aspects noted above: whether there are other initiatives seen only in certain regions/areas and whether indeed there are 'policy issues that have scarcely found their way on to the agenda'. We will return to these issues in Chapter 7.

When you turn to the following chapters you will find that although there are many new initiatives, provision of education and care is 'patchy', they may be too expensive, or may not meet the needs of many women, for example lone mothers who of necessity must work (see Ball and Vincent, 2005). There is ample evidence of this in the stories of those children born in 2000 that start each of the following chapters of this book – how fragile was the provision for many, how easily it could terminate or cease to meet their family's needs. Many of these children had numerous transitions to face by the age of six. Some, as you will see, had to attend several pre-school settings, some of these even concurrently, whilst other families had to call on the support of grandparents at short notice to fill the gaps.

We now have further evidence, from a longitudinal study in the UK, of the positive benefits of high-quality pre-school provision (Sylva et al., 2004; see also Clark, 2005). The findings of the EPPE research (The Effective Provision of Pre-school Education) by Sylva et al. are cited as an additional reason by policymakers for expenditure on expanding the provision of early childhood education and care, and for improving the training of practitioners. Well before entering school, young children have acquired what Sylva and Pugh refer to as 'learning dispositions' as well as key cognitive skills (Sylva and Pugh, 2005). Numerous research studies have illustrated the powerful effect of early education on children's readiness for school and their later success. However, the word 'quality' has now entered the debate with the finding that poor quality childcare may have no effect, negative or otherwise.

The EPPE study has not only confirmed the positive effect of high quality early education, it also 'points to a significant positive influence of the home learning environment' (quoted in Clark, 2005: 80). The design of the research made it possible to go further and look at the particular pedagogic models and practices in the most effective settings. It was found that the children tended to make better intellectual progress in fully integrated centres that combine care and education, in nursery schools and in settings with staff who have higher qualifications, especially where a large proportion are trained teachers (Siraj-Blatchford and Sylva, 2004, as discussed in Clark, 2005: 81–2).

> Many publications are now available based on the EPPE and linked researches in England, Northern Ireland and Wales. You will find these provide a helpful framework against which to assess current developments, the relative quality of different types of provision and pedagogical approaches (see www.ioe.ac.uk/projects).

A CURRICULUM FOR THE EARLY YEARS

In his keynote address to the EECERA conference in 2004, John Bennett, programme manager of the OECD early childhood reviews, presented an analysis of curriculum issues in national policy making (Bennett, 2004). According to Bennett in the early childhood context it is probably not appropriate to consider the curriculum in the traditional sense – as a plan of instructional activities; however, he stresses that in the last decade a greater awareness has developed of the need for curricular or pedagogical guidelines. From the evidence in the review he suggests that there is some agreement that programmes should be active, play-based and encourage a wide range of key learning experiences, a view also expressed by the EPPE researchers referred to earlier. First however there are, Bennett argues, two broad types of curriculum along a continuum from broad developmental goals to focussed cognitive goals. Second, he indicates that there is a growing interest in a curriculum for children under three. Thus when considering developments in early education and care in any country one important consideration is the recommended curriculum for the early years, to examine where it lies on this continuum and the consequences for transition to the later stages of education.

Over recent years many Early Years professionals have been concerned that the introduction of written curricular documents for the pre-school years may formalise and narrow the experiences provided for young children (for example, as noted earlier in the Nordic countries). Professionals in England in particular have been concerned that the balance and breadth of the curriculum in the early years in primary schools were being sacrificed in attempts to raise standards of literacy and numeracy, and a demand for primary schools, in England at least, to rank highly in league tables (see Chapter 2). We can take some comfort not only from pledges of massive increases in funding, but also the content of some of the more recent curricular documents, and the stated aim to improve the qualifications of those involved in the education and care of young children.

You will see from Chapters 2–6 that the curriculum in the early years in primary schools differs greatly across the UK; in its breadth, its formality and the extent of continuity with pre-school settings and play-based learning. The transitions faced by young children such as those whose stories we will highlight here, from birth to six years of age – and some even born on the same day – must still give cause for concern, as must the possible trauma faced by the young child whose initial experience of 'formal' education is within the first year in primary school.

As you will find, there appears to be little discussion in the UK or the Republic of Ireland as to whether children might be starting school at too young an age, and certainly much earlier than in most other countries. Variation exists in the precise ages of the children entering primary school in the five countries discussed here, however, in all cases it is well before the children are six years of age. In England the introduction of the Foundation Stage in 2000, which in 2006 now lasts for two years, may delay the introduction of more formal curriculum 'subjects', though the abrupt change that could follow still gives cause for concern. As you will find discussed in Chapter 6, in Wales the Foundation Phase lasts for longer. In Scotland, in an attempt to achieve continuity in children's learning, plans for a 3–18 curriculum are being piloted that will shortly replace the national guidelines for ages 5–14.

> For comparisons of policy and developments with regard to age when starting formal schooling as described by the 20 participating countries in the OECD (2006) study, see the OECD website (www.oecd.org/edu/earlychildhood).

UNDERSTANDING EARLY YEARS POLICY

> Policy documents often contain statements as facts as though there can be no argument about them, when indeed they may well reflect personal beliefs, cultural norms of the country concerned, or the political leanings of those involved in drafting the documents. Be cautious about accepting statements in documents as facts even where there appears to be a general consensus.

In their recent publication *Understanding Early Years Policy* (Baldock et al., 2005), the authors stress the major impact that policy decisions have on the daily life of Early Years practitioners and the need for practitioners, and particularly those in managerial positions, to understand the process by which policies are developed and implemented. Every setting has its own policies;

however, the policies of central and local government determine both the level of resources provided and also the constraints on how these are spent.

Some of the developments referred to by Baldock and his colleagues are specific to England, and as they remind readers, Scotland and Wales now have greater autonomy in this area of policy as well as in many others. Their book is proving a valuable resource to all those interested in Early Years policy.

The authors define policy as:

> an attempt by those working inside an organization to think in a coherent way about what it is trying to achieve (either in general or in relation to a specific issue) and what it needs to do to achieve it. (Baldock et al., 2005: 3)

There is an inevitable tension between central government wishing to set policies for the nation and local authorities having to implement said policies. Baldock et al. give examples of where there can be a lack of clarity, an inconsistency between policies arising from different contexts, or even conflict (see p. 5). Broad objectives may be set; however, for these objectives to be achieved there may be a need for changes in the law and not merely the provision of resources. Furthermore, new organisational structures may have to be put in place and new funding found.

> The policies of government are heavily influenced by the views of a wide range of organisations, the media and the general public and even short-term political expediency. The government is then dependent on many different agencies and the general public for successful implementation.
>
> How many different departments are likely to be involved in the successful implementation of policy initiatives? (See Baldock et al. (2005: 8) for a list.)

It is important to bear in mind the warning by Baldock and his colleagues that those outlining a policy may be clear as to the identity of those it is hoped to benefit, *but less clear on the identity of those who may be put at a disadvantage.* They claim that a consensus across political parties in the UK on the importance of Early Years services is a new thing. They also list policies they think will continue over the next ten years at least, regardless of whichever political party is in government in the UK (see p. 12 for details).

> Make your own list and consider what developments are likely to have priority, then compare your list with that given by Baldock et al.

Baldock and his colleagues argue that the current UK Labour government's Early Years policy in their first term was aimed, to a significant extent, at getting people off welfare and into work. Some might claim this was placing the needs of children second; others might claim that reducing child poverty, which has had a high priority, did put children centre stage. However, one outcome of the policies so far had meant that the expansion was more targeted than inclusive (with the latter being applicable in the Nordic countries). It may be that some of the new developments currently under way are creating more state structures with a focus on the needs of children and their families; others may indeed be having a negative impact on family life.

Some of the posts now being established in the UK mirror posts established much earlier in the Nordic countries, where childcare was based on more gender equality and equal opportunities for all children rather than on targeted priorities for deprived areas or families.

OUTLINE OF THE BOOK

This book is about developments in policy and practice in the early education and care of children from birth to eight years of age. In Chapters 1 and 7 we consider general issues and indicate ways in which the information in Chapters 2–6 can be used to develop an appreciation of the similarities and differences in policy and practice across the four constituent parts of the United Kingdom (England, Northern Ireland, Scotland and Wales) and in the Republic of Ireland. The authors of these chapters are intimately concerned with developments in early education and care in their respective countries. Each chapter is introduced and brought alive by two case studies, or stories, describing the experiences of children born in that country in 2000. The authors relate the experiences of these children to recent policy initiatives and in the final section of each chapter they discuss how the experiences might differ for children born in 2006 and for their families.

We hope this book will give you an appreciation that there are real differences in the historical background and many aspects of early education and care in these five areas. As you read the 'stories' about the selected children you should hopefully come to appreciate just how dangerous it is to make generalisations about early education and care in the United Kingdom, as is so frequently done even in recent textbooks, in some official publications and often in the media.

No superiority is intended for England from the fact that it is the first country to be considered; the countries are presented in alphabetical order! In Chapter 2 on England, the scene is also set for the subsequent chapters with a number of general references; these you will find of relevance for a broader consideration of policy elsewhere. In Chapters 3–6 you will find details of official publications and websites particular to Northern Ireland, Scotland, the Republic of Ireland and Wales, to enable you to obtain more detail on the policy developments in these countries; these websites will provide sources to enable you to continue to update your knowledge.

TOPICS FOR DISCUSSION

What are the implications for young children and their families of the expansion of early education and care? Consider the advantages and disadvantages.

What effects might there be on family life as a result of the encouragement in many countries for the mothers of young children to return to work?

What is the evidence that 'Early schooling robs kids of childhood'?

What kind of curricular documents might reflect a child-centred approach to early education and care?

Curricular documents are now appearing covering children from birth to three years of age. How might these affect the self-esteem of mothers of young children?

We will return to these issues when you have read Chapters 2–6.

You might find it helpful before you turn to a detailed study of Chapters 2–6 to read the ten case studies as tasters to set the scene for what is to follow.

REFERENCES

Baldock, P., Fitzgerald, D. and Kay, J. (2005) *Understanding Early Years Policy*. London: Paul Chapman.

Ball, S.J. and Vincent, C. (2005) 'The 'childcare champion'? New Labour, social justice and the childcare market', *British Educational Research Journal*, 31 (5): 557–70.

Bennett, J. (2003) 'Starting Strong', *Journal of Early Childhood Research*, 1 (1): 21–48.

Bennett, J. (2004) *Curriculum Issues in National Policy-making*. Keynote address, EECERA conference, Malta. Paris: OECD.

Bertram, T. and Pascal, C. (2000) *The OECD Thematic Review of Early Childhood Education and Care: Background report for the United Kingdom*. Available at: www.oecd.org/edu/earlychildhood

Clark, M.M. (2003) 'Education in Scotland: what can we learn from the census?', *Primary Practice*, (35): 31–3.

Clark, M.M. (2004) 'Education in England and Wales: what can we learn from the census?', *Primary Practice*, (36): 35–8.

Clark, M.M. (2005) *Understanding Research in Early Education: The relevance for the future of lessons from the past*. Abingdon: Routledge.

Cohen, B., Moss, P., Petrie, P. and Wallace, J. (2004) *A New Deal for Children? Re-forming education and care in England, Scotland and Sweden*. Bristol: Policy.

Einarsdottir, J. and Wagner, J. (eds) (2006) *Nordic Childhoods and Early Education*. Greenwich, CI: Information Age.

Moser, T. (2006) 'The Nordic Early Childhood Education and Care Systems (ECEC) in a Pan-European Perspective'. Oral presentation EECERA conference, Reykjavik.

Organisation for Economic Co-operation and Development (OECD) (2001) *Starting Strong: Early childhood education and care*. Paris: OECD.

Organisation for Economic Co-operation and Development (OECD) (2006) *Starting Strong II: Early childhood education and care*. Paris: OECD.

Sylva, K. and Pugh, G. (2005) 'Transforming the Early Years in England', *Oxford Review of Education,* 31 (1): 11–27.

Sylva, K., Melhuish, E., Sammons, P., Siraj-Blatchford, I. and Taggart, B. (2004) *The Effective Provision of Pre-school Education (EPPE) Project: Final Report. A longitudinal study funded by the DfES 1997–2004.* London: SureStart/DfES. Available at: www.ioe.ac.uk/projects/eppe

Waller, T. (ed.) (2005) *An Introduction to Early Childhood: A multidisciplinary approach.* London: Paul Chapman.

Zigler, E., Gilliam, W.S. and Jones, S.M. (2006) *A Vision for Universal Preschool Education.* New York: Cambridge University Press.

ENGLAND

Gill McGillivray

A CHILD BORN IN ENGLAND IN 2000: MICHAEL'S STORY

Michael was born in May 2000. His mother, Suzanne, had a normal delivery. He lives with both parents and an elder (by two years) brother, Samuel. Both parents are educated to graduate level; mother to postgraduate level. Both parents are employed and have their own car; Michael's mother took extended maternity leave for both children, and his father, Paul, took five days paternity leave when Michael was born. Extended maternity leave would have meant some loss of income.

Michael lives in a rural part of the south west region of England in a village with a population of approximately 800. Suzanne returned to part-time work when he was ten months old (having previously worked full-time). Michael had already been attending a privately run nursery, for two days each week, from the age of nine months, in order to settle him before being left for three days each week when his mother was working. Samuel attended the same nursery, for the same sessions. The nursery was located in the town where Suzanne was employed. Suzanne worked varying days each week, and she had difficulty in finding daycare that would accommodate such variation. Nursery managers preferred a regular pattern of attendance in order to fill places, but this setting kept a specific number of places open for flexible hours to meet parents' needs.

When Samuel started school in September 2002, and Michael was two years four months old, childcare arrangements had to be reviewed to meet Michael's parents' needs, Samuel's schooling arrangements and availability in a rural area. The outcome was that Samuel was in the care of a childminder for before and after school care (the childminder lived locally to the school), and Michael continued to attend the privately run nursery, 12 miles away from Samuel's school. The arrangements for transporting the children to their settings and the cost of childcare for both children placed significant financial and time demands on both parents.

To alleviate this, Michael's parents decided to change Michael's childcare arrangements slightly when he was three years old, by placing him with the same childminder as his brother for one day each week, but staying with the private setting for the remaining two days when his mother worked.

When Michael was three years six months, his parents decided to withdraw him from the privately run nursery, and move him to a voluntary pre-school that operated in a village several miles from both the family home and the village where Samuel went to school. The decision was predicated on the preference for the setting's ethos and approach to play-based learning taken by staff working at the pre-school. Suzanne sensed a change in ethos at the privately run nursery that reduced flexibility for parents at the expense of predictable income, as well as an unsatisfactory approach to play in her view. The children who attended the pre-school would be likely to attend the same infant school as Michael (and his older brother), so attendance at the pre-school would allow Michael opportunities to establish friendships with children he could later be with in Reception class. (There was no nursery school or class provision locally for Michael.)

Attendance at pre-school seemed to suit Michael's needs. The demands on Suzanne were challenging however. Although the admissions policy of the pre-school was able to offer flexibility for parents who worked variable hours each week, the expectation was that parents would volunteer to work on a rota basis to support the pre-school. Such support allowed the setting to minimise staffing costs, but failed to recognise the needs of working parents and the difficulties they may have in being available for rota duty. Such arrangements necessitated Suzanne taking time off work. Michael was in the care of a childminder when he was not at the pre-school – a different childminder from his brother, as their childcare was in different villages.

School holidays presented significant challenges for Michael's parents in terms of childcare arrangements in the summer of 2004. Michael's childminder was not available during school holidays as she had her own children to care for. The school which Samuel attended and the pre-school both closed during Christmas, Easter and the summer holidays, operating for 39 weeks of the year. Paul and Suzanne 'muddled through', juggling annual leave taken by each of them, and grandparents travelling to stay with the family for short periods of time to provide childcare. Neither of Michael's parents had family relatives living nearby.

Michael started primary school in September 2004, attending the same school as his brother. He had had access to the first year of the Foundation Stage curriculum during his time at the pre-school and accessed the second year of the Foundation Stage in a mixed Reception, Year 1 and Year 2 class of 31 children who lived in those local villages within a radius of approximately ten miles. From May to June 2005, his teacher completed the Foundation Stage Profile to record Michael's assessment against the Stepping Stones and Early Learning Goals in the Curriculum Guidance for the Foundation Stage. Michael had achieved most Stepping Stones and Early Learning Goals in all six areas of learning. His profile was passed on to the local education authority.

Michael's parents took leave to look after Michael and his brother during the Christmas and Easter holidays of Michael's first year at school. During the summer of 2005, Michael was old enough to be enrolled at a summer playscheme that operated locally. The hours were limited however to 10am to 3pm, and did not allow Suzanne to work a full day; the alternative playscheme was too far to travel to and was expensive. The solution was to ask friends and family to help out in taking and fetching Michael and his brother to and from the playscheme when their parents were not able to take leave.

Michael has now come to the end of his Year 1 National Curriculum education. His teacher has assessed him to be achieving higher than average levels so far in English, Mathematics and Science.

He has friends in his class who also go to the same childminder for before and after school care on the days that Suzanne is working. Michael continues to be an active child, with interests in football and swimming. His parents take it in turns to drive Michael to local venues in order to allow him to participate in sessions at the nearest sports centre (ten miles away from their home). Children from other families in the same village may not be as fortunate as Michael if they do not have access to their own transport. Buses to the nearest town are caught from a bus stop a mile away from the village, and are therefore difficult to access with young children. Employment in the region is close to the national average, but transport may create difficulties for families. There are no shops or other facilities in the village, so access to leisure, health and childcare is limited for some.

A CHILD BORN IN ENGLAND IN 2000: SURAYA'S STORY

Suraya was born in August 2000. She was born prematurely at 34 weeks when her mother, Zainab, was admitted to hospital with acute appendicitis. Suraya was delivered by Caesarean section and put into an incubator for ten days due to her low birth weight. She gained weight rapidly and appeared to be developing well at discharge.

She lives with both parents and has two younger brothers (Iftakar born in 2002, Mahmood in 2004). Her father, Ahmed, is educated to HND level in accountancy and has worked part-time for the local authority since 1998. Her mother had a limited education in rural Pakistan, but is very interested in further training in order to develop a small business related to her sewing and embroidery skills. At present she works from home doing piecework for a local employer and is paid the minimum wage. This is a recent development, as when Suraya and the younger children were born she was unemployed, having made the decision to stay at home to look after them. Neither parent has family relatives living close by. Both parents rely on public transport for economic reasons, although father holds a current driving licence.

Suraya has lived in two different inner city suburbs of Birmingham in central England. Her first home was in a first floor flat in private, rented accommodation. She attended a voluntary church pre-school two miles from her home twice weekly with her mother from the age of 12 months. This was on the advice of the health visitor who was concerned at the lack of play space in the home and her mother's social isolation. This may have been partly due to a lack of community language (Mirpuri) support in the area. Zainab attended regularly and gained in confidence over the period of a year from her contact with other mothers in her community and staff at the pre-school. She was offered support and advice with her subsequent pregnancy which progressed to full term with no complications in November 2002.

At the age of two years six months, Suraya was able to attend three part-time (two and a half hours) sessions weekly without her mother. There was a small sessional fee, not always easy for the family with a new baby to afford. The journey to the playgroup was also problematic in inclement weather as the bus service was erratic and added to weekly financial outlay. By the time Zainab had returned home, there was often less than 20 minutes before she had to set out to collect Suraya at the end of the session. Consequently, Suraya ceased attending the playgroup in March 2003 and there was no more convenient setting available in the local area.

In August 2003, the family relocated to a Housing Association property in a different Birmingham suburb in a local SureStart area. This presented a wider range of educational and care opportunities for Suraya and her brother.

When the family moved into their new accommodation they were visited by an Outreach Worker from SureStart who identified their particular needs through the help of a Mirpuri-speaking Family Support Worker. Zainab and the children were encouraged to attend the local school (half a mile from their home) that hosted a daily mother and baby group and classes for mothers in a range of subjects. These were heavily subsidised by the local authority and only required a small donation to cover refreshments. (Other activities were available for those fathers who wanted them.)

Suraya was registered for a part-time morning place at the 45-place nursery class in the school and attended daily from September 2003. As this was within the statutory sector there was no charge other than a voluntary contribution to the school fund.

For six months, Zainab and Iftakar attended the mother and baby group at the SureStart setting, and Suraya settled well at nursery. In March 2004, mother's third pregnancy began to make life problematic. Constant sickness prevented her from attending regularly. The Family Support Worker suggested that she would benefit from the intervention of a Home-Start Worker (via SureStart) to help with the temporary difficulties. Home Start is a charitable organisation to support mothers with young children in the home. Ahmed was initially concerned that this would cause expense but was delighted to discover that this was a free service staffed by volunteers in the area.

A Home-Start worker, Farida, was allocated to fetch and collect Suraya daily from home and school and to take Iftakar to the mother and baby group twice weekly in order to provide some respite for mother. As the pregnancy progressed, mother developed health complications which meant that she needed constant bed rest, so the services of Farida were extended to help with dressing and feeding the children on days when father was unavailable to help. An acquaintance from the mother and baby group (Shaheena) also became involved by providing support with shopping and general help and subsequently became a close family friend.

Suraya continued to make good progress through the play-based nursery Foundation Stage curriculum. She particularly enjoyed imaginative play and had many friends. She was fortunate to be taught by a teacher who used her own bilingual skills in English and Mirpuri to support learning. She was offered a full-time nursery class place in the summer term of 2004 when Zainab was in the later stages of her third pregnancy. Mahmood was born with no complications in July 2004 but mother remained unwell and was diagnosed with postnatal depression.

In the Autumn term of 2004, Suraya transferred to the Reception year in the same primary school, where she was the youngest in the class of 30 children. Suraya was aged four years one month. The Foundation Stage Curriculum was closely followed but there was also a strong emphasis on preparing for more formal work in Year 1 in the Spring term of 2005. Suraya found learning to read via a phonics approach very challenging and this seemed to result in her 'feeling poorly' on frequent occasions. Her attendance was quite poor during the Spring term which caused her reading to fall behind even more. Her mother continued to feel unwell; she had continued support from Farida and her friend Shaheena.

Both parents were sufficiently concerned at Suraya's lack of progress and enthusiasm that was reported to them at the parents' consultation evening at the end of Suraya's Reception year, that they began to make enquiries about another local school with a nursery class recommended by Shaheena. Suraya's parents visited the school. They felt it had a very different ethos with an emphasis on child-centred approaches throughout Key Stage One. They decided to transfer Suraya to begin Year 1 at the new school in September 2005. Iftakar also joined the school nursery, within easy walking distance.

Zainab continued to attend sessions at the SureStart setting with her new baby and with encouragement from staff and friends made a gradual recovery from postnatal depression. Her sewing skills had long been recognised through her contribution in making role play clothes and puppets for the group. An opportunity for home-based employment arose from contact with another parent. Zainab began this in December 2004. Although this enabled flexible working around the needs of the children, she found that she required at least one day per week when she could work uninterrupted for seven hours.

Fortunately, Shaheena had recently become a registered childminder and was willing to look after the baby and collect the two older children from school and nursery. This, combined with Ahmed's help, has meant that Zainab is able to make a very small profit after paying for childcare in term time. She has recently enrolled on an evening class at SureStart to learn how to set up her own business and intends to achieve this by 2008. By this time, all three children will be in full-time education at school, which intends to offer full service extended provision in term time from September 2007.

The only difficulty Zainab is facing is during the summer holidays, when she still needs to work to maintain her employment and income. Although Shaheena is willing to take all three children for as many hours as necessary, the cost would be prohibitive. Suraya is now old enough to attend a subsidised playscheme run by the school for two weeks of each vacation; this would help, but there has to be a reliance on family, friends and professionals to help with childcare.

(Thanks to Karen Argent who prepared Suraya's story.)

BACKGROUND

England, one of the four countries that form the United Kingdom and with a population of 50 million by 2004, has 83.7 per cent of the population of the UK (Office for National Statistics, 2006). Between 1951 and the latest census in 2001 the population of England had already increased by 19 per cent and was more culturally diverse than ever before. A growth of a further 7 million in the UK population is predicted by 2031, much of that in England as a consequence of inward migration. Contrasts are to be found in the landscape of England as some areas are distinctly rural, but three in four of the population live in a city, (7 million in London, the capital, and a further million in Birmingham in the Midlands).

To appreciate the culturally diverse population of England, it is useful to understand the history of immigration patterns. The first large-scale migration of people of minority ethnic origin came from the Caribbean during the 1950s. Immigrants from India and Pakistan arrived mainly in the 1960s, refugees from Uganda during the 1970s and immigrants from China and Bangladesh came during the 1980s and 1990s. The minority ethnic population for England was given as between 7 and 9 per cent at the time of the 2001 census, and in Great Britain had grown by 53 per cent between 1991 and 2001 (see Clark, 2004).

Refugees, asylum seekers and migrant workers continue to increase the cultural diversity of the population. Government figures show that over 400,000 from the eight Eastern European countries most recently admitted to the European Union have registered as migrant workers since 2004 (Home Office, 2006). As minority ethnic groups are proportionately younger than the white population, the proportion of children from ethnic minority groups will increase.

London has the highest proportion of people from most minority ethnic groups and in two areas of London, Newham (the most economically deprived local authority in England) and Brent, white people already were in the minority by 2001. It was reported that more than 300 languages were spoken by children in London`s schools, making the capital the most linguistically diverse city in the world at the time of the census. It is difficult to obtain precise figures for the number of community languages represented in local authorities, or the impact of the diversity of languages spoken by asylum seekers.

One interesting statistic is that in Southampton among a group of asylum seekers housed by the National Asylum Support Service, 63 different countries were represented with 68 community languages (Clark, 2004). One primary school in Newham, London, when inspected by Ofsted in 2006, was judged to be outstanding; it was noted that 30 languages were spoken by pupils in the school. This example illustrates how some settings are managing the experiences of learners successfully, with the rich tapestry of languages and cultures contributing to learning. Changes in the population have significant implications for many aspects of life, in particular early education and care as practitioners develop strategies to meet the needs of local families.

> Families who are asylum seekers or refugees may need to make several moves in the first few years after they arrive in England, before they find more permanent accommodation. This could be unsettling for the young children. What challenges do you think it will present for those planning early education and care in a local area?

Administration

England is subject to the administration of the UK's government in Westminster. Some government departments have responsibility solely for affairs in England (such as the Department for Education and Skills); others have responsibility across the UK (such as the Department for Defence). The UK joined the European Community (now the European Union) in 1973. The impact of membership of the EU is explored by Ruxton (2001) in the context of Early Years education and childcare, but the most recent and relevant change is the introduction of the Work and Families Act 2006, which aligns England with European partners in, for example, parental entitlement to extended maternity and paternity leave. The act provides legislation for one of the principles enshrined in *Choice for Parents, the Best Start for Children: A Ten Year Strategy*, (HM Treasury, 2004; frequently referred to as the *Ten Year Strategy*), namely the need to respond to changing patterns of employment and ensure that parents, particularly mothers, can work and progress their careers with access to affordable and flexible childcare.

In England, the Department for Education and Skills (DfES) was established 'with the purpose of creating opportunity, releasing potential and achieving excellence for all' (DfES, 2006a). The drive to improve services for children, young people and their families, as communicated in *Every Child Matters, Change for Children* (DfES, 2004a) has signatories from many government departments. Responsibility for the implementation of *Every Child Matters, Change for Children* is held by the SureStart Unit within the DfES. Key roles relating to children and families appointed for England are the Minister for Children, Young People and Families, the Minister for Social Exclusion and the Children's Commissioner for England. Child and family health and social care are under the remit of the Department of Health, and the Department of Work and Pensions is responsible for the government's welfare reform agenda, supporting people of working age, employers, disabled people, pensioners, families and children.

These various structures indicate how aspects of early years education and care remain split across different government departments. For further exploration of the relationship between national and local level responsibility in recent years see Cohen et al. (2004).

Healthcare and socio-economic issues

England, as part of the UK, signed up to the United Nations Convention on the Rights of the Child (UNCRC) in 1992. The Children's Rights Alliance for England (CRAE) is critical of the current government's lack of progress in the full implementation of the UNCRC. Some health and care issues for young children and families are illustrated by the following statistics: the West Midlands region has the highest infant mortality rate (8.6 deaths per thousand live births) among health authorities in England. The perinatal mortality rates in England and Wales increased in 2003, and there is significant variation by region, social class and profession of parents (Horton, 2005). Additional health issues are apparent in child obesity data: England had the fourth highest level of obesity in 2004, after Malta, the USA, and Canada (WHO, 2004). Three and a half million children in England were living in relative poverty in 2003–4: these children are more likely to be injured in household accidents, are more likely to be obese, and are more likely to suffer ill-health such as bronchitis (CRAE, 2005).

Child health issues contribute to the concerns of those working in childcare and education settings. Recent media and public attention has been drawn to the poor nutrition offered in school meals, and the 'Healthy Schools' initiative is intended to address issues of obesity. The high cost of housing and childcare in England contributes to poverty levels, and the number of children in a family, the presence of disabled children or adults, ethnicity and unemployment exacerbate health issues.

One in four dependent children lives in a lone parent family (Clark, 2004). Women's choices about work and childcare are influenced by their culture and ethnicity (Bryson et al., 2005). Families want flexible provision if they work unusual hours, staff who represent and understand different cultures within the community, and information that is readily available and accessible (Daycare Trust, 2006). Barn et al. (2006) report findings from parents (272 mothers and 113 fathers) from a variety of ethnic groups in England who participated in a study of parenting. The authors suggest that those working with families must be aware of the complexity of 'migration, ethnicity, socio-economic circumstances, multiculturalism, and racism' (Barn et al., 2006: 1). The proximity of grandparents was important for some, and parents recognised both the challenges of sociali-sation and also of language learning for their children.

Children's experiences will be different for other reasons too: there were 60,000 looked-after children in England; 68 per cent were in foster care in 2004–5, and there were 2,900 unaccompanied asylum-seeking children in England (DfES, 2005b). Mental health data for children in Great Britain iden-tify that one in ten children aged five to 16 years had a clinically diagnosed mental health disorder in 2004 (DH, 2004). Such data portray the scale of inequality amongst children, young people and their families, and offer a con-text for the stated aims of *Every Child Matters, Change for Children* (DfES, 2004a). Inequalities are evident for children in England in many aspects of their lives and experiences in the home, childcare and education.

> Think of the health problems faced by Suraya's mother, and the support she received in coping with her three young children. Had the family lived in a more rural area, or indeed in another town, to what extent might such a range of sup-port have been available?

POLICY AND PRACTICE IN EARLY CHILDHOOD EDUCATION AND CARE

The context

What is it like to be a child growing up in England? The diversity of socio-economic factors creates a multiplicity of childhoods. *The Good Childhood Inquiry*, the UK's first independent national inquiry into childhood led by Lord Layard, was announced in July 2006. Its aims are 'to renew soci-ety's understanding of childhood for the twenty-first century to inform, improve and inspire all our relationships with children' (Children's Society, 2006).

The UK's government spent 0.3 per cent Gross Domestic Product (GDP) on childcare; Sweden spent 2 per cent in 2003 (Cohen et al., 2004). What does this mean for children in childcare in England? Might there be a dichotomy here between the ideology of improving childhood but with-out the financial investment to make it a reality?

In England, the pace of change in early childhood education and care has been rapid in recent years. Some of the demographic changes already identified, child protection and economic forces are key drivers in the transformation. Some changes in Early Years education and care are recurring themes, such as the provision of flexible childcare by the Ministry of Labour during the Second World War to allow mothers to work on the land and in munitions factories. The fact that the nation's economy seems to be the driving force, as opposed to social need, has met with criticism. A history of early education in the UK is presented in the OECD Thematic Review for the UK (Bertram and Pascal, 2001), and debates about constructs of childhood have pertinence in the context of historical images, perceptions and policy (see Aries, 1962 and Waller, 2005.) The media, specifically via television programmes shown in the UK, have tended to problematise children (Cohen et al., 2004) and portray parents as inadequate in providing for their children's nutritional needs and dealing with challenging behaviour.

A recent policy that has had an impact on the provision of early childhood education and care in England is the introduction of *Curriculum Guidance for the Foundation Stage* (QCA, 2000), *Birth to Three Matters* (SureStart, 2003) – to be combined to become the *Early Years Foundation Stage* from 2008) – and the Children Act 2004, preceded by the Green Paper *Every Child Matters* (DfES, 2003). The framework for *Every Child Matters, Change for Children* (DfES, 2004a) is underpinned by five outcomes for all children and young people that are intended to be achieved by all departments, agencies and professionals working together. The five outcomes are: to be healthy, to stay safe, to enjoy and achieve, to make a positive contribution and to achieve economic well-being. The structures needed to deliver these outcomes are creating a radical re-organisation across local government departments, as they bring together all those working with children, young people and families across health, social care and education: for example, early years practitioners, youth workers, health professionals, teachers and those working with looked-after children.

Policy

The newly-elected Labour government in 1997 made it clear that childcare was one of its priorities. *The Plowden Report* (DES, 1967) had recommended an expansion of nursery education, but on a mostly part-time basis to minimise children's separation from their mothers. In 1972 it triggered the plans of Margaret Thatcher, then Secretary of State for Education, who promised a nursery education place for all four-year-olds whose parents wanted it, within ten years. This was not delivered, and an attempt in 1996 to implement a nursery voucher system also failed.

There was a sharp decline in birth rates in the 1970s and 1980s, and primary schools felt the impact. To compensate, children who were four years old were taken into Reception classes, thus removed from pre-school education. Serious concerns were voiced about the lack of policy and debate regarding four year old children in primary school, and the suitability of the education they were receiving (Clark, 1988; David, 1990).

In the National Childcare Strategy (DfEE, 1998) the stated intention was to raise the number of childcare places available, to improve the quality of childcare provision, to make childcare more affordable and provide free education for every four-year-old whose parents wanted it (this was later extended to three- and then two-year-old children in 2006). Early Years Development and Childcare Partnerships were created in each local authority, 'charged with delivering integrated early education and childcare' (DfEE, 1998: 7; see also Cohen et al., 2004 for further analysis.) Eleven Early Excellence Centres were already in place at this time, and an additional 40,000 'out of school' care places were to be made available as part of the National Childcare Strategy. The variety of settings available as well as the job titles of those people who work with young children and their families had been confusing (see Michael's story), and the National Childcare Strategy aimed to rationalise qualifications and the quality assurance systems that monitored settings (see Ball and Vincent, 2005).

The SureStart initiative announced in 1998 was designed to target families with babies and young children living in the most deprived areas of England and was the current Labour government's attempt to alleviate the high number of children and families living in poverty. Its aims were to offer outreach services; support for children and families, such as childcare, primary health care and support for those with special needs. There were 250 SureStart projects in operation by 1999 (Baldock et al., 2005), and despite its critics, the government was determined to continue with its expansion. Research in both the UK and the USA has shown that intervention and inclusion in the most deprived regions improve the outcomes for families with babies and young children, and removes families from relative poverty (Sylva and Pugh, 2005).

> Suraya's family benefited from SureStart services through the courses and childcare that helped Suraya's mother, as well as contact with a Home-Start volunteer. How important do you feel the support was to the family, and in what ways?

The National Evaluation of SureStart (Tunstill et al., 2005) reported findings that indicated that the programme was not reaching some of the most disadvantaged families and that the work in some local programmes was not having the impact it should. Critics suggest that more time is needed for the impact of SureStart to be assessed. Penn, however, is critical of SureStart in its 'vague and grandiose' aims; she suggests that the well being of the child has not been at the heart of the initiative (Penn, 2006: 10). The issues of stigmatisation and access remain as challenges, however, for those who are committed to ensuring SureStart delivers on its original aims.

Birth to Three Matters (SureStart, 2003) sets out a framework to support practitioners working with babies and young children from birth to three years. The focus is on four aspects of development: a strong child, a skilful communicator, a competent learner and a healthy child. The framework supports an holistic approach to working with babies and young children, develops reflective practice and recognises the challenges of working with this age range. The principles that underpin the framework emphasise relationships and the role of the adult in caring for a baby or young child, as well as focusing on placing the child centre stage at the begining.

Similar principles are mirrored in *Curriculum Guidance for the Foundation Stage* (QCA, 2000). Practitioners (including childminders and those in private, voluntary and statutory settings) are offered training in *Birth to Three Matters* and *Curriculum Guidance for the Foundation Stage* through their local Early Years Development and Childcare Partnerships (EYDCPs), local childminding networks and private training organisations, for example, to support the effective implementation of both frameworks.

In 2006, consultation was taking place regarding the proposed merging of *Birth to Three Matters* with *Curriculum Guidance for the Foundation Stage* to become the *Early Years Foundation Stage* from 2008. The aim is to create a single framework 'for care, learning and development for children in all early years settings from birth to the August after their fifth birthday', so that settings are able to offer continuity in their provision and opportunities for learning (DfES, 2006b: i). (See Baldock et al., 2005: 35–8 for key dates in policy development.)

Provision

Table 2.1 illustrates the types of childcare usually available to parents in England. For the youngest children, the childcare offered includes childminders, privately run nurseries, nannies and informal care (such as grandparents). Children from two years nine months are able to attend pre-schools, which are usually run on a voluntary basis. All local authorities provide some nursery education (nursery class, nursery unit or nursery school) for children in the year before they start school, but provision is patchy. Each nursery or pre-school session is usually two or two-and-a-half hours long and may not match parents' working patterns, or fit with other childcare available. Mothers may find arrangements difficult if they have a baby to care for too, as in Suraya's case. Nursery education settings offer some full-time places if this is needed by a family. The variation in childcare provision and its associated aspects, for example the pay and conditions of staff, exacerbates the range and quality of childcare and thus any inequalities for children and their families.

The development of provision for 'out of school' care continued beyond the initial announcement in the National Childcare Strategy (DfEE, 1998) with the introduction of extended schools as part of the *Every Child Matters* Green Paper. Extended schools were to act 'as the hub for services for children, families and other members of the community' (DfES, 2003: 29). The target was for each local education authority to have at least one extended school fully functional in 2006 and for all schools to have extended provision by 2010. Cummings and colleagues reported on the

TABLE 2.1   Types of Early Years care and education provision in England

Statutory/ Maintained	Private/ Independent	Voluntary	Combined/ partnership
Nursery school	Privately owned and run nurseries	Pre-schools	SureStart programmes – often partnerships between charitable organisations (NCH, Barnardos) with statutory provision (Primary Care Trusts, for example).
Nursery Class	Crèches	Crèches	
Foundation Stage Unit	Childminders		
	Nannies		

findings of an evaluation of the Full Service Extended Schools Project for 2003–4, and noted variability in management and organisation, services offered to families and in relationships with the communities the extended schools were serving (Cummings et al., 2005).

Approximately half a million full daycare places (in private or statutory settings, see Table 2.1) existed in England in 2005 (Ofsted, 2006a), and this created a third of all places available. Other places were provided by child-minders and 'out of school' care (each approximately 300,000 places), ses-sional care (pre-schools) and crèches. The typical cost of childcare in 2003 was approximately £512 per month for a child under two years (Cohen et al., 2004.) Costs vary according to where parents live (fees are higher in London) and whether it is for a first child or siblings. Childcare tax credits and vouchers are intended to allow parents some choice and access to child-care, but at just over £50 per week per child in 2003, parents are still expected to make a substantial contribution (Cohen et al., 2004).

> Look again at the early history of Michael and Suraya and the range of early education and care they were able to access. Michael lived in a rural area and had well-qualified parents, yet even his family struggled to meet their needs for early education and care. What additional problems might be faced by other families in such a situation? Suraya and her family lived in a large city where they had a range of support, including helpful neighbours and someone who could converse in Mirpuri with her mother. In your experience, how widely available is the range of support experienced by Michael's and Suraya's families?

TRANSITIONS

Transitions for children in England are most likely to be when starting nursery, starting school, or moving to and from different places of care for a child aged two to four years. A young child may need to cope with several transitions simultaneously as well as consecutively, between settings and carers in each day (as both case studies illustrate), due to the fragmented structure of provision. The increased involvement of parents and children is recognised as a way to support children's transitions in settings in England.

Transitions allow opportunities for personal growth and development for any individual. How children are supported in their development of new relationships and deal with the possible closure of others will influence how they cope and develop future resilience in new situations. The issue of transition between Reception year and Year 1 in schools in England has been the subject of research, local policy initiatives and guidance (Fabian, 2002; Ofsted, 2004) as the contrasts between the curriculum and approaches to learning and teaching needed to be reconciled (Clark, 2005). There is variability in provision for children making the transition into school and staff may not acknowledge the range of experiences that children can bring with them, such as the influence of their pre-school (Sylva and Pugh, 2005).

Children move from various types of daycare, depending on local availability, parents' working patterns and shifts, and access to free or low-cost childcare. The role of extended schools is intended to reduce such fragmentation and support parents through the development of full service provision, offering care before and after school for school-age children as well as other services. Michael's story illustrates the number and nature of the several transitions that a child, particularly of two, three and four years of age, could typically experience where there is limited but continuous childcare available.

Birth to Three Matters (SureStart, 2003) advocates a key worker system. An effective key worker system recognises the needs of both the child and the parents, and should provide also for communication requirements (by having an interpreter and materials in appropriate languages if needed) that would support transition, particularly as a child begins in a new setting.

Sanders et al. (2005) report that for children moving from Reception year (four to five years) into Year 1 (five to six years) in primary school, there must be greater consideration for the needs of younger children in the cohort, as well as children with English as an Additional Language (EAL) and Special Educational Needs (SEN). They recommend that teachers have more training on how to support the transition from Reception to Y1, and that the issue of transition may be a target for developing a shared understanding between professionals in health, care and education.

Good practice is typified by prioritising transition, arranging opportunities for familiarisation, making home visits (sometimes controversial for reasons of invasion of privacy, for example), as well as adopting a key worker system. Pen Green Children's Centre was one of the first Early Excellence Centres, starting in 1983 in Corby, Northamptonshire, in an area of severe deprivation. Staff (known as Family Workers) operate closely with parents; there is a policy of 'sitting in' – for parents to stay with their child for the first two weeks that they attend Pen Green. This allows family workers to gain a genuine understanding of the culture, needs and individuality of each family, easing the transition for both parents and children (Community Playthings, 2006).

The role for parents is variable from setting to setting, despite the recent emphasis on promoting genuine partnership with parents. School settings, particularly Reception classes as part of a larger organisation, have to operate as such, and may not be able to offer as much flexibility and choice to parents, or indeed children, as to what routines and learning take place (Clark, 2005). Accountability and regulation may have forced practices to look quite different, but with the advent of a common regulatory framework and the Early Years Foundation Stage for all children from birth to five, flexibility and choice may ease transition for children and parents in the future.

> To what extent do you think that parents are able to exercise any influence on their children's early education, and in what ways? Do you feel there should be more choice available to parents and how could this be developed?

SCHOOLING

Context

Approximately 93 per cent of children educated in England attend maintained schools, with the remaining 7 per cent attending either private (public) schools or receiving home-tutored education (Yeo and Lovell, 2002). Governing bodies for schools have responsibility for standards, education, recruiting staff and managing the premises of the school they govern.

The 1944 Education Act provided education for all children aged five to fifteen years (since raised to sixteen). The Education Reform Act (1988) introduced the National Curriculum in England, and a whole new vocabulary (Key Stages, Statutory Assessment Tasks or Tests, Attainment Levels and Targets, core subjects, foundation subjects) had to be acquired by education practitioners.

Table 2.2 indicates the organisation of types of setting, ages and Key Stages within the National Curriculum framework in England. Some children will start school in the term of their fifth birthday; others will start in the year they will be five. A child who has a birthday in August could begin school when aged four years one month, like Suraya. Policy is determined by the local authority, even an individual school, thus creating inequalities in educational experience for children as they enter Year 1 and begin Key Stage 1 education (Gelder and Savage, 2004).

In England, children start school in the Reception year, which is the second year of the Foundation Stage. Parents will often want their child to

TABLE 2.2   National Curriculum: Key Stages, ages and types of setting in England

Type of setting	Key Stage	Age Years
Nursery school, nursery class, nursery unit, pre-school*, childminder*, private nursery*	Foundation Stage (Year 1)	3–4
Reception class in an infant, primary or first school	Foundation Stage (Year 2)	4–5
Infant school, primary school or first school (5 to 9 years)	Key Stage 1	5–7
Junior, primary or middle school (9 to 13 years)	Key Stage 2	7–11
Secondary school or middle school	Key Stage 3	11–14
Secondary school	Key Stage 4	14–16/18

* if in receipt of a Nursery Education Grant from their local authority to support delivery of the Foundation Stage Curriculum

start school in September if their place is jeopardised by starting later in the academic year; this contributes to the continuing increase in the number of four year old children in Reception classes (57 per cent of all four-year-olds were in Reception classes in 1999; 61 per cent in 2004, and 1 per cent of all three year olds; DfES, 2004b).

Some schools have Foundation Stage units, where the Foundation Stage Curriculum has integrated delivery across Nursery and Reception classes. Others may have a separate nursery school in the vicinity, where children receive the first year of the Foundation Stage before moving to their new school for the Reception year. There is variability in how the Foundation Stage is provided for, depending on the availability of nursery school or pre-school education or childminders drawing on the Nursery Education grant. Michael's story illustrates how there was only pre-school provision for him to receive the Foundation Stage curriculum; nursery education was not available to him.

Curriculum guidance for the Foundation Stage

When *Curriculum Guidance for the Foundation Stage* (QCA, 2000) was introduced, it was generally welcomed by those working with children aged three to five years. It was seen as an endorsement of a play-based approach to learning and teaching in nursery schools, nursery units, Nursery classes and Reception classes, although ambiguity remains as to interpretation of the guidance (Adams et al., 2004). Emphasis on a play-based approach to Early

Years education had been lacking in the *Desirable Outcomes* (SCAA,1996) that had preceded *Curriculum Guidance for the Foundation Stage*. The language within the Desirable Outcomes guidance conveyed preparation for the National Curriculum, indeed with a focus on literacy and numeracy, but did not convey the principles and practice to which Early Years educators generallysubscribe (Adams et al., 2004).

The guidance sets out six areas of learning (personal, social and emotional development; communication, language and literacy; mathematical development; knowledge and understanding of the world; physical development and creative development) with a range of stepping stones leading to early learning goals within each area of learning. In the Education Act 2002, *Curriculum Guidance for the Foundation Stage* (QCA, 2000) became statutory as part of the National Curriculum.

The *Foundation Stage Profile* (QCA, 2003) was introduced in January 2003, and the first set of profiles that recorded children's achievements against the stepping stones and early learning goals had to be sent to local authorities in the summer term of that year. The Foundation Stage Profile was met with a mixed response; some condemned it as a mere checklist, others welcomed the emphasis on child observation as a tool for assessment.

Conflict remains between the ethos and the approach taken by those who advocate an Early Years curriculum that endorses learning through play – childhood as a stage in its own right and holistic learning with an emphasis on diversity and cultural understanding – as opposed to those who see the early years as preparation (Adams et al., 2004). The controversy surrounding the place of phonics in the early stages of the teaching of reading illustrates such tension and conflict. Clark (2006) offers a critique of the Rose Report that made recommendations to the DfES that an approach known as 'synthetic phonics' should be taught in England to young children on entry to school. Clark alerts readers to the worrying recommendation in the Rose Report that 'Engaging young children in interesting and worthwhile pre-reading activities paves the way for the great majority to make a good start on systematic phonic work by the age of five: indeed for some an earlier start may be possible and desirable' (quoted in Clark, 2006: 27).

The National Curriculum

The National Curriculum was introduced in 1988 with the following aims:

- To establish an entitlement for all pupils irrespective of background, race, culture, gender, differences in abilities or disabilities.
- To establish standards.
- To promote continuity and coherence.
- To promote public understanding.

When children move on to Key Stage 1 (see Table 2.2), the National Curriculum, National Literacy Strategy and National Numeracy Strategy direct the learning and teaching experiences in Year 1 and Year 2 classrooms. Children experience the Literacy Hour and Numeracy Hour daily, and are assessed at the end of Year 2 on their achievement in English and Mathematics. The other subjects taught as part of the National Curriculum in Key Stage 1 are Science, Design and Technology, Information Technology, History, Geography, Art, Music and Physical Education, with Religious Education as an additional statutory area and Personal, Social and Health Education as a non-statutory area of study.

Until 2005, children aged six to seven years were assessed by SATs (Standard Assessment Tasks) but policy changed following the Excellence and Enjoyment trial in 2004. Children's final levels of achievement in English and Mathematics at the end of Key Stage 1 are now teacher- assessed on the basis of their performance over the Key Stage. (Curriculum frameworks and guidance are available from www.qca.org.uk and www. teachernet.org.uk)

> A child in England is likely to have been in full-time education for two years by the age of six, whereas many European countries have a policy of starting school education when children are seven years of age. To what extent do you think the curriculum offered to children in England up to the age of eight is appropriate? In what ways do you think it should be modified? You would note that Suraya's family were able to transfer her to a different primary school when they became unhappy at the formality of the education she was receiving and its affect on her. How likely is it that such opportunity is widely available?

SPECIAL EDUCATIONAL NEEDS

The Warnock Report (DES, 1978) raised the profile of children with special educational needs (SEN) including those children under five years of age (see Clark, 1988). The Education Act 1981 legislated for the assessment of young children with SEN to be undertaken by local authorities (child development centres, for example) for early intervention and surveillance purposes. The Warnock Report's recommendations led to more children with SEN being integrated into mainstream schools as opposed to being educated in special schools. Special education, however, remains controversial: Warnock herself has reneged on her original recommendations and a report from the Select Committee on Special Educational Needs levels severe criticisms at government. It stated that the current government lacks vision and strategy for the education of children with SEN; that the direction of travel needs to be clearly communicated that policy needs to be child-centred; that the workforce needs to be developed and strategy needs to be brought to the core of policy as opposed to being marginalised (NCB, 2006).

The SEN *Code of Practice* (DfES, 2001) is based on inclusive principles, where children and parents are involved in the development of Individual Education Plans (IEPs), case conferences and other decision-making that has an impact on a child and their family. Settings have to have a regard for the SEN code of practice, but it is not statutory. Assessment may result in a Statement of Special Educational Need, in which the child's legal entitlement to support is set out. Early intervention for babies and very young children is considered essential, but depends on both the adults who care for and work with them and their families. The SureStart initiative is intended to provide support for early intervention in deprived areas, but could also be considered as contributing to the surveillance approach in helping children with SEN.

The Special Educational Needs and Disability Act (SENDA) in 2001 reinforced parental right in seeking a mainstream school for their child and also their right to ask for a place in a special school if they wanted it for their child. From September 2002, the Disability Discrimination Act (DDA) 1995 was extended to cover all education settings. Reasonable steps now have to be taken to ensure that disabled children are not disadvantaged in any way. The issues of segregation and integration have created contention amongst many, particularly as the publication of league tables for primary schools has become the focus of both media and public attention. Schools are expected to show, through league tables, how their pupils are continually raising their achievement through increased attainment levels in SATs (Standard Assessment Tasks and Tests). In the early days of league table publication, statistical data did not take account of socio-economic factors or the number of children with SEN attending a school. Headteachers experienced a tension between expectations to show increased achievement on the one hand, and supporting the integration of pupils with SEN on the other. As Ofsted admitted, inequalities still exist for children with SEN: 'Too little had been done nationally to focus schools' attention on improving the achievement of pupils in the lowest quartile' (Ofsted, 2006b: 15). Statistical data on pupil achievement have changed to include 'in school Performance and Assessment reports of factors such as social deprivation, SEN, and prior attainment' (Ofsted, 2006b: 17), but the damage has been done. Some schools still continue to grapple with inclusion.

> What are the issues for adults working with children from birth to eight with special educational needs in terms of integration and inclusion? How does this vary with the age of the child and the child's special needs? What problems arise as a consequence of the Standard Assessment Tasks/Test levels expected of children in England?

SAFEGUARDING CHILDREN

The discourse over recent years has changed from 'child protection' to 'safeguarding children'. What has created such change in England, and what are the implications? The Children Act 1948 created separate services for children, and the evolution of the welfare state following the Second World War promoted an interventionist approach. In the 1970s it became apparent that issues of child welfare were too complex for existing policy (Parton, 2006).

Reports into child abuse – following the deaths of Maria Colwell, aged seven in 1973, Jasmine Beckford, aged four in 1984, Tyra Henry and Kimberley Carlile (both in 1987) – contributed to the legislation set out in the Children Act 1989. Tensions between the rights of families and professional responsibilities needed to be acknowledged, and the ensuing principles of the Children Act 1989 were an attempt to recognise these and to promote negotiation, partnership and support (Parton, 2006). Key terms were 'a child in need' and 'significant harm'. However, the structures in place as a result of the Children Act 1989 failed to prevent the death of Victoria Climbié in 2000 aged eight. A key finding of the *Laming Report* (2003), following her death was that there were ineffective lines of communication between professionals and across agencies with responsibility for Victoria's welfare and safety. Also, preceding Lord Laming's report was a Department of Health publication *The National Service Framework for Children, Young People and Maternity Services* (DH, 2002). The concept of safeguarding children clearly demanded greater understanding. Both reports recommended a strategy to promote effective inter-agency working, with shared understanding of how to safeguard children at risk.

The subsequent Green Paper, *Every Child Matters* (DfES, 2003) was arrived at through consultation with children and young people and proposed five outcomes (being healthy, staying safe, enjoying and achieving, making a positive contribution, economic well-being). The provision for children and young people to achieve the five outcomes were SureStart Children's Centres; full service extended schools; the Young People's Fund, Child and Adolescent Mental Health Services (CAMHS); the *National Service Framework for Children* (DH, 2004) and tackling homelessness and reforms to the youth justice system. The focus here was on supporting parents and carers, early intervention and effective protection, accountability and integration, and workforce reform.

The Children Act 2004 legislated for the proposals in the Green Paper: key aspects were the duty on agencies to co-operate; the introduction of Local Safeguarding Children Boards; resources from health, care and education to come together to create Children's Trusts; appointing a Children's Commissioner for England; creating an integrated inspection framework for all children's and young people's services, and appointing a Director of Children's Services for each local authority. *Every Child Matters, Change for Children* (DfES, 2004a) sets out how services were to be integrated at local level and supported by the integrated inspection framework, alongside any funding allocations.

In April 2006, further guidance on how professionals would be supported in working together to safeguard children was published by the DfES. This included information sharing and the Information Sharing Index; the Common Assessment Framework and guidance on the role of the Lead Professional; and allowing standardised systems to be used in all children's services, by all who work with children and young people.

Significant questions still need to be asked about the role of children and families in the shifting landscape of children's welfare, and also how professionals are beginning to work together to safeguard children. Franks (2006) reports the findings from research carried out with African refugee families in Tyne and Wear, in the North East region of England. Although not representative of all communities and families with whom care and health professionals may work, these findings can provide some insight into the challenges for such professionals. The report states, 'The findings challenge us to understand that there are cultural differences which require understanding through the development of trusting relationships within an environment that is often experienced as confrontational and hostile' (Franks, 2006: iv).

The issues are complex and the summary here does not allow for debate and discussion of policy, systems and practice to safeguard children, but as Parton (2006) acknowledges:

> the current process of reconfiguration is explicitly transformational in its intent so that few vestiges will remain of what was put in place in the early 1970s. In the process, the use of both social work and the family as the primary mechanisms for ensuring the welfare of children is changing. (Parton, 2006: 28)

There is work to be done in moving from the interventionist approach of post-war welfare support in England to the preventive approach intended in present policy. New uncertainties and change may create shifting sand for such policy. It is important to ask whether the state, by taking on a surveillance role and threatening childhood by exercising control, through legislation for example, is allowing genuine participation and freedom. (See Parton, 2006, for a more detailed analysis of safeguarding children in England.)

> What are the implications of the recent measures in terms of children's human rights to privacy and to be kept safe? Study the Common Assessment Framework, the role of the Lead Professional and the Information Sharing Index on the *Every Child Matters* website (see Useful Websites information at the end of this chapter), and reflect on issues of recording and sharing information between professionals.

QUALITY ASSURANCE

The Education and Inspection Bill 2006 caused controversy in the popular media due to the creation of 'trust' schools and the autonomy associated with such a status. Other key changes within the bill are allowing more parental input; fairer admissions; free transport for the most disadvantaged families; new nutritional standards for food and drink in local authority maintained schools and the merging of existing inspectorates into a single inspectorate to cover the full range of services for children and young people. The latter changes particularly arise from the Green Paper *Every Child Matters* (DfES, 2003) and the Children Act 2004.

The Office for Standards in Education for England (Ofsted) took over the inspection of education and social services childcare provision (previously undertaken by social services) as part of the National Childcare Strategy in 1998, and this added to their role as the inspectorate for children and learners in England that started in 1993. Ofsted is independent of the government but accountable to it, appointing teams of staff to undertake inspections of childcare settings, schools, colleges, children's services, teacher training and youth work. Inspections are based on how settings work with the regulations that apply to them and how they perform within appropriate inspection frameworks. They inspect schools providing the National Curriculum at all key stages, including the Foundation Stage for children aged three to five years.

Daycare standards for five types of daycare – sessional (such as pre-schools), crèche, childminding, full daycare and 'out of school' care – were introduced in 2001 (Ofsted, 2001). There are 14 standards that settings are expected to meet, relating to suitable persons; organisation; care, learning and play; physical environment and equipment, for example. Private providers, such as childminders and pre-schools, may offer teaching and learning for the Foundation Stage and can receive a Nursery Education Grant for the children aged three to five years in their care, if the practitioners are able to show, when inspected, how they plan for learning and teaching within the Foundation Stage guidance (QCA, 2000).

Until April 2005, the inspection regime required separate inspections for nursery education and Foundation Stage settings conducted by teams of schools inspectors from Ofsted, and teams from the Early Years Directorate (a separate arm of Ofsted) who would inspect childcare settings working within daycare standards. An integrated system has now been introduced by Ofsted, and inspections take place with minimal notice. Settings are inspected soon after registration with Ofsted, and thereafter every three years unless the setting is judged to have weaknesses. The inspection framework is intended to assess what it is like to be a child in each setting, and uses a self-evaluation system. Settings are advised to use the self-evaluation system (linked to the five outcomes in *Every Child Matters* (DfES, 2003), as well as the relevant daycare standards, as a tool for ongoing quality assurance. Inspectors talk to everyone in the setting to inform their judgement, and the outcomes are categorised as unsatisfactory, satisfactory, good, or excellent. Ofsted regulates early education childcare through a regime of registration, inspection, investigation (following complaints, for example) and enforcement.

PROFESSIONAL DEVELOPMENT AND TRAINING

A wide range of people work with children in education and childcare settings, in England: nursery nurses, childminders, classroom assistants, teachers and nursery assistants, for example. There is a tradition that people who work in education and childcare are generally women, and pay and status are low (DfES, 2002). The challenge to bring about change in the gender balance in the childcare workforce, in all settings including primary schools in England, is one yet to be overcome, as well as retaining the workforce (Cameron et al., 2001). Childcare workers earn £6 per hour on average, as compared to nursing auxiliaries and assistants in the health sector who earned £6.70 per hour in England in 2003 (DfES, 2005a). The level of training for those working in childcare (indeed the care sector in general) has also remained low (Cohen et al., 2004; Bertram and Pascal, 2001) and perpetuates the low status and esteem of the profession.

The National Childcare Strategy (DfEE, 1998) set out the newly-elected Labour government's vision for raising the qualifications profile of the childcare workforce. As part of the initial reorganisation, when care and education came together under local authority control, the gap between the pay and conditions of those working in school nurseries and those working in social services day nurseries became apparent (Sylva and Pugh, 2005). The government introduced a national framework for accredited qualifications to explain levels, occupational areas and nominal standards and to promote a more transparent, and accessible, range of qualifications (QCA, 1999).

The Ten Year Strategy (HM Treasury, 2004), building on the National Childcare Strategy, outlined the vision for ensuring quality through workforce reform. Elements of the strategy included

> a new qualification and career structure; offering access to professional support and continuous professional development to childminders and other home-based childcarers; a reformed regulatory framework and inspection regime; local authorities working in partnership with childcare providers to support continued improvement. (TEN, 2004: 4–5)

The Childcare Act 2006 has now legislated for the inspection framework, for local authorities to provide affordable and flexible childcare, and for having strategies in place to promote all providers (whether private, voluntary or independent) to work together.

Some reports into the Early Years and childcare workforce in England explore possibilities for development and reformation, concepts of pedagogy (drawing on Scandinavian models), and universality and integration (such as Moss, 2003, and Cameron, 2004). Others provide insight into statistics and outcomes from surveys involving members of the workforce (Cameron et al., 2001; Sauve Bell, 2004). Conclusions from these papers are unanimous in their agreement that the childcare workforce in England needs to be reformed. Results from the Effective Provision of Pre-School Education (EPPE) research show not only the importance of a well-qualified workforce in supporting effective early learning for young children, but also that the workforce will benefit in its own self-esteem as its qualifications profiles are raised (Sylva et al., 2003). There is also a debate about the extent to which effective early learning for young children is merely 'preparatory' or acts as a time for immersion and being a child of two, three or four years of age.

The Children's and Young People's Workforce Development Council (CWDC) was launched in April 2005 with a remit to improve the lives of children and young people by ensuring that those working with children have the best possible training, qualifications, support and advice. *The Common Core* (DfES, 2005c) aims to promote skills and knowledge that will be needed by the children's and young people's workforce, as part of the workforce reform in England. It sets out six areas of expertise: effective communication and engagement; child and young person development; safeguarding and promoting the welfare of the child; supporting transitions; multi-agency working and sharing information. These areas of expertise are intended to develop knowledge and practice to 'promote equality, respect diversity and challenge diversity helping to improve life chances' (DfES, 2005c: 4).

As part of the children's workforce reform, the Integrated Qualifications Framework (IQF) is intended to allow progression for those who work with children and young people in health, education and care professions in vertical and horizontal dimensions. It is envisaged that there will be specialist routes within the IQF (Early Years, School Workforce, for example) and that routes will allow progression from level 1 to Masters level. The range of courses available currently to the childcare workforce begins at Entry level (pre-Level 1) to specialist Foundation Degrees (including the SureStart Sector Endorsed Foundation Degree in Early Years) at level 5, Honours degree at level 6, and the National Professional Qualification for Integrated Centre Leadership (NPQICL) at Masters level (level 7).

In March 2006, the DfES published a consultation document asking for views on proposed workforce reform, including having an Early Years graduate in every Children's Centre by 2010, and every childcare setting by 2015. The proposal is to create an Early Years Professional who will be assessed against national standards in order to be given the title and status of Early Years Professional (EYP). The first cohort of graduates is being assessed during 2006, and the national standards may be modified as a result of the pilot. The current government has allocated a transformation fund to support financial demands on private, voluntary and independent settings, for example, in paying for training and increased salaries for graduates and retaining well-qualified staff.

It remains to be seen how the workforce reform is implemented at local level. Early Years Development and Childcare Partnerships (EYDCPs) are currently working with their local partners to provide information and guidance about government strategies and funding. Schools, further education colleges, higher education institutions, and Connexions advisers (who offer career and employment advice to young people) are all involved in ensuring that there are opportunities for those school leavers considering, or training for, a career working with children and young people that meet the overall vision. Some may find the workforce reforms challenge deepseated attitudes about what working with young children means.

What impact will the intention to raise the qualification profile of the workforce in England have on young people making career choices, as well as those (some childminders for example) who may decide later in life to take up childcare as a career?

Note the important role played by childminders in supporting the families of both Michael and Suraya. Investigate the extent to which childminders and their role have been taken into account in plans for the future of early education and care in England.

Some childcare, health and social care practitioners may be joining a multi-professional team for the first time in a Children's Centre, for example. What challenges may face them?

FUTURE AND IMMINENT CHANGES

Imagine a child born in 2006: she is called Maisie, and she lives in Newham in London. Maisie should, if policy is delivered, have some different experiences from Suraya and Michael. Maisie should be able to be cared for in a setting that her parents have chosen for its affordability and proximity. If Maisie attends a Children's Centre, the number of transitions she will experience in her early childhood should be reduced as care is more continuous than the fragmented experiences of Michael and Suraya. Maisie will have access to a single curriculum framework from birth to when she starts school. Maisie should be cared for by a childcarer who is qualified to at least level 2, in a setting that is led by a graduate. Maisie's parents should have easier access to health care and support in seeking employment and training, if they want it.

I fear that Maisie may still have to start school at four years of age in England, however, and in 2006 the government had shown no sign of abolishing the National Curriculum. Maisie will have to be content with the transition from the Early Years Foundation Stage to Key Stage 1. It will be a challenge for the reforming Early Years workforce to ensure that there is not a 'top down' influence exerted on the Early Years Foundation Stage, but instead a flow from 'bottom up' with early childhood experiences and learning informing the initial learning in Key Stage 1.

Maisie will more likely be in a lone parent household, yet the chances that she will be living in poverty may be reduced. Tax credits and childcare vouchers should provide financial support for Maisie's parents. When Maisie starts school in 2010, her parents may choose to use the full service provision available if they are in employment, offering care for Maisie from 8 am to 6 pm before and after school. Maisie should have healthy meals, drinks and snacks available to her in school and in her childcare setting.

In what ways do you think children such as Maisie, born in 2006 in England, will experience improved early education and care in England as a consequence of the anticipated changes? How positively do you view the imminent changes proposed in early education and care in England? What challenges do you consider there are for family life and children's early childhood as a result of the proposed developments?

TOPICS FOR DISCUSSION

Early Years Foundation Stage

Will the Early Years Foundation Stage from 2008 be implemented as a 'curriculum for babies' as feared by some observers? How will one framework for all Early Years settings impact on the broad range of provision currently on offer? How will practitioners work with, and understand, the principles within the framework? Will there continue to be downward pressure exerted on the Early Years Foundation Stage from the National Curriculum to ensure children are 'prepared' for formal education at five years, as opposed to having an opportunity to be immersed in childhood (*Education*, 2006)? What will be the impact of the 'synthetic phonics' approach to teaching reading endorsed by the government in 2006?

Early Years Professional Status

How will the implementation of the Early Years Professional be received by the workforce? How well informed is the workforce of the changes being imposed at national level? What will be the impact of having Early Years Professionals leading Early Years Foundation Stage settings on nursery and Reception teachers? How will the Integrated Qualifications Framework support workers from health and care moving into the Early Years workforce and vice versa? Will there be more men, more workers from minority ethnic backgrounds, better retention in the workforce?

Children's Centres and Children's Services

Will the national targets for Children's Centres and established extended schools by 2010 be achieved? Will the challenge of multi-agency working be embraced so that there will be clearer communication and awareness of the varying cultures and protocol within health, education and care? Will local children's services be successful in developing and facilitating the childcare market? Will Children's Centres in deprived and disadvantaged areas deliver the flexible entitlement to Early Years education? Will the reconfiguration of services ensure that children are safeguarded, with none slipping through the safety net?

Language of Early Years Care and Education

How will the language of Early Years care and education evolve? Will the language maintain the concept of difference between 'care' and 'education' that has had such an historical and fundamental influence on the evolution of services for young children and their families in England? Will 'pedagogy' be assimilated more into the language of Early Years education? Will there be a shared language between and across professionals working in children's services? Will participation become an accepted and expected experience for children, young people and parents, or will the language of policy and practice convey an implicit sense of children and young people having policy 'done to them'?

KEY MILESTONES IN GOVERNMENT STRATEGY FOR EARLY CHILDHOOD EDUCATION AND CARE IN ENGLAND

2006

- increase in the maximum proportion of eligible childcare costs covered by the childcare element of Working Tax Credit to 80 per cent
- entitlement to 12.5 hours free early education and childcare to increase to 38 weeks a year for all three and four year olds
- £250 million 'Transformation Fund' to come on stream from April 2006 until August 2008
- most local authorities to have Directors of Children's Services and Children's Trusts in place
- consultation on proposals for a new quality framework for the care and education of children from birth to five.

2007

- paid maternity leave extended to 39 weeks
- entitlement to free early education and childcare for three and four year olds extended to 15 hours a week for first cohort of children.

2008

- Children's Centres in 2,500 communities
- half of all families to have access to school-based care for five to eleven year olds
- one third of secondary schools open from 8 am to 6 pm offering extended services
- new legal framework for local authorities (Children's Services) to be in place
- reformed regulation and inspection system for the early years and childcare to be in place supported by a new birth to five quality framework
- all local authorities to have Directors of Children's Services and Children's Trusts.

2010

- all parents of three and four year olds offered access to wrap-around childcare, linked to the early education offer and available all year round from 8 am to 6 pm weekdays
- 15 hours a week free Early Years provision for all three and four year olds, for 38 weeks a year
- all parents of children aged 5–11 to have access to childcare from 8 am to 6 pm weekdays all year round, based in their school or early education provider, or nearby with supervised transfer arrangements
- all secondary schools open from 8 am to 6 pm weekdays providing extended services
- Children's Centres in 3,500 communities, with Early Years provision led by an Early Years Professional graduate
- goal of 12 months paid maternity leave, transferable to the father by the end of the next parliament.
  (Adapted from TEN, 2004)

REFERENCES

Adams S., Alexander E., Drummond M.J. and Moyles, J. (2004) *Inside the Foundation Stage: Recreating the reception year*. London: Association of Teachers and Lecturers.

Aries, P. (1962) *Centuries of Childhood*. London: Cape.

Baldock P., Fitzgerald, D. and Kay, J. (2005) *Understanding Early Years Policy*. London: Paul Chapman.

Ball, S. J. and Vincent, C. (2005) 'The children's champion? New Labour, social justice and the childcare market', *British Educational Research Journal*, 31 (5): 557–70.

Barn, R. with Ladino, C. and Rogers, B. (2006) *Parenting in Multi-racial Britain*. York: Joseph Rowntree Foundation. Available online at www.jrf.org.uk/knowledge/findings

Bertram, T. and Pascal, C. (2001) *The OECD Thematic Review of Early Childhood Education and Care: Background report for the UK*. Available online at www.oecd.org/

Bryson, C., Bell, A., La Valle, I., Barnes, M. and O'Shea, R. (2005) *Use of Childcare Among Families from Minority Ethnic Backgrounds and Among Families with Children with Special Educational Needs*. National Centre for Social Research. DfES London: SureStart.

Cameron, C. (2004) *Building an Integrated Workforce for a Long Term Vision of Universal Early Education and Care*. Policy Paper Number 3. Available at www.daycare trust.org.uk

Cameron, C., Owen, C. and Moss, C. (2001) *Entry, Retention and Loss: A study of childcare students and workers*. Research Brief Number 275. London: DfES.

Children's Rights Alliance for England (CRAE) (2005) *The State of Children's Rights in England*. London: CRAE.

Children's Society (2006) *The Good Childhood Inquiry*. Available online at www.childrenssociety.org.uk/goodchildhood/

Clark, M.M. (1988) *Children Under Five: Educational research and evidence*. London: Gordon and Breach.

Clark, M.M. (2004) 'Education in England and Wales: what can we learn from the census?', *Primary Practice*, No 36, Spring: 35–8.

Clark, M.M. (2005) *Understanding Research in Early Education: The relevance for the future of lessons from the past* (2nd edn). Abingdon: Routledge.

Clark, M.M. (2006) 'The Rose Report in context: what will be its impact on the teaching of reading?', *Education Journal*, Issue 97: 26–9.

Cohen, B., Moss, P., Petrie, P. and Wallace, J. (2004) *A New Deal for Children? Re-forming education and care in England, Scotland and Sweden*. Bristol: The Policy Press.

Community Playthings (2006) *Pen Green: A Case Study of a Centre of Excellence*. Available online at www.communityplaythings.co.uk

Cummings, C., Dyson, A., Papps, I., Pearson, D., Raffo, C. and Todd, L. (2005) *Evaluation of the Full Service Extended Schools Project: End of year report*. Research Brief Number 680. London: DfES.

David, T. (1990) *Under Five – Under-educated?* Buckingham: Open University Press.

Daycare Trust (2006) *Ensuring Equality: Black and minority ethnic families' view on childcare*. London: National Centre for Social Research.

Department for Education and Employment (DfEE) (1998) *Meeting the Childcare Challenge*. London: The Stationery Office.

Department for Education and Skills (DfES) (2001) *Code of Practice for Children with Special Educational Needs*. London: DfES.

Department for Education and Skills (DfES) (2002) *Childcare Workforce Surveys 2001: Overview*. London: DfES.

Department for Educations and Skills (DfES) (2003) *Every Child Matters. The Green Paper*. London: The Stationery Office.

Department for Education and Skills (DfES) (2004a) *Every Child Matters, Change for Children*. London: DfES.

Department for Education and Skills (DfES) (2004b) *Provision for Children Under 5 years of Age in England – January 2004* (provisional). Available online at www.dfes.gov.uk/rsgateway/DB/SFR/

Department for Education and Skills (DfES) (2005a) *Labour Force Survey,* (Winter 2003). London: DfES.

Department for Education and Skills (DfES) (2005b) *Children looked after in England (including adoptions and care leavers) 2004–5*. London. National Statistics.

Department for Education and Skills (DfES) (2005c) *The Common Core of Skills and Knowledge for the Children's Workforce*. London: DfES.

Department for Education and Skills (DfES) (2006a) *About the Department*. Available online at www.dfes.gov.uk/aboutus/

Department for Education and Skills (DfES) (2006b) *The Early Years Foundation Stage*. London: DfES.

Department of Education and Science (DES) (1967) *Children and their Primary Schools: A report of the Central Advisory Council for Education (England) Vol 1,* (The Plowden Report). London: HMSO.

Department of Education and Science (DES) (1978) *Report of the Committee of Inquiry into the Education of Handicapped Children and Young People* (The Warnock Report). London: HMSO.

DH (2002) *Safeguarding Children: A joint chief inspectors' report on arrangements to safeguard children.* London: Department of Health.

DH (2003) *What To Do If You're Worried a Child is Being Abused.* London: Department of Health.

DH (2004) *The National Service Framework for Children, Young People and Maternity Services.* London: Department of Health.

Education (2006) 'Early schooling robs kids of childhood', *Education* No: 232, 4th August.

Fabian, H. (2002) *Children Starting School: A guide to successful transitions and transfers for teachers and assistants.* London: David Fulton.

Franks, M. (2006) *Safeguarding and Promoting the Welfare of Children in the African Refugee Community in Newcastle.* London: The Children's Society Research Unit.

Gelder, U. and Savage, J. (2004) 'Children and social policy: a case study of four year olds in school', in J. Willan, R. Parker-Ress and J. Savage (eds), *Early Childhood Studies,* Chapter 5. Exeter: Learning Matters.

Home Office (2006) Accession Monitoring Report May 2004–June 2006. Available online at news.bbc.co.uk/1/shared/bsp/hi/pdfs/22_08_06_migrant workers.pdf

HM Treasury (2004) *Choice for Parents, the Best Start for Children: A ten year strategy for Childcare.* London: The Stationery Office.

Horton, C. (ed.) (2005) *Working with Children 2006–07: Facts, figures and information.* London: Sage/Guardian Books.

Laming Report (2003) *The Victoria Climbié Inquiry: Report of an inquiry by Lord Laming* (Cm 5730). London: The Stationery Office.

Moss, P. (2003) *Beyond Caring: The case for reforming the childcare and early years workforce.* (Policy Paper No: 5). Available at: www.daycaretrust.org.uk

National Children's Bureau (NCB) (2006) 'Select Committee on Special Educational Needs', *Bulletin of the Early Childhood Unit,* July.

Office for National Statistics (2006) *The 2001 Census.* Available online at www.nso.gov.uk

Ofsted (2001) *Guidance to the National Standards.* London: Ofsted.

Ofsted (2004) *Transition from Reception Year to Year One* (HMI Report No: 2221). London: Ofsted.

Ofsted (2006a) *Quarterly Childcare Statistics as at 30th June 2006.* London: Ofsted. Available online at www.ofsted.org.uk

Ofsted (2006b) *Inclusion: Does it matter where pupils are taught?* (HMI Report No: 2535). London: Ofsted.

Parton, N. (2006) *Safeguarding Childhood.* Basingstoke: Palgrave.

Penn, H. (2006) 'Poor Show', *Nursery World,* 22 June.

Qualifications and Curriculum Authority (QCA) (1999) *Early Years Education, Childcare and Playwork: A framework of nationally accredited qualifications.* London: QCA.

Qualifications and Curriculum Authority (QCA) (2000) *Curriculum Guidance for the Foundation Stage.* London: QCA.

Qualifications and Curriculum Authority (QCA) (2003) *The Foundation Stage Profile.* London: QCA.

Rose, J. (2006) *Independent Review of the Teaching of Early Reading* (Final Report). Available online at www.standards.dfes.gov.uk/rosereview/

Ruxton, S. (2001) 'Towards a 'Children's Policy' for the European Union?' in P. Foley, J. Roche and S. Tucker (eds), *Children in Society*. Basingstoke: Palgrave.

Sanders, D., White, G., Burge, B., Sharp, C., Eames, A., McEune, R. and Grayson, H. (2005) *A Study of the Transition from the Foundation Stage to Key Stage 1* (DfES Research Report SSU/2005/FR/013). London: DfES.

Sauve Bell (2004) *Early Years Childcare and Playwork Workforce Development* (Final Report). Ampthill: Sauve Bell Associates.

School Curriculum and Assessment Authority (SCAA) (1996) *Nursery Education: Desirable Outcomes for Children's Learning*. London: DfEE.

SureStart (2003) *Birth to Three Matters: A framework to support children in their earliest years*. London: DfES/SureStart.

Sylva, K. and Pugh, G. (2005) 'Transforming the Early Years in England', *Oxford Review of Education*, 31(1): 11–27.

Sylva, K., Melhuish, E., Sammons, P., Siraj-Blatchford, I., Taggart, B. and Elliott, K. (2003) *The Effective Provision of Pre-School Education (EPPE) Project: Findings from the Pre-school Period* (Research Report Brief 2503). London: DfES.

The Education Network (TEN) (2004) *Policy Briefing on the Ten Year Strategy*. (No: 54/04). 10th December.

Tunstill, J., Meadows, P., Alnock, D., Akhurst, S., Chryanthou, J., Garbers, C., Morley, A. and van de Velde, T. (2005) *Implementing SureStart Local Programmes: An In Depth Study*. London: SureStart Unit.

Waller, T. (2005) 'Modern Childhood: contemporary theories and children's lives', in T. Waller (ed.), *An Introduction to Early Childhood*. London: Paul Chapman.

World Health Organisation (WHO) (2004) *Young People's Health in Context, Health Behaviour in School-aged Children (HBSC) Study*. London: WHO.

Yeo, A. and Lovell, T. (2002) *Sociology and Social Policy for the Early Years*. London: Hodder and Stoughton.

USEFUL WEBSITES

www.childrennow.co.uk   Weekly journal for the young people's and children's workforce

www.crae.org.uk   Children's Rights Alliance for England website

www.dfes.gov.uk   Department for Education and Skills website

www.everychildmatters.gov.uk   Website with useful information, policy and links relating to the government policy headed *Every Child Matters*

www.oecd.org   Organisation for Economic Co-operation and Development website, for information on *Starting Strong* (2001) and *Starting Strong II: Early childhood education and care* (2006)

www.ofsted.org.uk   Non-governmental organisation with responsibility for inspection and regulation of Early Years care and education in England

www.ncb.org.uk   National Children's Bureau website

www.nurseryworld.co.uk   Weekly journal for the Early Years workforce

www.qca.org.uk   Non-governmental organisation with responsibility for qualifications and assessment website

www.surestart.gov.uk   Information, policy and links relating to the national SureStart initiative and local SureStart information

www.teachernet.org.uk   Information for teachers and school managers

NORTHERN 3 IRELAND

Glenda Walsh

A CHILD BORN IN NORTHERN IRELAND IN 2000: HOLLY'S STORY

Holly was born in February 2000. Her family consists of her mother (Margaret), her father (John) and one older brother (Matthew), who was four years old when Holly was born. They also enjoy a large extended family, with both sets of grandparents living close by. They live in a detached, four bedroom dwelling in a small village in County Tyrone. John is an accountant by profession and Margaret is a primary school teacher. Both are qualified to degree level; John has a BSc in Chartered Accountancy and Margaret has a BEd, specialising in English. Both have been working on a full-time basis. Margaret returned to full-time employment when Matthew was four months old, and as a consequence the family could be described as being reasonably comfortable financially. They also receive child benefit for the two children.

After Holly's birth, Margaret returned to work in August 2000. Margaret's maternity leave lasted a period of 18 weeks. John also took one week's unpaid paternity leave, the first week after Holly returned from hospital. When Holly was six months old and Matthew was about to go into P1 (the first year of primary school in Northern Ireland) Margaret returned to the P5 classroom. Initially, Holly was looked after by Margaret's mother but unfortunately, in late 2000, Margaret's father suffered a stroke and so her mother could no longer look after the children. For the first time Margaret and John had to seek alternative childcare arrangements. They decided upon a registered childminder who lived in the local village and who would be willing to collect Matthew from school. Margaret was able to bring Matthew to school and Margaret's mother was able to assist whenever the children were poorly.

When Holly was three years old, she attended the playgroup in the nearby village. John and Margaret had high academic aspirations for their children but Margaret knew that Holly would probably not get a place in a local nursery school because of where they lived and more importantly because of their financial circumstances. Also the playgroup would be more practical in terms of getting Holly collected. Holly spent one and a half years at the playgroup. She started there when she had just turned three, on an afternoon basis three days per week 12:30–2 pm, and attended on a full-time basis Monday to Friday from 9am–12 noon from September 2003.

There were four members of staff at the playgroup – one playgroup leader who had an Early Childhood Studies degree and three playgroup assistants, one of whom was trained to NVQ Level 3 and the others to NVQ Level 2. Another young girl assisted in the playgroup, but as yet she was unqualified. Holly's parents had to pay £5.00 per day for the afternoon session and as Holly had received a funded place, only £5.00 per week for the full-time session. This reduced the childcare costs, to some extent, for the family. The care and education that Holly received at the local playgroup were provided in line with the Curricular Guidance for Pre-school Education, issued in 1997 (DHSS, CCEA and DENI, 1997). It is based on the premise that children learn best through play.

Holly began compulsory schooling in September 2004 at four and a half years old at the same primary school as Matthew. Holly and Matthew are lucky that their mother teaches at the school they attend which means that they can play in their mum's classroom until school commences at 8:45 am. As there is no Breakfast Club at the school, other working parents have much more difficulty as children are not allowed on the premises until 8:40 am. The school has approximately 170 pupils and Holly was taught in a class of 26 in both P1 and P2. The school has a good academic reputation in terms of the 11+ (an examination taken in early P7 which determines whether children attend grammar or secondary schooling) and conforms to a formal style of classroom management where the children are expected to sit for the majority of the day and the teacher is principally in control. The school follows the Northern Ireland Curriculum (DENI, 1996) and focuses particularly on the 3Rs, Reading, wRiting and aRithmetic. Holly has received reading homework from the October of her first year at school and at the end of P2 she appears to be progressing well. Her teacher has informed her parents that she is above average in the class in English, Mathematics and Science, however she did express a concern that Holly can be over anxious about certain activities and afraid of getting the wrong answer. Formal activities assume priority throughout the day.

In P1 and P2 the school begins four days per week with approximately 45 minutes of structured play (with the other morning being PE day), whilst the teacher on several of these occasions hears individual or groups of children read. These play activities tend to be followed by more reading- or writing- related tasks, which in many cases consist of colouring in, copying from the board, or completing simple worksheets. A break of approximately 15 minutes then follows during which the children eat a snack, go to the toilet and if the weather permits play outdoors. After this short pause the children return to a maths-related activity that tends to involve them in completing some form of worksheet. A phonic activity or handwriting exercise then follows. Lunch tends to take place at around 12:15 pm and lasts approximately 45 minutes.

After lunch the activities are less demanding, for example listening to a story, watching television, participating in songs and rhymes or completing an unfinished activity. School ends at 2 pm for most of Key Stage 1 (that is P1–3) and both Holly and Matthew are picked up by the childminder. Matthew has been staying later at school until 4 pm to undertake preparation for the 11+ and on a Thursday and Friday afternoons both Holly and Matthew stay late to take part in afternoon clubs (French and football respectively).

Holly's parents are fortunate, given the support they receive from their extended family in the upbringing of their children. Holly continues to do very well at school, despite her shy and reserved disposition. Her parents are trying to overcome this by ensuring that she becomes involved in local church activities such as Brownies and she has also recently been enrolled in swimming lessons at the local leisure centre as well as dancing sessions.

A CHILD BORN IN NORTHERN IRELAND IN 2000: RYAN'S STORY

Ryan was born on 1st July 2000. He lives with his mother (Sue) and his father (Mark). Sue and Mark were married for six months when Ryan arrived. Sue was 18 and Mark 21 when Ryan was born. Both parents left school at 16. Sue worked as a shop assistant in a large supermarket on a part-time basis and Mark works as a taxi driver. They live in a terraced house in a housing estate in north Belfast. Ryan was not planned but both Sue and Mark are committed to doing the best for him. Sue has given up work to look after Ryan as they would not be able to afford childcare arrangements. As for extended family support, Mark's mother and father are divorced and although his mother lives close by, she works on a regular basis and therefore cannot provide much support. Sue's family provides some help at the weekends, but both grandparents work on a full-time basis during the week.

As Mark's income is less than £12,000 per annum, they are eligible for government support initially by means of the Working Families Tax Credit and more recently the Working Tax Credit and Child Tax Credit. They are also eligible for child benefit.

Although Sue was responsible for caring for Ryan, she wanted to have the opportunity for both Ryan and herself to mix with others. For this reason she attended a local parent and toddler group and there learned about the Greater Shankill Partnership's Early Years Project (see the Greater Shankill Early Years Project website at www.earlyyears.org.uk/forward.htm for more details). The project offers personal support to families in the area on a voluntary self-referral basis, the purpose of which is to help parents and children alike. Sue found this project to be very worthwhile, and when Ryan began nursery school she decided to take up the opportunity to gain a qualification in childcare.

Ryan commenced nursery school in October 2002 at the age of two years and three months. In the area where he lives there is a surplus of nursery places and because of Ryan's circumstances he was eligible for two years in nursery. The nursery unit he attended is attached to the local primary school and has two classes. One class of 25 is full of rising four year olds and half of the other class consists of two and three year old children. In Ryan's class there was one qualified nursery teacher and a classroom assistant with a NVQ Level 2. The nursery followed the Pre-school Curricular Guidance for Northern Ireland (DHSS, CCEA and DENI, 1997) but no guidance material was available for the two year olds. The nursery teacher possessed a BEd qualification; however, she had specialised in KS2 and therefore had little experience of nursery-aged children when she commenced her job in September 2002, and no professional experience of working with two year olds. Sue walked Ryan to and from school daily.

In September 2004 Ryan commenced compulsory schooling at the age of four years and two months (the earliest possible school starting age in NI, as the cut-off point is 1 July of any given year). Ryan attends a local primary school with approximately 400 pupils – and three classes of about 20 pupils in each year group. It is involved in piloting an intervention known as the Enriched Curriculum (CCEA, NES and BELB, 2002). In this curriculum children experience a more play-based and practical approach to their early years of schooling in contrast to the more traditional Northern Ireland curriculum. A more varied curriculum is delivered, where the activities are shorter in duration.

In both P1 and P2 the day generally begins with a play session, where the children have some degree of choice as to their activity. The teacher (BA in Early Childhood Studies and PGCE in Early Years) and classroom assistant (NVQ Level 2) are both involved in the play session to assist learning, which lasts about one and a half hours. A plenary session concludes the play, encouraging the children to reflect on the play activities just completed. After playtime, a shared reading activity tends to take place. Using a large format book, the teacher focuses the children's attention on a particular reading skill, such as phonological awareness. Break-time follows where children have the opportunity to eat something and to play freely with their friends. The children then play outdoors, with time being spent on developing their gross motor skills. On returning to the classroom, practical mathematics usually begins involving a puppet, maths games and the computer. As the activities tend to be short and snappy there is usually time before lunch for a story and/or some rhymes.

Shared writing usually follows lunch where the emphasis is placed on the creative aspect of writing rather than the secretarial, although the teaching of letter formation is not ignored. The teacher acts as scribe on several occasions, encouraging the children to think imaginatively whereby they are responsible for creating the story, recipe, comic strip and so on. The day finishes in a relaxed fashion in the form of circle or story time with songs and rhymes.

Ryan is now in P3. Although he is not the most academic, he loves school and gives of his best. His mother has just finished her NVQ Level 3 in childcare and is about to start as a classroom assistant in Ryan's primary school.

Northern Ireland (NI) is one of the four constituent parts of the United Kingdom (UK). It is part of the island of Ireland, consisting of six counties: Antrim, Tyrone, Fermanagh, Armagh, Londonderry and Down. It covers 14,139 square kilometres and it has an estimated population of 1,710,300 (NISRA, 2005a). English is the native language, but recently (as a result of the Belfast Agreement; see NIO, 1998), Irish and Ulster-Scots have also been granted official recognition. At the same time there has been an increase of people from minority ethnic groups moving to NI (Save the Children, 2005) and it is anticipated that there will be a further increase in the next few years. The population is almost equally distributed between Protestant (45.5 per cent) and Roman Catholic (40.3 per cent) (Census, 2001). This political and religious divide has resulted in much contention and dispute throughout the province.

For over three decades Northern Ireland has been fraught with political and sectarian conflict. The region's community divisions can be traced back to the seventeeth century and the plantation of Ulster, when Protestant settlers were introduced from England and Scotland in an attempt by the English Crown to subdue Ireland's most Gaelic and Catholic province. Tensions between planter and Gael were sharpened by the religious warfare of the later 1600s. The future of the plantation scheme was finally secured by the Williamite victory at the Boyne in 1690 which placed power in the hands of an ascendancy-based Irish parliament.

In 1801, however, following the United Irish Rebellion against British rule, the British government passed the Act of Union, abolishing the Irish parliament and imposing 'direct rule' from Westminster. The nineteenth century saw the Irish Nationalist demand for Home Rule paralleled by the rise of Unionism among the Protestant population of the industrial north. A series of rebellions by the physical force section of Irish separatism culminated in the Easter rising of 1916, orchestrated by the Irish Republican Brotherhood (IRB). Although the rising was defeated, the subsequent execution of its leaders secured a wave of nationalist sympathy for an Irish republic. The Anglo-Irish War of 1919–21 resulted in the partitioning of Ireland into two states, the Irish Free State and Northern Ireland, in 1921.

Northern Ireland remained part of the UK under a Unionist-controlled devolved government at Stormont from 1921 until 1972. The Roman Catholic minority opposed partition and effectively formed 'a state within a state' with its own social infrastructure of Church, schools and cultural activities, while Unionist governments tended to favour their own supporters. Sectarian tensions erupted into violence in the 1920s and 1930s while the illegal Irish Republican Army (IRA) remained a threat to the state's existence. Such unrest came to the fore in Northern Ireland in August 1969, requiring the deployment of British troops. The 'Troubles' had begun. This period saw the birth of the Provisional IRA which launched a campaign of violence in pursuit of a united Irish Republic. The escalation of violence, involving the IRA, loyalist paramilitaries and the security forces, led the Conservative government in March 1972 to suspend the Northern Ireland parliament and to impose direct rule from London.

This did not end the bloodshed, however, and a series of attempted solutions in the 1970s and 1980s proved abortive. It was not until the paramilitary ceasefires of 1994 that Northern Ireland began to return to normality. (For an in-depth account of the history of the 'Troubles' in Northern Ireland see Phoenix, 1989).

The unremitting violence of 1968–94 resulted in the deaths of 391 children under 18 and 875 young people aged 18–24 (Save the Children, 2005). In addition many children and young people have experienced trauma in several ways including the loss of family members, the witnessing of violence and murder and the experience of riots and bombs (Ewart and Schubotz, 2004). Such conflict has resulted in widespread residential, educational and social segregation, reflected in the fact that 95 per cent of children attend schools segregated by religion and 80 per cent of social housing is also segregated (Kelly and Sinclair, 2003). Similarly such 'Troubles' have impacted on the local economy, whereby government monies have been invested in defending the country, and outside investors have been disinterested as a consequence of the violence. Moreover Northern Ireland children suffer high levels of poverty (32 per cent as compared to 19 per cent in the UK who are living in families totally dependent on benefits) and for many years there have been low levels of family support services (Horgan, 2005).

The picture however is not perhaps as bleak as it seems, particularly towards the latter part of the 1990s. In 1994 the combined Irish Republican Army and Loyalist ceasefires brought European investment through a special support programme for peace and reconciliation. From 1996 Northern Ireland has enjoyed a special relationship with the European Union and the International Fund for Ireland that provide it with increased financial investment. Furthermore the Belfast Agreement of 1998, granting devolved government, was envisaged as an 'historic milestone in recent political history in NI towards achieving lasting peace' (Donnelly et al., 2006: 1). This agreement brought hope not only in terms of economic growth and prosperity but also in its commitment to promoting a culture of tolerance, respect and inclusion. Despite the fragility of the peace process and the fact that the Assembly was still suspended in 2006 with direct rule once again reinstated, a number of policy developments has taken place that directly impact on young children's care and education. These will be considered later in this chapter.

Context

Although, as with England, Northern Ireland is still in 2006 subject to the administration of the United Kingdom's government in Westminster, it does have a number of distinctive features that influence Early Years education and care. It is necessary to highlight these differences at the beginning of this chapter to avoid any misunderstanding. Children in Northern Ireland are obliged to commence formal education in the September after their fourth birthday. Unlike children in England who attend Reception classes at this age, Northern Ireland children start in Primary 1 and are required, at present, to follow the requirements of the Northern Ireland Curriculum (DENI, 1996). Furthermore, unlike England, all children must commence primary school in the September of any given year.

> Refer to Holly's and Ryan's stories for details of just how different the curriculum could be for children in their first years at primary school. What would be the implications for the families and the children were all schools to offer a play-based curriculum such as Ryan was offered in the experimental project?

Northern Ireland's education system, although under review, is presently governed by a process of selection at the end of primary school known as the 11+. Early in Primary 7 the majority of children undertake an examination to determine whether they attend grammar school, if successful, or secondary school. Parents have the right to exempt their child from such an examination. If this happens the child will automatically attend the local secondary school; however, only a very small number of parents decide to do so. This examination focuses on English, Mathematics and more recently Science and, as a result, it could be argued that traditionally there has been a downward pressure on teachers in Northern Ireland to focus on the 3Rs, (Reading, wRiting and aRithmetic) from the outset of a child's primary education.

A further distinctive feature of the Northern Ireland education system is its segregated nature. Although pre-school education tends to be integrated in terms of religion, primary schools have been principally monocultural in that Protestants attend controlled schools governed by the state, and Catholics attend maintained schools partly maintained by the Roman Catholic church. The implications of this 'divided' education system for young children might be that their neighbour, particularly if in a rural community, or a pre-school peer might attend a different primary school simply because of their religious belief.

> Segregated schooling is a controversial topic, with the pros and cons of 'faith' schools being hotly debated in the UK. What dangers are there in the separation of primary schools by religion as in Northern Ireland? What challenges would Early Years practitioners/teachers face in playing a part in tackling sectarianism and prejudice in an Early years setting/classroom?

Northern Ireland is a society emerging from a history of conflict that has had major implications for young children growing up there. Not only has pre-school education and care suffered financially until very recently, but also many young children have experienced trauma that has impacted greatly on their emotional, social and physical well-being.

POLICY AND PRACTICE IN EARLY CHILDHOOD EDUCATION AND CARE

Pre-school developments

Early Years Education and Care (EYEC) in Northern Ireland has for many years been equated with pre-school education, that is, the period before formal schooling commences. Pre-school in Northern Ireland is provided in a range of settings in the statutory, voluntary and private sectors and falls principally under two departmental bodies, namely the Department of Education which oversees the statutory sectors and the Department of Health, Social Services and Public Safety which has responsibility for the private and voluntary sectors. Unlike England, health and social services are merged into one department in Northern Ireland. Provision has however, for many years, tended to be uneven and poorly co-ordinated, falling far short of the necessary requirements (DHSS, TEA and DENI, 1999). Before 1998 funded pre-school places were provided solely by the statutory sector in a combination of nursery schools and nursery units attached to primary schools. A number of primary schools, particularly in rural areas, also provided Reception classes for children in their pre-school year, provision that has been highlighted as being inappropriate for this age group (see Pascal, 1990, and Pinkerton, 1990). At that time organised childcare was the preserve of voluntary/private playgroups and day nurseries that did not receive any government funding (DENI, 2004a). Government interaction on this matter was limited whereby the early years of education and care in Northern Ireland were considered principally to be a parental concern.

Like the rest of the United Kingdom, things began to take a turn for the better during the 1990s. Government interest in the pre-school sector began to grow, stemming principally from the positive findings from an array of research literature highlighting the benefits for children, families, communities, society and the economy as a whole (see for example Schweinhart and Weikart, 1997). Radical social, economic and demographic changes have also been taking place in the last twenty years, the most significant for EYEC being the increase in the number of working mothers (the economic activity rate for women of working age with dependent children is currently 65 per cent in Northern Ireland as compared to 69 per cent in Great Britain; NISRA, 2006). Set in this context the government could no longer ignore the need for policy developments in this area. Fitzpatrick (2005) argues that the 1990s were also particularly significant for the politics of Northern Ireland. The Early Years sector benefited from the European investment granted as a result of the 1994 combined Irish Republican Army and Loyalist ceasefires. Approximately £42 million was allocated to Northern Ireland during 1994–2005 for pre-school places, training, staffing, buildings and innovative programmes.

Following significant reports such as *Starting with Quality*, more commonly known as *The Rumbold Report* (DES, 1990) and the *Start Right report* (Ball, 1994), the DHSS and the Department of Education for Northern Ireland jointly published in 1994 a report entitled *Policy on Early*

Years Provision for NI (DHSS and DENI, 1994). This report set out an array of principles and policy objectives in an attempt to maximise the quality and scope of pre-school provision. It also recommended that one year of pre-school provision should be made available for all those children under compulsory age whose parents wished to avail of it, taking account of the lower age limit for compulsory schooling that exists in Northern Ireland. In the subsequent year *The Children (Northern Ireland) Order* (Great Britian, 1995) was published. In essence the principal features of the order replicated those of the Children Act in England and Wales (Statutes in Force, 1989), referring to the care, upbringing and protection of children, particularly those considered 'in need'. A duty was placed on local authorities to regulate pre-school services in the private and voluntary sectors and to undertake a review of daycare facilities once every three years.

Such initiatives culminated in the publication of two major reports, *Investing in Early Learning* (DENI and DHSS, 1998) and *Children First* (DENI, TEA and DHSS, 1999), which launched the Pre-school Education Expansion Programme (PEEP) and the overall Childcare Strategy for NI respectively. These efforts comprise not only an aim to raise the quality of care and to provide more childcare provision, but also attempt to make childcare more affordable and accessible to all parents and children. In light of the recognised differences between Northern Ireland and England (for example, the lower compulsory school starting age and the single entry to compulsory schooling in the September of each year), the current government introduced a programme for pre-school expansion. This programme, phased according to the availability of resources and targeted towards particular groups of children, was experienced by both Holly and Ryan. Preference was given to socially disadvantaged children aged four before the first of September in their final pre-school year (DENI, 1999). Such criteria prevented Holly from getting a place in a nursery setting. The preference given to the older children has been overruled by the recent publication of *Outcomes from the Review of Pre-school Education* (DENI, 2006).

> Parents, such as those of Holly, had to find a substantial sum of money for their children to be looked after by a childminder, without any assurance of quality. What changes in provision might ensure for such parents a better guarantee of value for money?

The Review of Pre-school Education in NI (DENI, 2004a) highlights how the PEEP has not only achieved its set targets, but has surpassed them. Sufficient places were available in 2003–4 for 95 per cent of children in their immediate pre-school year; the target had been 90 per cent. The review also draws attention to a 60 per cent decline in Reception classes as a result of the PEEP. In fact the recent document detailing the outcomes of the review (DENI, 2006a) indicates that the Department of Education in Northern Ireland intends to bring forward legislation to prevent a school offering Reception places, in an effort to encourage parents to avail of more pre-school provision. Such a decision is evidence of the current government's perceived support for more practical and play-based activity in the early years of schooling. It would appear therefore that pre-school services have increased such that currently there is a surplus of appropriate provision in Northern Ireland. With the birth rate falling (a drop of 2.6 per cent in the first quarter of 2005; NISRA, 2005b), there is growing concern that amount of provision outweighs requirement. Several statutory nursery schools and units particularly in the cities and large towns have been obliged to fill their places with two year old children.

> Ryan is an example of a two year old placed in a nursery school. Reflect on the impact such an arrangement might have on children and practitioners.

Many playgroups in certain areas of Northern Ireland are also finding it difficult to meet their quota (DENI, 2004a). Currently there is much debate as to how these excess facilities may be best used in the future but as yet there is no consensus as to the way forward.

> There has been anecdotal evidence that such excess provision may be used for the purposes of after-school facilities in Northern Ireland. How do you feel such excess provision could best be used?

Integration of services

In the past pre-school services in Northern Ireland tended to be disintegrated and poorly co-ordinated. Education and care providers were totally separate and little harmonisation was in evidence until, as Sutherland (2006) argues, the 1994 policy paper when inter-agency and multi-disciplinary Early Years Committees were established in each Health and Social Services (HSS) area, co-ordinated by a new Inter-Departmental Group on Early Years (IDGEY). Further small policy initiatives have been taking place since the PEEP that reveal a slight shift in policy thinking. Not only has the expansion pro-gramme 'created a new educational phase incorporating the statutory and voluntary/private sector. This phase has a curriculum taught across both sec-tors, and common inspection standards' (DENI, 2004a: 23).

> Look again at Holly's and Ryan's stories: both experienced the same pre-school cur-riculum despite attending different types of pre-school setting.

As part of the expansion programme, pre-school education advisory groups representing both sectors have been set up to take forward the planning of said expansion programme. A key aspect of the Northern Ireland Childcare Strategy (DENI, TEA and DHSS, 1999) was the establishment of four new childcare partnerships to take forward the strategy. These partnerships comprised representation from government departments, statutory agencies, employers, parents, voluntary and community organisations and childcare providers. The culmination of these developments is evidenced in the *Children and Young People's Funding Package* (DENI, 2006b) that represents an effort on the part of government to address children's social, health and educational issues cohesively in one package. Furthermore an integral feature of the Education Minister's vision for EYEC is to provide more co-ordinated services, whereby the Department of Education will assume centralised responsibility for all of the childcare services previously dealt with by the Department of Health and Social Services, starting with the SureStart programme from 2007. Despite these developments, it would appear that much still remains to be done before integrated services built around children's needs rather than professional structures are available.

The Pre-school Curriculum

Curricular Guidance for Pre-school Education, issued in 1997 by the Northern Ireland's Council for the Curriculum, Examinations and Assessment (CCEA), represents a shared view of what constitutes good quality pre-school provision in the education and care sectors in Northern Ireland (DHSS, TEA and DENI, 1999). Representatives from both the DHSS and the DENI worked together on the document to plan curricular guidance that could be applied across a range of pre-school settings. All pre-school settings, both statutory and voluntary and funded by the government, are required to follow the *Curricular Guidance for Pre-school Education* (DHSS, CCEA and DENI, 1997) as part of the Pre-school Expansion Programme (DENI and DHSS, 1998). The document is based on the premise that young children require a curriculum that 'meets their physical, social, emotional and cognitive needs …; motivates, challenges and stimulates them' and 'is broad and balanced allowing them to make choices and providing them with opportunities through play and other experiences …' (DHSS, CCEA and DENI, 1997: 7).

It could be argued that the *Curricular Guidance for Pre-school Education* in Northern Ireland is process-based and child-centred in perspective (see for example Guimarães and McSherry, 2002, and Melhuish et al., 1999), whereby the emphasis is not on what young children should have achieved before entering formal schooling but rather describes the kind of learning opportunities which young children should have through play and other relevant experiences, and the characteristics that the majority of children who have experienced appropriate pre-school education will have displayed.

To reflect ongoing changes in the primary sector, particularly with regard to the introduction of a Foundation Stage, the *Curricular Guidance for*

Pre-School Education has been revised to ensure an easier transition for our youngest children (DHSS&PS, CCEA and DENI, 2006). The revised version reflects the same child-centred approach of the traditional guidance, prioritising play as the medium by which young children learn. It could be argued that it actually goes one step further, emphasising a need for the curriculum to be enjoyable and to provide equality of opportunity, whereby young children feel included, secure and valued. More emphasis is also placed on the role of assessment, reflection and evaluation of children's learning and a section is included on providing for younger children, as well as the transition to primary school.

> Compare the experience of Holly and Ryan on entry to primary school. Which do you think better met the needs of young children aged between four and five years of age, and in what ways?

Developments for 0–3 Year Old Children

However, despite these developments both in terms of provision and quality for three and four year old children, Northern Ireland falls far short of its counterparts in the UK in terms of meeting the needs of the youngest children in our society – the under-threes. Unlike England and Scotland, a single framework or guidance document focusing on both the care and education of the under-threes does not exist in Northern Ireland in 2006. The under-threes experience a variety of Early Years provision in the education sector (nursery schools and classes), the private sector (full and part-time daycare, childminders) and the voluntary sector (crèches). As a result there is little consistency in the guidance/curriculum followed and arguably in the quality of the experience on offer for children under three.

> Both case studies exemplify this, Holly being looked after by a childminder and Ryan by his mother and then a nursery. What are the implications for mothers and children of the lack of consistency in services for children from birth to three in Northern Ireland, particularly those children whose mothers work full-time?

As part of the NI Childcare Strategy the current government has invested a sum of money into the implementation of SureStart programmes. According to the strategy 'This programme aims to work with parents and children under four years of age in areas of social disadvantage to promote the physical, intellectual and social development of pre-school children to ensure they have the best start in life' (DHSS, TEA and DENI, 1999: 14). The Children and Young People's Funding Package (£0.75 to £2 million) has also been set aside for a planned developmental programme for two year old children which will focus on 'constructive play in group settings to enhance children's social development, build on their communication and language skills, and encourage their imagination through play' (DENI, 2006b: 6).

Despite the latter's progress, it would appear that this is an area that requires much more of the government's support and interest to ensure a high and consistent level of quality of provision for this age group of children.

Health and Well-being

Previous policies concerning young children have principally dealt with their education and care. There is growing concern within some areas of Northern Ireland about young children's health and well-being. For example, in north and west Belfast patterns of children's health and well-being are considerably worse than other parts of Northern Ireland (Rooney, 2002). Rooney argues that coupled with the social and economic disadvantage of these areas is the impact of the conflict in the past three decades. It is estimated that 37 per cent of children in Northern Ireland are affected by poverty and 32,000 children are living in severe poverty that contributes significantly to ill health such as poor dental care, malnutrition and increasing levels of asthma (Save the Children, 2005). There has also been an upsurge in the level of child obesity in Northern Ireland that has consequences for children's health and well-being. It is reported by the Health Promotion Agency (2003) that approximately a third of boys and a quarter of girls are overweight by the age of twelve. In fact it was found that Northern Ireland children aged between 8–15 are the biggest television addicts in the UK, such sedentary behaviour contributing further to the obesity problem (McDonald, 2006).

Furthermore, the rate of deteriorating mental health in Northern Ireland is approximately a third higher than in England and Wales (Gosling, 2004). Of particular concern is the aftermath of the 'Troubles'. Whilst the number of deaths and casualties has declined since the signing of the Belfast Agreement, sectarianism is still affecting the lives of many children (OFMDFM, 2006). Research conducted by Connolly and Healy (2004) indicates that some children as young as three hold sectarian prejudices which can develop into deeply-engrained sectarian attitudes by the age of seven or eight years.

> Can you suggest ways that Early Years practitioners can help to prevent sectarian prejudices developing in young children?

At a practical level projects such as the Greater Shankill Early Years Project, as experienced by Ryan and his mother, have been successful to some extent across the fields of education, training, employment, health, the environment and sports, contributing to the overall physical, social and economic regeneration of the community. However, as highlighted by OFMDFM (2006), 'despite significant investment by government over many years, there is insufficient progress being made to improve the lives of our most marginalised and disadvantaged children and young people' (p.3).

See Ryan's story for details of the Greater Shankhill Early Years Project.

Several policies have attempted to address these health and well-being issues, such as *Investing for Health* (DHSS & PS, 2002b) and *Promoting Mental Health – Strategy and Action Plan 2003–2008* (DHSS&PS, 2003) and culminating in the publication of the ten year strategy entitled *Our Children and Young People – Our Pledge* (OFMDFM, 2006) whereby children's health and well-being have been prioritised, together with the *Children's and Young People's Funding Package* (DENI, 2006b). In an effort to reduce underachievement and improve the life-chances of children and young people, £20 million has been granted to schools for before- and after-school activities; £3.5 million for counselling services; £10.8 million for SureStart; £5.6 million for additional support for children in care; £1.7 million for youth outreach to marginalised young people; £4 million for child protection and £12.5 million for services for children with special needs. The package therefore attempts to focus on supporting learning, creativity and healthy lifestyles; its impact is still some way off.

Children's health and well-being issues do not exclude those working in childcare and education settings. In Northern Ireland, Early Years practitioners not only need to address young children's nutritional habits, safety and well-being but, as recommended by Connolly and Healy (2004), children as young as three should be encouraged to appreciate and respect diversity and difference in an effort to build a more stable and secure society for the future.

TRANSITIONS

'Transition' is currently a topical issue in EYEC discourse, but as yet few policy developments in Northern Ireland have been seen to respond to the challenge. The transition from pre-school to primary school has been given some recognition in the revised *Curricular Guidance for Pre-School Education* (DHSS & PS, CCEA and DENI, 2006) where a section entitled 'Transition to the Primary School' provides guidance as to how this might be effectively ensured. The content of the curriculum itself is structured under six areas, namely: the Arts; Language Development; Early Mathematical Experiences; Personal, Social and Emotional Development; Physical Development and Movement, and the World Around Us, and these are synonymous with the structure of the revised curriculum for the Foundation Stage (CCEA, 2005). From this it could be argued that a smoother transition from pre-school to primary school will be facilitated. The fact that all funded pre-school centres are obliged to fulfil the requirements of *Curricular Guidance for Pre-School Education* (DHSS & PS, CCEA and DENI, 2006) and that pre-school education is plentiful will to some extent ensure that in the future children such as Holly and Ryan, despite their diverse backgrounds, will begin primary schooling on an equal footing.

The emphasis placed on promoting a positive home-school liaison (see for example *Curricular Guidance for Pre-School Education,* (DHSS & PS, CCEA, and DENI, 2006) and *Planning for the Foundation Stage* (CCEA, 2004) in an effort to involve parents in the education of their child may to some extent play a part in ensuring a more effective transition between home and school. *Children First: The NI Childcare Strategy* (DHSS, TEA & DENI, 1999) also recognised the instrumental role that parents play in their child's education and a sum of £600,000 was granted to establish pilot parenting groups across Northern Ireland. The fact that parents are perhaps more knowledgeable about their child's education and also have a say in the education of their children may ensure that both children and parents alike are less aggrieved about the whole education process.

As in England, from April 2007 the plan is to extend maternity leave and pay from six to nine months, as part of the Work and Families Northern Ireland Order 2006, with the intention of a year's paid leave by April 2008. There will be a new right of 26 weeks paternity leave, some of which might be paid. This could be considered an effort by the government to ease the transition for working parents who are leaving their new baby to return to work.

Despite these efforts on the part of government, they appear to fall far short of the requirements to ensure effective transitions for all concerned.

> Many young children such as Holly and her brother, can find themselves in the care of several guardians in any given day including for example, parents, grandparents, childminders, Early Years practitioners. How can such 'transitions' be eased for such children?

'Wrap-around' care should be foremost on the government's agenda to meet the needs of children and working parents in Northern Ireland. A study conducted by Gray and Bruegel (2003) on the availability, use of, and demand for childcare services in Northern Ireland for the Equality Commission in Northern Ireland, found that childcare provision per thousand children is much lower in Northern Ireland as a whole than in England, especially in terms of provision for the under-fives. Despite the Pre-school Expansion Programme which has given rise to placements in a pre-school setting for all children in their pre-school year, such placements tend to be part-time and can result in working parents such as Holly's, seeking alternative arrangements before and after school. This shortage of childcare places with extended hours is reflected in the extensive use of unregistered childminders in Northern Ireland, as indicated by Gray and

Bruegel (2003). Their study also highlighted that in order for both parents to maintain their jobs a complex 'juggling act' of alternating their working hours had to be undertaken, in some cases resulting in one partner working days and the other nights.

In 2006 the *Children and Young People's Funding Package* (DENI, 2006b) has made some attempt to respond to this need by investing a sum of approximately £13.3 million in extended schools (8am–6pm). These extended schools will provide activities based on particular circumstances and needs, such as Breakfast Clubs, after-school study support and after-school youth, sport and leisure activities; programmes for parents and community use of schools will also be included. The initiative will be targeted on nursery, primary, post-primary and special schools located in disadvantaged areas and will play a part in easing the transitions for children and their parents. Yet how these transitions will be eased for children and parents remains the question – one that remains unanswered.

SCHOOLING

Since the Education Reform (Northern Ireland) Order (Great Britain, 1989), children there have been obliged to commence formal schooling in the school year of their fifth birthday (with no Reception class).

> As the school year is calculated from 1st July, some children begin formal schooling as early as four years and two months, such as Ryan, and remain in primary school until they are eleven years old. Contrast this with the situation in Scotland and in England.

Table 3.1 details the present progression through primary and secondary education in Northern Ireland.

While the majority of their European counterparts follow a play-based and practical approach towards teaching and learning, four to five year olds (such as Holly) are obliged to follow the demands of the Northern Ireland version of the National Curriculum, which has been described as focusing too heavily on academic achievement, detracting from the enjoyment of learning, and lacking relevance and coherence for everyday life (Harland et al., 1999). Such evidence has been reinforced by further studies, such as that of Walsh (2000) and Sheehy et al. (2000), which focused particularly on Early Years children. The various findings suggest that the formal Year 1 curriculum was not meeting the needs of four and five year old children, particularly those from areas of social disadvantage.

In light of European practice and a review of Early Years research, the NI Council for the Curriculum, Examinations and Assessment (CCEA) has been revising the existing curriculum since early in 1999, in an attempt to make it

TABLE 3.1   Ages and stages of schooling in Northern Ireland

Key Stage	Age (years)	Type of setting
Key Stage 1 (comprising primaries 1–4)	4–8 years	Primary school
Key Stage 2 (comprising primaries 5–7)	8–11 years	Primary school
Key Stage 3	11–14 years	Secondary or grammar school*
Key Stage 4	14–16/18 years	Secondary school, grammar school or further education college

* The examination, known as the 11+, determines whether children attend a grammar school (i.e. if successful) or secondary school. This selection process is currently under review. (See DENI, 2004b, for more information.)

'more explicitly relevant and meaningful to young people, the society and the economy' (CCEA, 1999: 4). One of their key goals is to ensure that the early years of schooling in Northern Ireland should become less formal in perspective, offering instead a more developmentally appropriate, play-based and child-led approach to teaching and learning.

This change in pedagogical approach has become known as the 'Enriched Curriculum' and is now being piloted in more than 120 schools throughout Northern Ireland. Ryan attended one of these pilot schools and appeared to enjoy it and learn from the experience. An evaluation of this intervention, known as the Enriched Curriculum (EC), was commissioned by the CCEA in 1999 and is still ongoing. Findings from the evaluation at the end of Key Stage 1 (that is, after the first four years of primary schooling) would suggest that despite a later start to the formal teaching of reading and writing, there is no substantial difference between the EC and traditional settings by the end of Year 4. Furthermore both teachers and parents tend to be positive about the EC and the quality of the learning experience, feeling that children's social, emotional and learning dispositions are enhanced in EC classrooms particularly in Years 1 and 2 (Sproule et al., 2005; Walsh, Sproule et al., 2006).

Widespread consultation, supported by the research above, has culminated in the CCEA proposing a Foundation Stage approach to Early Years education, encompassing Years 1 and 2 of primary schooling that:

> is concerned with removing the early experience of failure and the concomitant promotion of children's self-esteem by: concentrating on oral language, shared reading, phonological awareness and emergent literacy activities to lay the basis for phonic skills; laying the foundations for a strong sense of number through sorting, matching, counting and other basic activities; promoting good motor development at gross and fine levels through appropriate indoor and outdoor activities; encouraging confidence, curiosity and creativity through activities such as circle time, structured play, role-play, art and music-making; and encouraging children to take responsibility for their own learning. (CCEA, 2005: 1)

This Foundation Stage will then be followed by Key Stage 1, comprising Years 3 and 4, and then Key Stage 2 (Years 5, 6 and 7), whereby a much more integrated and topic-based approach is being proposed (see CCEA, 2006). The rolling out of the Revised Curriculum begins in September 2007 with Year 1 and Year 5 classes and all classes will be expected to follow the requirements for the Revised Curriculum from September 2010.

Such a curricular change represents a huge landmark in the education system of Northern Ireland that has been renowned in the past for its conservatism and traditionalism (see for example Caul, 1990, and Gallagher and Dunn, 1991). Such a development paves the way for an exciting but challenging future for Early Years education in general.

SPECIAL EDUCATIONAL NEEDS

Much of Northern Ireland's legislation regarding special educational needs has generally replicated what has been happening in England. Although Northern Ireland has its own Code of Practice on the Identification and Assessment of Special Educational Needs (DfNI, 1998) and a Special Educational Disability Needs Order (SENDO) (DENI, 2005), rather than a Special Educational Needs Act (SENDA) (DfES, 2001), these are similar to the English documentation. Both the English and Northern Ireland Codes of Practice give detailed guidance on effective processes for the identification and assessment of pupils with SEN and the SENDA and SENDO both go some way in promoting and facilitating effective inclusion of SEN pupils into mainstream classes, which now appears to have become a priority for both contexts.

The issue of inclusion is recognised in the Northern Ireland pre-school curricular guidance (DHSS&PS, CCEA and DENI, 2006) where it describes the inclusion of children with SEN in mainstream classes as an 'enriching experience' (p.15) for everyone concerned, that is, other children, parents and staff alike. It does stress however that such an emphasis on inclusive practice 'requires careful and detailed planning before and following admission' (p.15) while at the same time promoting the importance of staff and parents working in close collaboration with other appropriate professionals in the field. Emphasis is also placed on a need for the earliest identification possible of any difficulties experienced by a child and for careful observation and assessment through close liaison with other professionals. The importance of adhering to the Code of Practice for children with special educational needs is also highlighted, as is allowing for flexibility both in the settling-in process and the length of session to meet with individual children's needs and requirements.

It could also be argued that the introduction of a Revised Northern Ireland Curriculum (from September 2007) into primary classes will play an instrumental part in facilitating effective inclusion in the primary education system (see Hunter and O'Connor, 2006). The Revised Curriculum strongly emphasises the need for schools to provide a curriculum that will meet the needs of all children, with an underpinning aim to empower (all) young people to develop their potential and make informed and responsible choices and decisions throughout their lives. Inherent within the Revised Curriculum is the notion that all children, irrespective of culture, ethnicity, linguistic and social background, gender and special educational need, should be offered the same range of learning pathways where individual needs will be met by greater differentiation of tasks. Fact-findings from the evaluation of the Enriched Curriculum, which has informed the Foundation Stage of the Revised Curriculum, would suggest that the more practical and play-based approach adopted by the EC in the early years provides a more inclusive curriculum for all children (Sproule et al., 2002).

> Reflect on what you have learned about the nature and approach of the Revised Curriculum in the early years of primary school. In what ways do you feel it might help to cater better for SEN children in mainstream classes?

The move towards more inclusive practice within Northern Ireland comes to the fore even more with the proposals embedded within the *Costello Report* (DENI, 2004b), as indicated by Hunter and O'Connor (2006), which aims to eradicate the system of academic selection at 11 years of age, commonly known as the 11+. As highlighted earlier in this chapter, at present the future of a child's education (that is, whether they attend a grammar or secondary school) is decided on the basis of a transfer test conducted at the age of 11. Such a system has inevitably resulted in much division and the Costello Report has responded by proposing a more equitable approach whereby any future post-primary arrangements should be based on the principles of equality, quality, relevance, access, choice, respect and partnership. Although transfer is proposed to continue at the age of 11, it will be on the basis of choice by parents and pupils and supported by appropriate information including a pupil profile conducted throughout a child's primary education. Such proposals will therefore facilitate a more inclusive approach from the outset within the primary education system where the specific needs of individual children, including those with SEN, will be at the core of the curriculum rather than being content to prepare children to meet with the challenges and demands of the 11+.

However, like England, despite this forward movement in terms of policy development, it would appear that translating the rhetoric into practice is much more problematic. Lundy and Kilpatrick (2006), commenting on the findings from research conducted for the Northern Ireland Commissioner for Children and Young People, argue that despite the fact that there is widespread support for inclusion within education circles, such support is tempered by concerns regarding, for example, the capacity of mainstream schools to cope with the ever increasing numbers of children with special educational needs entering their classrooms and the associated problems of bullying and child protection. The lack of appropriate resources and support facilities was also identified, as were unacceptable delays in the statementing process and the need for earlier intervention. Research conducted by Winter (2006) adds fuel to these concerns, where many teachers feel inadequately prepared by their initial teacher education to take on board the challenges they face to enable them to facilitate inclusive practice in their classrooms. In fact the Chief Inspector of Schools in Northern Ireland (ETI , 2003) stressed the need to address variations in the quality and nature of provision for children with special educational needs in most mainstream schools.

> Consider the implications of inclusion of SEN children for the Early Years practitioner and the other Early Years children. What help and support does the teacher need to ensure effective inclusion? What role does the government need to play? How can the needs of mainstream children be safeguarded?

SAFEGUARDING CHILDREN

It could be argued, particularly at the beginning of the twenty-first century, that young children are coming higher on Northern Ireland's policy agenda. Not only was the PEEP (DENI and DHSS, 1998) perhaps the first time that real government monies were being invested in the youngest children (money that was enjoyed both by Holly and Ryan), but as part of the Northern Ireland Childcare Strategy, childcare partnerships were charged with meeting 'the needs of all children from all communities, including those with special social and educational needs and those with a disability' (DHSS, TEA and DENI, 1999: 19) as well as ensuring that the voice of parents is being heard both in service delivery and policy development. Likewise the forthcoming implementation of a Foundation/KS1 Curriculum with children's needs and interests at its heart provides evidence of the current government's perceived commitment to a better future for its children.

Inherent within an array of recent government policies is the underlying message, in rhetoric at least, that young children have rights that need to be adhered to and needs that require protecting. In response to policy developments in England on this issue, such as the publication of the document *Tomorrow's Future – Building a Strategy for Children and Young People* (DfES and CYPU, 2001) and *Every Child Matters (DfES, 2003)*, Northern Ireland too has made some progress. The appointments of a Commissioner for Children and Young People and more recently a Minister for Children and Young People, as part of the over-arching Ten Year Strategy for Children and Young People (OFMDFM, 2006), also stress the emphasis being placed in Northern Ireland on ensuring that the needs of children and young people are met, their rights upheld and their voices respected and listened to.

Such thinking culminated in a recent publication entitled *Our Children and Young People – Our Pledge: a ten year strategy for Children and Young People in NI 2006–2016* (OFMDFM, 2006), which stresses that each child and young person should be 'healthy; enjoying, learning and achieving; living in safety and with stability; experiencing economic and environmental well-being; contributing positively to community and society; and living in a society which respects their rights' (OFMDFM, 2006: 7). The strategy identifies that 'currently in the vast majority of cases, adults act effectively in the interest of children and young people. However it remains the case that children and young people have decisions made about them for and against their interests, without their views being taken into account, or their needs properly considered'. Eide and Wenger (2005: 20) highlight how many professionals claim that they are constantly acting in the best interests of young children but what adults consider as 'the child's perspective is not necessarily the same as the child's own point of view or perspective' (p.73). Research by Cunningham et al. (2004) and Walsh et al. (2006) confirms this thinking. Their studies, conducted in an effort to access the views and interests of three and four year old children, found that parents and Early Years practitioners are not always in tune with children's thinking.

The Ten Year Strategy (OFMDFM, 2006) also stresses the importance of working in partnership with and a need to secure the support of the parents, carers and communities in which our children and young people live. The strategy also recognises that this is a country slowly emerging from conflict, and pledges to ensure that its children and young people are 'supported to grow together in a shared, inclusive society where they respect diversity and difference' (p.17). Although this is certainly a step in the right direction and a commendable response to a very urgent need, a sceptic might ask 'Will it really make a difference?' The pledges are certainly very worthy but in some respect philanthropic in perspective whereby there is an underlying assumption that everyone is going to work together for the best interests of children and young people. It could be argued that the practical implications of changing mindsets, from a society where children have been undervalued to one where they are placed at its heart, have largely been ignored.

As highlighted in Chapter 2 on England, the current government's more proactive role in safeguarding children could be envisaged in many respects as controlling. Although the Ten Year Strategy promotes the image of children as active participants in their own lives, who have interests and rights, evident by the fact that children were involved in the development of such a strategy, the government's interference on childhood issues may be interpreted as threatening children's freedom, their privacy and to some extent their innocence. This argument has also been put forward by Moss et al. who stress that listening to children's views and perspectives can be a means 'of governing the child more effectively, behind a mask of child-centredness and children's rights, as part of the process of bringing the child ever more constantly under the adult gaze' (2005: 11).

> The government is presented with a vicious circle: interfering in children's lives to ensure their safety may be interpreted as 'controlling', but no interference could be considered 'negligence'. How can such issues be resolved?

QUALITY ASSURANCE

A growing issue within all aspects of EYEC is the emphasis placed on assuring quality in an effort to raise standards. The Northern Ireland Childcare Strategy stressed the need for high quality Early Years services to be available to all children, based on the findings of a longitudinal study known as the *Effective Pre-school Provision in NI* Project which found that quality provision does make a difference (Melhuish et al., 2003). Quality of the curriculum in primary schools is currently assured by an inspection procedure organised and managed by the DENI's Education and Training Inspectorate (ETI). During the inspection the inspection team, by means of direct observation, evaluates three key areas, namely: ethos, learning and teaching, and leadership and management. Each school is also encouraged to engage in a process of self- evaluation to assist in overall progress and development.

The quality of services for pre-school children (both statutory and voluntary/ private, funded by the Department as part of the PEEP) is also assured by an inspection conducted by the Education and Training Inspectorate (ETI). The inspection criteria used are set out in the document *Evaluating Pre-school Education* (ETI, 2000) and fall under three main headings: the ethos of the setting, the quality of the educational provision, and the children's responses and management arrangements including leadership, organisation and teamwork, staff development and links with parents.

The voluntary and private sector (that is funded and non-funded settings) is also required to have an annual inspection under *The Children (Northern Ireland) Order* (1995) arrangements which apply to both pre-school children and under. Criteria assessed are contained within the document *Standards for Pre-school Settings* (DHSS&PS, 2002a) and concentrate on health and safety; child protection; the physical environment and the care and learning environment. As a result funded pre-school centres are subject to two inspection processes. In addition to these standards, other organisations such as the Northern Ireland Childminding Association (NICMA), the Northern Ireland Early Years Organisation (NIPPA) and Play Board have provided a range of guidance material as well as accreditation programmes in an attempt to enhance the quality of the provision.

Under-threes, such as Ryan, who find themselves in the education sector have no guidance/standards specific to them. Although these settings follow the requirements of the *Curricular Guidance for Pre-school Education* (DHSS& PS, CCEA and DENI, 1997) and guidance material and quality are assured through a formal inspection conducted by members of the Education and

Training Inspectorate (ETI), the under-three age range has tended to be overlooked. The revised *Curricular Guidance for Pre-school Education* (DHSSPS, CCEA and DENI, 2006) has included a very short section entitled 'Providing for Younger Children' (pp.16–17) that highlights how staff should 'recognise the stages of development of the younger children and have realistic expectations of them' and 'they need to ensure that appropriate resources and activities are provided to meet the children's needs' (p.16). Reference is also made as to how staff might provide an appropriate adult/child ratio for younger children and the necessity of a flexible approach to cater for their needs. However little advice as to how such needs should be met is provided. A reference to the publication by SureStart entitled *Birth to Three Matters* (Abbott, 2005) is given, but without any follow-up explanation.

A more integrated approach towards assuring quality throughout all EYEC services, particularly for the under-threes, is necessary. It could be argued that most of the above criteria preclude what Katz (1995) describes as the 'bottom-up' perspective of quality, namely how it feels to be a child in a particular setting. Criteria that address for example children's motivation, concentration, confidence and independence, such as those described in the *Quality Learning Instrument* (Walsh and Gardner, 2005), would perhaps provide a greater insight into the quality of a setting in terms of the child's perspective.

PROFESSIONAL DEVELOPMENT AND TRAINING

Since the Northern Ireland Childcare Strategy was implemented in 1999 there has been a growing emphasis placed on the need for Early Years practitioners in Northern Ireland to be appropriately educated. The importance of a suitably trained workforce has been further reinforced by the Effective Pre-school Project in Northern Ireland (EPPNI) research which found that staff qualifications in pre-school centres are associated with higher quality provision and better outcomes for children (see Melhuish et al., 2003).

Nursery school teachers and Foundation/Key Stage 1 teachers are already required by law to be educated to degree level and to possess qualified teacher status by means either of a Bachelor of Education (BEd) degree or a degree plus a Postgraduate Certificate in Education (PGCE). In the voluntary/private sector minimum qualification levels were set as part of the PEEP (DENI and DHSS, 1998) in an effort to raise standards. At least half the staff must hold a relevant qualification in education or childcare. Relevant qualifications are classified as NVQ Level 3 or the equivalent (for at least one member of staff) and all other qualified members of staff must have a NVQ Level 2 or its equivalent.

How appropriate were the qualifications and experience of Ryan's nursery teacher for teaching very young children? What additional aspects do you feel would be required?

The need for support to be given by an Early Years specialist to providers who are not qualified teachers, in helping to raise standards and to prepare children for school, has been stressed by the PEEP (DENI and DHSS, 1998). Holly's playgroup leader benefited from this facility. This role is distinct to Northern Ireland and is envisaged as providing support to settings in: planning curricular activities; assessing children's progress; assisting in the development of self-improvement programmes and action planning; and preparing children for the transition to compulsory education. The requirements demanded for such a specialist role include: a qualified teacher who has taught for two of their last five years either in a Nursery, Reception, Year 1 or Year 2 class in a grant-aided school; a qualified teacher who has taught pre-school children in the voluntary/private sector for two of their last five years; or a qualified Early Years specialist (Early Childhood Studies/Early Years Specialist diploma/degree or its equivalent i.e. NVQ Level 4).

NIPPA, the Early Years organisation (Northern Ireland Pre-school Playgroup Association) is committed to a graduate workforce throughout EYEC but based on the pedagogue tradition, rather than a teacher-led profession. Controversy around this issue has been taking place ever since the introduction of the Pre-school Education and Expansion Programme within Northern Ireland whereby the promise of a year of 'nursery education' (DHSS and DENI, 1994) was replaced by one of 'pre-school education' (DENI and DHSS, 1998). Sutherland (2006) highlights how this caused grave concerns particularly amongst the spokespersons for the British Association for Early Childhood Education, now known as Early Education, at the prospect of other than qualified teachers delivering Early Years education. It would appear, however, with the changing focus towards much more play-based practice in both the Pre-school and Foundation stages of schooling that a different type of 'teacher' may be required to implement the curriculum effectively. Findings from *The Early Years Enriched Curriculum Evaluation Project* (Sproule et al., 2006) have indicated the need for initial teacher training programmes to prepare student teachers better to take on board the challenges of a more developmentally appropriate Early Years curriculum.

Currently there is some concern amongst Early Years teachers that if a new role other than 'teacher' is adopted the current status and salary scale may change accordingly. Nursery school and Foundation teachers might no longer enjoy the equality they have with the rest of the teaching workforce. However, the needs of other Early Years practitioners, such as playgroup staff who are expected to fulfil the same requirements as nursery teachers for much less pay and status, need to be considered urgently. What aspects of the proposed developments are likely to be of concern to Early Years teachers?

Although the professional development of primary school teachers is currently facilitated through the Curriculum Advisory and Support Services, that is the five education and library boards (presently under review), such support is not granted to the statutory nursery sector. The training and on-going professional development of the voluntary/private sector are principally catered for by NIPPA, the Early Years organisation. With the Review of Public Administration some major changes will be taking place within this field and it has been recognised by the DENI (2006a) that providing support and training for all pre-school settings is clearly an issue. With the prospect of more integrated services, perhaps a more co-ordinated approach to the training and professional development of all Early Years practitioners will be implemented.

What are the implications for the Early Years practitioner of a more 'children's rights-based' society? How might they become more in tune with the thinking of young children in their care?

FUTURE AND IMMINENT CHANGES

Northern Ireland, as a society emerging from conflict, would appear to have made great strides over the past decade in the field of EYEC. Imagine a child born today in 2006, called Joshua. Will his education and care experiences differ greatly from those of Holly and Ryan? If policy is delivered Joshua will enjoy a pre-school place of his parents' choosing, particularly if he lives in a city or large town. Joshua will be following the requirements of the revised version of the Northern Ireland Curriculum, a curriculum that is less pre-scriptive in style and more developmentally appropriate in perspective.

In his first two years of primary school he will enjoy a more practical and play-based approach to his education, ensuring an easier transition on his part from pre-school to primary. Furthermore Joshua should be living in a more stable and secure society where his chances of living in poverty should be reduced. He should be experiencing a healthier lifestyle and be less exposed to sectarianism and terrorism. Depending on where Joshua lives, he might find himself in a school with children from different minority ethnic groups, as a consequence of the high number of people from Eastern Europe moving into Northern Ireland. Such a situation may be beneficial in terms of developing cultural awareness in Northern Ireland's children. It may, how-ever, present many challenges for the Early Years practitioner.

Joshua's parents may still experience some degree of struggle in ensuring effective and appropriate childcare arrangements for their son. Although some developments should have taken place in the form of extended school-ing and the expansion of SureStart, particularly for disadvantaged families, Joshua might still be experiencing a number of transitions in any given day as 'wrap-around' care still appears to be a long way off. The present and future for EYEC are challenging but exciting. Although in practical terms Joshua's childcare and education arrangements will not have changed dramatically from those of Holly and Ryan, the future certainly looks more hopeful as finally children in Northern Ireland are beginning to be valued and the education and care system appears to be responding to this. Now it is time for Northern Ireland society to ensure that the rhetoric becomes reality.

TOPICS FOR DISCUSSION

The Revised Early Years Curriculum

Will the revised Northern Ireland curriculum be able to maintain the high academic standards within its schools? Many sceptics are of the opinion that the more play-based and practical approach to be introduced into Years 1 and 2 will ensure a watered-down version of the existing curriculum. Will this be the case? Will teachers be willing to abandon their more formal ways and allow the curriculum in the early years to be more play-based and practical in approach when it begins to come into effect from September 2007? Will teachers be prepared to change? Who will effectively monitor whether their approach to teaching young children has appropriately changed? How will parents respond? Will the revised Early Years curriculum allow for more collaboration between pre-school and primary school? How will such collaboration be ensured as the pre-school year is not considered as part of the Foundation Stage? What about two year old children – will they still largely be ignored, or will we have begun to think of some form of curriculum for them? Do two year old children simply need care or do they also need to be educated? What might the implications of a form of 0–3 curriculum be for all those concerned, that is parents, carers and children?

The Early Years Practitioner versus The Teacher

What is the most appropriate training/education for an Early Years practitioner to take on board the challenges of the revised curriculum and the pre-school curriculum? Is qualified teacher status necessary? If not how can we guarantee high status for practitioners working with this age group? Will a graduate workforce be guaranteed in the early years? What impact might a graduate workforce have on salaries? How can we ensure a more equitable workforce? Will all Early Years practitioners be educated in the same way or those in pre-school and early primary schooling differently? What about those who work with two year old children and under – what in your opinion is the most appropriate training for them?

More integrated services

What will be the impact of the Department of Education assuming full responsibility for all matters concerning young children be like in practice? Will care still have its place within pre-school and early primary classes? Will all Early Years services be able to work together effectively to ensure the best possible future for children in Northern Ireland? How will we begin to translate such thinking into Children's Centres in Northern Ireland? Will extended schooling have an impact on the number of transitions the children of working parents have to make? How could the anxieties of working parents and their children be effectively addressed?

Children's health and well-being

Will children be healthier and wealthier as a result of the Ten Year Strategy? Will the peace settlement be maintained? If so what impact might a more peaceful society have on young children in Northern Ireland? Will pre-school and the early years of primary schooling have begun to respond to the wider requirements of education – for example children's health in terms of healthy meals and well-being, and in terms of tackling sectarianism and racism in the classroom? What will be the impact of the inclusion of children from minority ethnic groups in the Early Years system of education and care? Can classrooms both in pre-school and early primary schooling be more inclusive in terms of special educational needs and ethic minorities? If so, what shape and form might this take? What will be the impact on our young children if Northern Ireland's schools remain segregated in terms of religion? As for children's rights, will the voice of the child in policy formation be effectively translated into Early Years practice and if so in what shape or form? How might teachers and parents have to change?

KEY MILESTONES IN GOVERNMENT STRATEGY FOR EARLY CHILDHOOD EDUCATION AND CASE IN NORTHERN IRELAND

- **1994** – the Irish Republican Army and the Loyalist ceasefires
- **1996** – recognition and investment by the European Union and the International Fund for Ireland
- **1997** – the Labour Party's commitment to universal pre-school provision in the voluntary, independent and private sectors
- **1998** – the Belfast Agreement, a Rights-based Agenda and the Children's Commission Office established, plus the launch of the pre-school expansion programme for Northern Ireland

- **1999** – the Children First Childcare Strategy with a focus on inclusion, social justice, affordability, accessibility, quality, economic objectives and the expansion of the SureStart Programme to include 20 per cent of 0–4 year olds
- **1999** – the Enriched Curriculum Pilot and the revision of the Northern Ireland Curriculum begin
- **2003** – maternity and paternity leave increased
- **2004** – the Review of Pre-School Education is launched
- **2006** – Outcomes of the Review of Pre-School Education are published
- **2006** – the publication of a Ten Year Strategy for Children and Young People in Northern Ireland
- **2006** – the Children and Young People's Funding Package (monies being invested in extended schooling; the expansion of SureStart with a focus on two year olds, child protection, counselling services and children with special needs)
- **2006** – Revised Pre-School Curricular Guidance
- **2008** – maternity and paternity leave further increased
- **2010** – the Revised Curriculum being implemented in all primary school classes in Northern Ireland
- **2016** – The Ten Year Strategy for Children and Young People fully in place. (Adapted from Fitzpatrick, 2006)

REFERENCES

Abbott, L. (2005) *Birth to Three Matters*. Maidenhead: OUP.
Ball, C. (1994) *Start Right: The importance of early learning*. London: Royal Society for the Encouragement of the Arts, Manufacturers and Commerce (RSA).
Caul, L. (ed.) (1990) *Schools Under Scrutiny: The case of NI*. London: MacMillan Education.
Census (2001) *Population in Northern Ireland: Breakdown by religious denominations*. Available at cain.ulst.ac.uk/ni/religion.htm (Accessed 1 April 2006.)
Connolly, P. and Healy, J. (2004) *Children and the Conflict in Northern Ireland: The experiences and perspectives of 3–11 year olds*. Belfast: OFMDFM.
Council for the Curriculum, Examinations and Assessment (CCEA) (1999) *Developing the Northern Ireland Curriculum to Meet the Needs of Young People, Society and the Economy in the 21st Century*. Belfast: CCEA.
Council for the Curriculum, Examinations and Assessment (CCEA) (2004) *Planning for the Foundation Stage*. Belfast: DENI.
Council for the Curriculum, Examinations and Assessment (CCEA) (2005) *Update on the Proposed Foundation Stage*. Belfast: CCEA. Available at www.rewarding learning.com/development/foundation/docs/foundationstage_update.pdf (Accessed 9 January 2006.)
Council for the Curriculum, Examinations and Assessment (CCEA) (2006) *The Revised NI Primary Curriculum*. Belfast: DENI.
Council for the Curriculum, Examinations and Assessment (CCEA), NES Arnold (NES) and Belfast Education and Library Board (BELB) (2002) *Enriched Curriculum: The beginning*. Belfast: CCEA.
Cunningham, J., Walsh, G., Dunn, J., Mitchell, D. and McAlister, M. (2004) *Giving Children a Voice: Accessing the views of 3–4 year old children in playgroups*. Belfast: DHSSPS.

DENI (Department of Education for NI) (1996) *The Northern Ireland Curriculum. Key Stages 1 and 2. Programmes of study and attainment targets.* Belfast: HMSO.

DENI (1998) *Code of Practice on the Identification and Assessment of Special Educational Needs.* Bangor: DENI.

DENI (1999) *Pre-School Education in Schools (Admission Criteria) Regulations (NI) 1998, Circular 1999/2.* Bangor: DENI.

DENI (2004a) *The Review of Pre-School Education in Northern Ireland.* Belfast: DENI.

DENI (2004b) *The Costello Report: Future post primary arrangements.* Available at www.deni.gov.uk/22-ppa_costelloreport.pdf (Accessed 4 September 2006.)

DENI (2005) *The Special Educational Needs Disability Order (SENDO).* Bangor: DENI.

DENI (2006a) *Outcomes of the Review of Pre-school Education in NI.* Belfast: DENI.

DENI (2006b) *Children and Young People's Funding Package.* Belfast: DENI.

DENI and DHSS (Department of Health and Social Services) (1998) *Investing in Early Learning: Pre-school education in Northern Ireland.* Bangor: DENI and DHSS.

DES (Department for Education and Science) (1990) *Starting with Quality (The Rumbold Report).* London: HMSO.

DfEE (Department for Education and Employment) and (QCA) Qualifications and Curriculum Authority (1999) *Early Learning Goals.* London: HMSO.

DfEE and SCAA (School Curriculum and Assessment Authority) (1996) *Nursery Education: Desirable outcomes for children's learning on entering compulsory education.* London: HMSO.

DfES (Department for Education and Skills) (2001) *Special Educational Needs and Disability Act (SENDA).* London: HMSO.

DfES (2003) *Every Child Matters.* London: TSO.

DfES and CYPU (Children and Young People's Unit) (2001) *Tomorrow's Future – Building a Strategy for Children and Young People.* London: TSO.

DHSS and DENI (1994) *Policy on Early Years Provision for Northern Ireland.* Belfast: HMSO.

DHSS&PS (Department of Health, Social Services and Public Safety) (2002a) *Standards for Pre-School Settings.* Belfast: DHSS&PS.

DHSS&PS (2002b) *Investing for Health.* Belfast: DHSS&PS.

DHSS&PS (2003) *Promoting Mental Health.* Belfast: DHSS&PS.

DHSS, CCEA and DENI (1997) *Curricular Guidance for Pre-School Education.* Belfast: CCEA.

DHSS&PS, CCEA and DENI (2006) *Curricular Guidance for Pre-School Education.* Belfast: CCEA.

DHSS, TEA (Training and Employment Agency) and DENI (1999) *Children First: the Northern Ireland Childcare Strategy.* Belfast: DHSS, TEA and DENI.

Donnelly, C., McKeown, P. and Osborne, B. (eds) (2006) *Devolution and Pluralism in Education in NI.* Manchester: Manchester University Press.

Eide, B.J. and Wenger, N. (2005) 'From the Children's Point of View: Methodological and ethical challenges', in A. Clark, A. T. Kjørholt and P. Moss (eds), *Beyond Listening: Children's perspectives on Early Childhood services.* pp. 71–90. Bristol: The Policy Press.

ETI (Education and Training Inspectorate) (2000) *Evaluating Pre-school Education.* Belfast: DENI.

ETI (2003) *Report of a Survey on the Inclusion of Pupils with Statements of Special Educational Needs in Mainstream Primary and Post-primary Schools in Northern Ireland.* Bangor: DENI.

Ewart, S. and Schubotz, D. (2004) *Voices behind the Statistics: Young children's views of sectarianism in NI.* London: NCB.

Fitzpatrick, S. (2005) 'A Vision for Early Childhood Services in Northern Ireland 2015: Challenges and opportunities'. Conference Paper presented at the Childcare in Practice conference at Stranmillis University College, Belfast, 22 March.

Fitzpatrick, S. (2006) 'Supporting Ongoing Quality Developments in Early Childhood Services in NI'. Conference paper presented at the Pre-School Matters conference at Stranmillis University College, Belfast, 29 April.

Gallagher, A.M. and Dunn, S. (1991) 'Community Relations in NI. Attitudes to contact and integration', in P. Stringer and G. Robinson (eds), *Social Attitudes in NI*. Belfast: Blackstaff.

Gosling, P. (2004) *Smoking Down but Drinking Up in Northern Ireland*. Available at www.medicalnewstoday.com/medicalnews.php?newsid=9051 (Accessed 25 July 2006.)

Gray, A. and Bruegel, I. (2003) *The Availability, Use of, and Demand for Childcare Services among the Parents of Children Aged 0–14 in Northern Ireland: Summary report*. Belfast: Equality Commission for Northern Ireland.

Great Britain (1989) *Education Reform (Northern Ireland) Order*. Belfast: HMSO.

Great Britain (1995) *The Children (Northern Ireland) Order*. Belfast: HMSO.

Guimarães, S. and McSherry, K. (2002) 'The Curriculum Experiences of Pre-School Children in NI: Classroom practices in terms of child-initiated and adult-directed Activities', *International Journal of Early Years Education*, 10(2): pp. 84–94.

Harland, J., Kinder, K., Ashworth, M., Montgomery, A., Moor, H. and Wilkin, A. (1999) *Real Curriculum: At the End of Key Stage 2: Report One from the Northern Ireland Curriculum Cohort Study*. Slough: National Foundation for Educational Research.

Health Promotion Agency (2003) 'Childhood Obesity – a Weighty Issue for Northern Ireland', press release 3 June. Available at www.healthpromotionagency.org.uk (Accessed 18 August 2006.)

Horgan, G. (2005) 'Child Poverty in Northern Ireland: The limits of welfare to work policies', *Social Policy and Administration*, 39(1): pp. 49–64.

Hunter, H. and O'Connor, U. (2006) 'In Search for Inclusion', *Support for Learning*, 21(2): pp. 53–6.

Katz, L.G. (1995) *Talks with Teachers of Young Children: A collection* (ED 380 232). Norwood, NJ: Ablex.

Kelly, B. and Sinclair, R. (2003) *Children from Cross-Community Families in Public Care in NI*. London: National Children's Bureau (NCB).

Lundy, L. and Kilpatrick, R. (2006) 'Children's Rights and Special Educational Needs: Findings from the research conducted for the Northern Ireland Commissioner for Children and Young People', *Support for Learning*, 21(2): pp. 57–63.

McDonald, H. (2006) 'Northern Ireland are Top TV Fans', *The Guardian*, 14 May. Available at www.guardian.co.uk/Northern_Ireland/Story, (Accessed 12 July 2006.)

Melhuish, E., Quinn, L., McSherry, K., Sylva, K., Sammons, P., Siraj-Blatchford, I., Taggart, B. and Guimarães, S. (1999) *Effective Pre-School Provision in Northern Ireland*. Belfast: Stranmillis University College.

Melhuish, E., Quinn, L., Sylva, K., Sammons, P., Siraj-Blatchford, I., Taggart, B., Hanna, K. and Sweeney, G. (2003) *Cognitive Development and Progress at the End of Year 1*. Belfast: Stranmillis University College.

Moss, P., Clark, A. and Kjørholt, A. T. (2005) 'Introduction', in A. Clark, A.T. Kjørholt and P. Moss (eds), *Beyond Listening: Children's Perspectives on Early Childhood Services*. Bristol: The Policy Press.

Northern Ireland Statistics and Research Agency (NISRA) (2005a) *Statistics Press Notice – Births and Deaths in Northern Ireland (2005): A National Statistics Publication*. Belfast: NISRA.

NISRA (2005b)*The Registrar General's Quarterly Report* (No.336). Available at census.nisra@dfpni.gov.uk (Accessed 8 May 2006.)

NISRA (2006) *Women in Northern Ireland*. Belfast: NISRA.

Northern Ireland Office (NIO) (1998) *The Belfast Agreement*. Available at www.nio.gov.uk/agreement.pdf (Accessed 2 September 2006.)

Office of the First Minister and Deputy First Minister (OFMDFM) (2006) *Our Children and Young People – Our Pledge*. Belfast: OFMDFM.

Pascal, C. (1990) *Under-Fives in Infant Classrooms*. Stoke-on-Trent: Trentham.

Phoenix, E. (1989) 'Northern Ireland: from birth pangs to disintegration 1920–72', in C. Brady, M. O'Dowd and B. Walker (eds), *Ulster:* An illustrated history. pp. 182–216. London: Batsford.

Pinkerton, D. (1990) 'Four Year Olds in Primary Schools in Northern Ireland', *OIDEAS,* 36: pp. 42–7.

Rooney, N. (2002) 'Where Progress is Built on Community Engagement', *The Journal of Health Promotion in NI*, 16: pp. 12–13.

Save the Children (2005) *Key Themes for Save the Children in NI*. Available at www.savethechildren.org.uk (Accessed 4 June 2006.)

Schweinhart, L. and Weikart, D. (1997) *Lasting Differences: the High/Scope Curriculum Comparison Study through Age 23*. Ypsilanti, MI: High/Scope Educational Press Foundation.

Sheehy, N., Trew, K., Rafferty, H., McShane, E., Quiery, N. and Curran, S. (2000) *The Greater Shankill Early Years Project: Evaluation Report*. Belfast: The Greater Shankill Partnership and CCEA.

Sproule, L., Trew, K., Rafferty, H., Walsh, G., McGuinness, C. and Sheehy, N. (2002) *The Early Years Enriched Curriculum Evaluation Project: Second Year Report*. Belfast: CCEA.

Sproule, L., Trew, K., Rafferty, H., Walsh, G., McGuinness, C. and Sheehy, N. (2005) *The Early Years Enriched Curriculum Evaluation Report: Final Phase 1 Report*. Belfast: CCEA.

Sproule, L., Trew, K., Rafferty, H., Walsh, G., McGuinness, C. and Sheehy, N. (2006) *The Early Years Enriched Curriculum Evaluation Report: Summary Report Year 5*. Belfast: CCEA.

Statutes in Force (1989) *The Children Act*. London: HMSO.

Sutherland, A. (2006) 'Including Pre-school Education', in C. Donnelly, P. McKeown, and B. Osborne, (eds), *Devolution and Pluralism in Education in NI*. Manchester: Manchester University Press.

Walsh, G. (2000) *The Play versus formal Debate: A study of Early Years provision in Northern Ireland and Denmark*. Unpublished PhD Thesis.

Walsh, G. and Gardner, J. (2005) 'Assessing the Quality of Early Years Learning Environments', *Early Childhood Research and Practice*, 7(1).

Walsh, G., Dunn, J., Mitchell, D., McAlister, M. and Cunningham, J. (2006) 'Giving Children a Voice: Accessing the views of 3–4 year old children in playgroups', *Representing Children*, 18(2): pp. 79–95.

Walsh, G., Sproule, L., McGuinness, C., Trew, K., Rafferty, H., and Sheehy, N. (2006) 'An Appropriate Curriculum for the 4–5 Year Old Child in Northern Ireland: Comparing play-based and formal approaches', *Early Years: An International Journal of Research and Development*, 26(2).

Winter, E. (2006) 'Preparing new teachers for inclusive schools and classrooms', *Support for Learning*, 21(2): pp. 85–91.

USEFUL WEBSITES

www.deni.gov.uk   the Department for Education in NI

www.dhssps.gov.uk   the Department for Health and Social Services in NI

www.ci-ni.org   the Children in NI website

www.nio.gov.uk   the Northern Ireland Office

www.nippa.org   NIPPA: the Early Years Organisation

www.ccea.org.uk   the Council for the Curriculum, Examinations and Assessment in NI

www.earlyyears.org.uk/forward.htm   the Greater Shankill Early Years Project

www.rewardinglearning.com/development/foundation/review.html   the Early Years Enriched Curriculum Project

Thanks to De Eamon Phoenix for his assistance with the historical information on 'The Troubles'.

Elections for the Northern Ireland Assembly have taken place and it will be reconvened on 8 May 2007.

THE REPUBLIC  OF IRELAND

Philomena Donnelly

A CHILD BORN IN THE REPUBLIC OF IRELAND IN 2000: AOIFE'S STORY

Aoife was born in February 2000. It was a home birth and a second child; it went very well and she was a healthy baby. Her sister Maeve was three years old at the time. The girls' parents, Una and Tim, grew up in Cork and met as business studies students at university there. They both graduated with honours degrees, and immediately found employment in the insurance and financial industry. The couple came to Dublin in 1994 and with the expanding Irish economy set up their own consultancy business in 1995 that they run from home. They believe that although they work very hard, they are still only modestly well-off. They have large debts, particularly mortgage repayments, but enjoy an income that allows them to take two holidays abroad each year. They live in a four-bedroom, detached house in a village in the Wicklow foothills that is rapidly becoming a select Dublin suburb. They have used one bedroom as a space for their home office; when the business is really strong they plan to build or rent more extensive office space that will be separate from their home.

Aoife was breast-fed. Her parents wanted to take a full year of shared parental leave, alternating their time away from the business, but they could not afford this. However, because she worked from home, Una could be flexible in scheduling her time with the baby and time in work. She took two months leave from the business and then returned gradually to full-time work. Tim and Una placed Aoife in the small local crèche/playgroup that Maeve had previously attended. It is a registered crèche with one qualified childcare worker and two assistants. The childcare worker, Orla, has FETAC Level 6 in childcare and she also owns the crèche. She employs two female school leavers, one of whom had recently begun a childcare course part-time. The other has no qualification. The crèche/playschool is a converted single story house and has a garden at the rear for outdoor play and activities. Una and Tim paid 1,600 euros per month for both their daughters until Maeve started primary school. They also employ a local woman, Mrs Foley, to help with housework in the afternoons; she does light housework and cares for the children after school until 6 pm every weekday.

Una and Tim found that the crèche/playgroup had prepared Maeve well for school, so Aoife stayed there until she was old enough to enrol in the local primary school. In September 2005 Aoife, aged four years and seven months old, joined a class of 28 boys and girls in that school. Maeve, who had stayed in the pre-school until she was five years old, attends the same school.

Maeve's extra time in pre-school happened because her parents had discussed her development with the pre-school leader, and agreed that she needed to stay for longer in the small, intimate environment where she felt secure, and for the sake of her language development she needed more immersion in an Early Years programme. Aoife, on the other hand, was more socially confident, had good language skills and loved being read to. She longed for 'big school', partly because Maeve was there but also because she wanted 'homework'.

Una and Tim are considering having Maeve assessed and expect that she may need learning support. They are also considering having the assessment privately as the public system has a long waiting list. They are very happy with Aoife's progress in school. Aoife's school day starts at 9 am and ends at 2 pm; she is now in Senior Infants – the second year of primary school. Aoife studies 11 subjects in school and her day is very structured and busy. She plays with games and activities from 9 am until 9.20 every morning. After roll call the teacher usually does Irish and some Maths. There is a ten-minute break when the children play on the yard if it is not raining. After break Aoife and her classmates study English that includes phonics work, some writing, reading, poetry and a story. According to the day, they then do some Science, Geography or History, Drama, Music or Computers. Aoife's teacher has just started using an interactive white board in the classroom. Twice a week they go to the hall for P.E.

Aoife eats her lunch with friends at her table in the classroom before going out for a half hour break to play. If it is raining they will have tabletop games and play activities in the classroom. Aoife is taught religion every day after big break and some days she does Art or Music or Drama. Most days her teacher reads a story before home time. Either Una or Tim takes the two girls to school and Mrs Foley collects them. Every weekend Aoife and Maeve attend horse riding and music lessons. They also have swimming lessons on Thursday evenings. Occasionally they visit their grandparents and cousins in Cork and regularly attend birthday parties for their friends.

Una and Tim work long hours and their business is thriving. They appreciate being able to work from home and thus avoiding the commute to Dublin with long traffic jams that many of their friends endure on a daily basis. They have a good lifestyle for themselves and their daughters and they are considering buying a small place in France as a holiday home. So far there have been no expensive health worries, but they do have private healthcare insurance.

Aoife is a happy child. She lives a busy life and her favourite activity is riding 'her' pony. Her favourite toy is her toy lamb which she has had since birth. Aoife wants to be a ballerina when she grows up.

A CHILD BORN IN THE REPUBLIC OF IRELAND IN 2000:
OWNEY'S STORY

Owney lives in a town in the west of Ireland and is a member of the traveller community. There are approximately 30,000 members of this indigenous minority community living in Ireland; they have been documented as being part of Irish society for centuries. They have their own language, customs and traditions. Despite a long-shared history they face ongoing individual and institutional discrimination and opposition to their way of life.

Owney is six and about to start big school (primary school) in September 2006. Owney's mammy, Winnie, and daddy, Small Thomas, are delighted. Owney made an introductory visit to school and it went well. Winnie and Small Thomas are pleased because they want Owney to get a good education and for him to be happy in school. They themselves didn't get much formal schooling. While they both attended primary school their experience was not always a positive one, as they were often segregated and suffered name calling. They want something different for Owney and know this means working closely with the school.

Small Thomas works in the markets and drives a van; Owney loves to go with his daddy in the van and for him it doesn't matter that his daddy cannot read or write. Winnie works in the primary healthcare project for travellers in her area, run by the local traveller support group and the Health Service Executive (HSE).

Owney was born in Ireland but moved with his family to England for a few years. They travelled around the country working in the markets. His sister Kathleen was born in England and the family came back to the west of Ireland for the birth of babbie (baby) Thomas. Back home they lived in a trailer on the side of a road for many months but recently they have been allocated a house in a local public housing estate. Owney has a large extended family living in the west and his grandparents are on an unofficial halting site near the town where Big Thomas, his grandfather, keeps lots of horses. Owney likes his house but prefers to go to the halting site where he can be with the horses and his cousins and can play football. Small Thomas's mother and sisters take care of Kathleen and babbie Thomas when Winnie is working and Owney goes to the pre-school.

He goes to the local traveller pre-school where he loves to play with the cars but especially the vans. The traveller pre-school was set up by the local parish priest and is run by an Early Childhood worker and three traveller assistants, funded under a Community Employment (CE) scheme. Traveller pre-schools are amongst the few initiatives grant-aided by the Department of Education and Science (DES). The initiative was set up with the aim of preparing traveller children for primary school. The services vary in quality as the DES does not take responsibility for the curriculum content or for professional supervision. This is a concern for traveller organisations which advocate that traveller children should attend integrated pre-school services.

Owney is one of 15 traveller children attending the pre-school in his town. He knew all the children well before he went to the pre-school; some of them are his cousins. He doesn't know any settled children (children from the majority community) as settled children cannot access this state-funded provision. Because of Owney's parents' experience of segregation in school they wanted Owney to attend an integrated community pre-school. However, this proved difficult because they were told there were no places available and anyway 'they had their own traveller pre-school up the road'.

Owney had a great experience in the pre-school and his parents were happy too. The session went from 9.30 am until 1 pm. His pre-school is a high quality setting that embraces diversity. His teacher is innovative and also engages is ongoing professional development, including diversity and equality training specific to early childhood. She is aware of the traveller children's and parents' (as former pupils) negative experiences within the education system and works hard to support the children's group and individual identity, giving them skills to deal with difficult situations as they arise. The environment is rich with the imagery of traveller culture. The children hear stories from their community and are encouraged to bring their cultural skills and knowledge into the setting, such as horses, cars and flower making. She also creates spaces for the children to talk about differences and similarities within the setting and broader community. The traveller assistants work side by side and support the use of the traveller language called 'Cant'.

Owney, like all traveller children, is growing up in a different cultural context from settled children. When traveller children go to school it is generally the first time they come into intimate contact with both settled adults and children. It may also be the first time they realise they are different, and different in a negative way. Owney's parents recognise the benefits the education system can bring to Owney but they also know that it can be difficult and that children can be hurt. The pre-school teacher works with the children to give them skills to deal with difficult situations that may arise for them in school, as well as working with a school to help with the transition into big school.

When Owney starts school in September the class will have 24 children. The day will go from 8.50 am until 2.30 pm and will be very structured with two 15-minute breaks and one 45-minute lunch break. All schools follow a standardised curriculum. However, the forthcoming Traveller Education Strategy will offer recommendations for greater support for the inclusion of traveller children at all levels of the education system. This will mean that traveller identity and culture would be addressed as part of the training and curriculum. Owney's parents hope that these new structures will give him the chances they didn't get and that he will continue confidently through the education system.

Travelling is part of Owneys family life but these days legislation, such as the Housing Miscellaneous Act 2002 (Trespass Legislation), has made it difficult to travel and halt so they only go on visits to their cousins up and down the country. Lots of times they visit priests, holy wells and healers around the country because Owney's babbie brother Little Thomas is often sick and needs prayers and blessings.

(Thanks to Colette Murray, Early Years Co-ordinator, Pavee Point, who prepared Owney's story.)

BACKGROUND

The Republic of Ireland covers about 80 per cent of the island of Ireland with the remaining 20 per cent in the north-east being Northern Ireland. Dublin is the capital city. It is a small landmass of 70,133 square kilometres; English and Irish are the official languages and the euro is the official currency. Ireland is a parliamentary democracy with a written constitution, the *Bunreacht na hÉireann* (Government of Ireland, 1937). Legislation is enacted through the *Dáil*, the house of elected representatives. Policy decisions are made by the Cabinet of Ministers chaired by the *Taoiseach* (Prime Minister). The local government structure consists of 29 county councils, five city councils, five borough councils and 75 town councils. There are eight regional authorities co-ordinating some of the county and city programmes. Each county and city council has a Childcare Committee.

The Republic has a population of about 4.2 million people (Central Statistics Office (CSO), 2006), 318,000 more than the previous census in 2002. This represents an 8.1 per cent increase in population over a four-year period, the highest the population has been since 1861. Ireland was previously a country from which people emigrated rather than a country to which people immigrated. Ten per cent of the population consists of foreign nationals, mostly citizens from Eastern Europe and countries like Poland that are now members of the European Union. It is estimated that there are approximately 150,000 Polish citizens living and working in Ireland and that Polish is now the second most commonly-spoken language in Ireland. The exact ethnic breakdown of the population will be available from the census in 2007. It is estimated there are 30,000 people in the travelling community (see Owney's story).

> Owney's story shows the isolation from the 'settled' community of many traveller children until they enter primary school. Look back at Owney and Aoife's stories and make a note of the most important ways in which their early lives differed.

In 2002 nearly 2,000 asylum seekers were recognised as refugees; this dropped to 966 in 2005. Many of these people are from African countries such as Nigeria. The decrease in refugee status is a result of an amendment to the Irish constitution that prior to 2005 recognised any child born in Ireland as Irish; this is no longer the case. The CSO officials suggest the increase in the birth rate is due mainly to the number of Irish women of childbearing age in the population rather than the arrival of immigrants. The annual excess of births over deaths is 33,000.

From the mid-1990s the Irish economy has been growing and expanding to such an extent that Ireland has, in 2006, one of the lowest levels of unemployment in Europe. Some of this economic revival has been attributed to an increase in the number of women in the workforce; hence to an increased demand for affordable, quality childcare. A growing awareness of the significance of early childhood education, particularly for children from disadvantaged backgrounds, has led to a demand for educational opportunities for young children.

The 2002 census reveals that there were 384,712 children between the ages of birth and six years in Ireland. The breakdown of these figures shows a total of 218,504 children in the three-to-six age group (CSO, 2002). The compulsory age for starting primary school in Ireland is six although the parents of most four year olds and nearly all five year olds opt to send their children to primary school. As a result of the compulsory age for school being six years of age early childhood in Ireland, unlike the international definition, is birth to six years rather than birth to eight years.

> In what ways might the very different early experiences of Aoife and Owney have affected their readiness for primary school, and in particular for the formality of the curriculum they would experience soon after entry?

History

Ireland has a long history of academic learning going back to the monastic tradition of the Middle-Ages. This tradition saw young men travelling to established colleges in mainland Europe to study. The penal laws in the late seventeenth century forbade Catholics from sending their children abroad for education or from setting up schools in Ireland. Despite this, however, unofficial schools often referred to as 'hedge schools' sprang up throughout the country and many of the teachers in these schools were poets and revered local people. Some still claim that the status of teaching in Ireland as a worthy profession springs from this time.

The penal laws against Catholics participating in education were repealed by 1793. An official commission in 1824 reported that there were 11,000 schools in Ireland catering for half a million children and with about 12,000 teachers. Lord Stanley, then Chief Secretary for Ireland, established the National School System in 1831. It was envisaged as an interdenominational system but because of pressure from all churches, by the mid-nineteenth century the system was increasingly evolving as a denominational system. Young children, some just three years of age, were catered for in the national school system. In 1871, 33 per cent of people over five years of age were illiterate; by 1901 this had been reduced to 14 per cent.

The Revised Programme for National Schools (1900) was a significant development in that for the first time the importance of what was referred to as 'infant' education, a title still used today, was emphasised. This was influenced by the Enlightenment in Europe led by Jean Jacques Rousseau and the ideas of Friedrich Froebel amongst others. It signified a new emphasis on the needs of young children and the consideration given to the environment in which they were educated.

The setting up of the Irish Free State in 1922 meant that Ireland, apart from Northern Ireland, was no longer ruled by Britain. This saw a strong, cultural revolution influencing the school system, with Irish becoming an obligatory subject taught for at least one hour per day and a renewed interest in Irish games and music. The Irish Republic was declared in 1948. A new National Primary Curriculum was introduced in 1971. It was based on a child-centred philosophy and its purpose was 'to enable the child to live a full life as a child and to equip him to avail of further education so that he may go on to live a full and useful life as an adult in society' (*Primary School Curriculum, Government of Ireland,* (1971), Book 1: 12). A revised Primary Curriculum was introduced into Irish schools in 1999.

POLICY AND PRACTICE IN EARLY CHILDHOOD EDUCATION AND CARE

Recent Irish governments have comprised centre-right coalition parties. The economy is mixed, with low direct taxation rates and significant inward investment from abroad. Social and economic stability has been due to a number of factors including the social partnership agreements between governments, trade unions and employers and representatives of community groups. These agreements set out programmes on a range of issues, such as ending poverty and agreeing wage increases over a specified period of time. Early childhood education has been referred to in these agreements but not in any great detail. *Sustaining Progress* (Government of Ireland, 2003–2005) called for priority for early education and childcare facilities for disadvantaged families.

The National Children's Office is a government agency set up to lead and co-ordinate the implementation of the *National Children's Strategy, 'Our Children: Their lives'* (Government of Ireland, 2000). The strategy is a ten-year plan to improve the lives of children from birth to 18 in Ireland and is a response to the *United Nations Convention on the Rights of the Child* (1989) ratified by Ireland in September 1992. Over 2,500 children and young people were involved in the development of the strategy.

> Note that in the Republic of Ireland many children and young people have been consulted and involved in the development of recent strategies. This is true in other European countries also. How would you attempt to involve young children in agency?

One of the difficulties involved in researching and managing Early Years services has been that until 2006 seven different government departments played a part in the lives of children. They collected their statistics in different ways, leaving it difficult to gain a clear overall picture about young children. However, this has changed with the setting up of one body under the Minister for Children to oversee and regulate the education and care of children prior to primary school, with additional functions such as policy work on child protection and the programmes and activities of the National Children's Office. The minister with responsibility for children is situated within the Department of Health and Children. The decision to locate the new body within the Department of Health and Children is unique to Western Europe, where such bodies are more often in the Departments of Education of relevant governments. However, a new Early Years Education Policy Unit has been established within the DES and is co-located with the Office of the Minister for Children. Representatives from the Department of Justice, Equality and Law Reform and the National Children's Office also participate in the new body.

Ireland has a high – by European standards – birth rate and a dramatic increase in the number of women participating in the workforce. In 1995 this figure was 483,000 women and by 2004 it had risen to 771,000 women – an increase of almost 60 per cent. This represents a significant change in Irish social and cultural life. To grasp the full importance of these changes, a knowledge of Irish social and economic life in the preceding decades is necessary.

In 1933 a bar was introduced banning women from working in the Civil Service and as primary school teachers after marriage. It was part of government policy to give priority of employment to men and restrict women's work to the home. In 1948 a radical Minister for Health in a coalition government, Dr Noel Browne, introduced a Health Bill in which he proposed a universal health scheme for mothers and children. This led to a bitter dispute and debate in which the Catholic bishops became directly involved. In a letter to the then *Taoiseach*, John A. Costello, the Catholic bishops pronounced:

> The Hierarchy cannot approve of any scheme which, in its general tendency, must foster undue control by the State in a sphere so delicate and so intimately concerned with morals as that which deals with gynaecology or obstetrics and with the relations between doctor and patient. (Kennedy, 2002: 200)

The scheme failed because it was contrary to Catholic social teaching. The marriage bar on women working as primary teachers was rescinded in 1958 and in 1973 for married women working in the Civil Service.

Other legal and social factors have also changed Irish society. Equal pay for women was introduced in 1974 and The Employment Equality Act came into operation in 1977, outlawing discrimination on grounds of gender or marital status in recruitment, training or provision for promotion. The Maternity Act (1981) provided for maternity leave and the right to return to work for pregnant employees. Divorce was introduced in Ireland as recently as 1995.

In what ways are the background factors listed above likely to have influenced family life and the recent development of early education and care in the Republic of Ireland?

Government policy for early childhood education

The White Paper on early childhood education *Ready to Learn* (Government of Ireland, 1999) is concerned with children from birth to six, and sets out the core objective of government policy as 'supporting the development and educational achievement of children through high quality early education, with particular focus on the target groups of the disadvantaged and those with special needs'. The guiding principles for this policy are

- Quality will underpin all aspects of early education provision.
- The state will build on existing provision and use the existing regulatory framework, where possible.
- Implementation will be undertaken on a gradual, phased basis to allow all the participants in the system to prepare adequately for the challenges that lie ahead.
- Progress will be achieved through a process of consultation, dialogue and partnership. (Government of Ireland, 1999: 15)

Early education providers who receive state funding for developmental/ educational places will be required to meet set standards. Other providers who satisfy the required standards can obtain special recognition through the awarding of a Quality in Education (QE) mark. The QE mark will apply to educational standards concerning curriculum, methodologies, staff qualifications and training. The existing childcare regulations will continue to apply.

Provision for children before formal schooling

There is a very limited public provision for early childhood education. The Republic is divided into four health authority areas, all of which are regulated by the Health Service Executive. Under The Child Care Act (1991) the local health authorities are responsible for the welfare and care of children attending pre-school services. For many years provision for children before formal schooling was generally unregulated and provided by private and voluntary providers. Now in some cases, there is limited public funding from the health authorities or the state training organisation (FÁS). Where there is state involvement the provisions are subject to the requirements of The Child Care Act. Voluntary providers, the majority of whom are members of the IPPA, the Irish Pre-school Playgroup Association, offer playgroup places to children on a sessional basis in local communities.

Childminding of one or two children by women in their own homes has been on an individual basis. Privately-run crèches have become a common feature in Irish cities and towns in recent years and some charges are prohibitive for many parents. On average, childcare can cost Irish parents 200 euros per week or 10,400 euros per year for one child. Child benefit payments were increased in the 2006 budget and an extra payment of 1,000 euros per year is now paid for each child under the age of six years.

As well as the increased demand for childcare places, there has been a growing awareness of the importance of good education for young children. Comparison of services with those in other European countries has been a contributing factor. Ireland has one of the lowest participating rates of three year olds in state-funded early education in Europe because the state does not invest directly in early education. Funding of public pre-primary education services is 0.44 per cent of GDP.

> You will have noted that by 2006 there was very limited state provision of early education and care, and little provision for children under three in the Republic of Ireland, compared with the countries in the UK discussed here. How is this likely to have affected the extent and type of provision? Are there any advantages in mainly private provision, and what are the disadvantages? Look at the experience of Aoife and her family.

Children from birth to three years of age who are cared for outside the home are typically accommodated in crèches or with childminders. The crèches offer a full-day service, with some also offering hourly sessions. The majority are privately owned although some are organised and run on a local community basis. Childminding is privately arranged between parents and childminders and varies according to the individual needs of particular families.

Pre-schools/playschools, Montessori schools and *Naíonraí* (playschools through the medium of Irish) are available for children from three to six years of age. The pre-school/playschool offers morning or afternoon sessions and is mainly privately owned, although some are community run and non-profit making. The Montessori and the *Naíonraí* facilities are sessional, usually mornings, and are privately and community run. Private individuals and some community-based bodies also run 'after–school' clubs and holiday camps for children from four years upwards.

The Department of Education and Science is involved in two intervention projects for targeted three to four year olds; the Early Start Programme which is attached to primary schools in some designated disadvantaged areas, and pre-schools for children from the travelling community. At present there are 1,680 children in Early Start classes and 600 children attending pre-schools for travellers facilities. The Early Start initiative is part of the National Anti-Poverty Strategy launched by the government in 1996. There are about 50 pre-schools for traveller children, organised by voluntary bodies with the DES providing the cost of transport and teacher salaries.

However, although the DES recommends the appointment of qualified primary teachers to traveller pre-schools, the conditions of service mean that in practice few take up these positions. The Department of Justice, Equality and Law Reform funds the Equal Opportunities Childcare Programme (EOCP) that aims to involve socially excluded parents in training, education and employment by supporting the development of community childcare facilities in disadvantaged areas.

The vast majority of Irish four, five and six year olds are enrolled in primary schools. These children are dealt with under the section on early childhood education within primary schools. There were 384,712 children under the age of six in Ireland at the time of the 2002 census. The most recent figures available estimate that 37,900 of them avail of childcare services. However, these figures (see Table 4.1) are probably quite conservative and do not reflect those services still operating in the black economy. 'Childcare' usually refers to children from three months to four or five years of age. In 2006 the government announced an increase in paid maternity leave to 26 weeks by March 2007 and unpaid maternity leave to 16 weeks if a mother wishes to avail herself of these.

TABLE 4.1   ECEC services in the childcare sector in the Republic of Ireland

Type of service	Sessional	Full-day	Total number of services
Playgroup/pre-school	1 276	252	1 528
Montessori school	402	229	631
Nursery/Daycare centre	–	414	414
'Other services'	113	118	231
Drop-in crèche	124	68	192
Naíonraí	159	3	162
Parent & toddler group	136	–	136
After school group	97	–	97
Workplace crèche	22	40	62
Homework club	43	–	43
Total			**3 496**
Total number of childminders (estimated)			**37 900**

Source: Forthcoming report of the ADM: *Notional Summary of the Country Childcare Census 1999/2000*, cited in the *Irish Background Report* 2002, adapted. The figure for childminders is taken from Government of Ireland, 1999a.

The Centre for Early Childhood Development and Education (CECDE)

Following the White Paper on early childhood education *Ready to Learn* (Government of Ireland, 1999), the DES established the Centre for early Childhood Development and Education (CECDE). It is jointly managed by

St Patrick's College, Dublin City University, and the Dublin Institute of Technology. The Centre has three main objectives: to develop quality standards for early years settings, to develop and implement targeted interventions in the areas of special needs and disadvantage for children in the birth to six years age group, and prepare the groundwork for the establishment of the Early Childhood Education Agency. This will become the new body mentioned previously under the remit of the Minister with Responsibility for Children. A quality framework *Síolta* (2006) published by the CECDE is now available. This is the first time that the ECCE sector in Ireland has an agreed set of national quality standards.

TRANSITIONS

Transition from a pre-school or home-based care to primary school is reasonably straightforward. Parents apply to their local parish school or to a school of their choice. Some schools do have waiting lists, for example many of the Educate Together schools have long waiting lists and children are often enrolled from birth. Churches give priority to children from their own faith.

> What problems may children face in transferring to primary schools in the Republic? Contrast Aoife and Owney's preparedness for life in primary school. Note that Aoife's sister Maeve was able to have her entry deferred. What would be the possible implications of such deferred entry for a child and their teacher?

SCHOOLING

Primary education

All primary schools come under the regulation of the DES in Dublin through the Education Act (1998). Schools are funded by the DES. It is a centralised system and although the regionalising of education services is regularly mooted, it has never been acted upon. However, primary schools are not managed by the state. The majority of primary schools come under the management of the Catholic church, with a smaller number under the Protestant church and a few under the Muslim faith. There is a board of management for each school comprising a chair, (often a local priest or minister), the principal, an elected teachers' representative, two elected parents' representatives and three bishops' nominees. There are also 125 *Gaelscoileanna* (Irish medium primary schools) that operate under this managerial system.

In the late 1970s a small, minority of urban parents began to object to the sectarian nature of the education system. They wanted a more integrated system and in the face of strong opposition from the Catholic Church and without support from the State, these parents set up a religiously integrated primary school in Dalkey, Dublin in 1980, called the Dalkey School Project. Others followed and were known as multi-denominational schools. In more recent years they have changed their name to 'Educate Together'. These schools are managed in a similar way to other primary schools, except there is greater parental involvement and no church managerial input. There has been an increasing demand for such schooling and in 2006 there were 39 Educate Together schools throughout Ireland. There are no fees in any of these schools, although parents raise funds to assist with the purchase of equipment and materials.

There is a National Parents Council that represents the interests of parents within the primary system. There is also a similar body for parents of second-level students, but as yet there is no such body for parents of younger children. Teachers in all of the above schools are paid by the DES.

> What are the possible benefits of schools such as 'Educate Together' that have developed recently in the Republic of Ireland? Compare them with similar developments in other European countries. In what ways do they differ from 'faith' schools that are a matter of controversy in England in 2006?

There is a very small number of private primary schools. These are expensive and teachers working in them do not enjoy the same remuneration as those working within the public sector. Altogether there are 3,278 primary schools with 26,039 teachers catering for 446,029 children between the ages of four to twelve in the Irish Republic. Just over 1,000 children are taught in small rural schools with no more than three teachers in each. There are 4,364 children between the ages of four to six, the first two years of primary schooling. There are 128 special schools for children with special educational needs. In recent years there has been a policy of integrating children with special needs into mainstream schooling.

Young children in primary school

Primary school in Ireland is an eight-year long programme. Children usually start primary education at four or five years of age. The first two years from four to six are considered 'early childhood' education and are referred to as 'infant education'. The first year of schooling is known as 'Junior Infants' and the second year is known as 'Senior Infants'.

TABLE 4.2   Grades and average ages of children in primary schools in the Republic of Ireland

Grades	Average ages (years)
Junior Infants	4–5
Senior Infants	5–6
First Class	6–7
Second Class	7–8
Third Class	8–9
Fourth Class	9–10
Fifth Class	10–11
Sixth Class	11–12

TABLE 4.3   Curriculum areas and subjects in primary schools in the Republic of Ireland

Curriculum Areas	Subjects
Mathematics	Mathematics
Language	Gaelige English
Social, environmental and scientific education	History, Geography, Science
Arts education	Visual arts, Music, Drama
Physical education	Physical education
Social, personal and health education	Social, personal and health education

Refer to Aoife's story to appreciate just how many subjects are covered in the early years in primary schools in the Republic. What problems might this cause for children like Owney, for a child who has not been to any form of pre-school, and for children like Aoife's sister Maeve?

There is a national curriculum for primary schools published by the National Council for Curriculum and Assessment (NCCA), a statutory body. This was developed by subject committees involving teachers, parents, school management, the DES and the main interests in primary education (including lecturers in colleges of education). There are seven curriculum areas. The curriculum for Religious Education remains the responsibility of the different church authorities and as such is not part of the state curriculum. The six curriculum areas and 11 subjects of the primary curriculum are shown in Table 4.3.

The children attending Junior and Senior Infants within primary school are educated in all 11 subject areas. There are three general aims of primary education in Ireland:

- To enable a child to live a full life as a child and to realise his or her potential as a unique individual.
- To enable a child to develop as a social being through living and co-operating with others and so contribute to the good of society.
- To prepare the child for further education and lifelong learning. (*Primary School Curriculum, Government of Ireland,* 1999: 7)

Children in Ireland are taught in classes of up to 30. When a child has been assessed and is stated as having special needs s/he may be appointed a classroom assistant. Outside of this, infant classes in primary schools do not have classroom assistants. The OECD's *Thematic Review of Early Childhood Education and Care Policy in Ireland* (Government of Ireland, 2004) is critical of the conditions for educating four and five year olds within the primary system. Two of the recommendations in the report are the employment of a trained classroom assistant in every infant class and the creation of a post of responsibility for a senior teacher to undertake the management of infant classes in each school. The Irish National Teacher Organisation (INTO), the union representing teachers at primary level and an influential body in Irish education, is currently demanding a reduction in the pupil-teacher ratio.

The National Council for Curriculum and Assessment (NCCA) is in the process of developing a framework document on curriculum content and methodologies for teaching children from three to six years. It is envisaged that this framework will dovetail with the primary curriculum and influence current work in the infant classrooms. There are four themes in the *Framework for Early Learning* (NCAA, forthcoming), namely: Well-being, Identity and Belonging, Communication and Exploring/Thinking. The NCCA Early Years team is also drawing up a document on Portraiture Studies to learn about children's experiences in early childhood settings. By listening to children, talking with them and sharing in their routines and activities, the NCCA aims to gain a greater understanding of what life for these children is like in a range of Early Years settings.

SPECIAL EDUCATIONAL NEEDS

The Education of Children with Special Educational Needs Act (2004) states that children with special learning needs should be educated alongside other children who do not have these needs. The Act applies to children under the age of 18. In 2002, there were 2,082 Early Years children with special learning needs in primary schools and 584 children in infant classes in special schools. The CSO figures which cover all disabilities show 2,029 children with some form of disability between the ages of birth to four, and 7,017 children between the ages of five to nine years. A Visiting Teacher service provides a support service for children with hearing or visual impairment from the time they are diagnosed, and this service remains with the child through formal schooling and into third-level education if necessary.

The Government of Ireland OECD Report (Government of Ireland, 2004) was highly critical of the overall lack of services for the majority of pre-school children with special needs and recommended urgent consideration be given to the creation of a comprehensive national system of Early Years services to provide structured, regular educational support to children and their families from time of birth or from diagnosis. A National Council for Special Education was established by ministerial order in December 2003, an independent statutory body with responsibility for planning and co-ordinating the provision and support services for children with special educational needs.

> Aoife's parents had the knowledge and experience to appreciate that her sister Maeve might need learning support, and they were prepared to have an assessment undertaken privately. What does this imply for less knowledgeable or poorer parents?

SAFEGUARDING CHILDREN

In 2006 the government appointed special rapporteurs with legal expertise to audit legal developments for the protection of children. This comes in the wake of a number of sexual abuse scandals, some involving institutions run by the Catholic church for the state in previous decades. There are increasing demands for the rights of children to be enshrined in the Irish constitution. Those working with children must now undergo a vetting process by the *garda* (police).

Garda vetting was introduced for new teachers and other new appointees who have unsupervised access to children and vulnerable adults from September 2006, through the Teaching Council. 'New' teachers are defined as those who are newly qualified or are re-entering the teaching profession after a period of three years or more. Vetting arrangements will be expanded on a phased basis over the coming years to include all 55,000 teachers currently in the system and the vetting process is now a condition of employment. Vetting for those working with children outside of the school system is to come into place in 2007 under the Child Care Regulations; the processes for implementation are not yet in place at the time of writing.

In November 2006 Mr Ahern, the current *Taoiseach*, announced that he plans to hold a constitutional referendum to protect the rights of children. The referendum will be designed to give greater protection to children in the areas of abuse, adoption and custody.

QUALITY ASSURANCE

Regulation in the childcare sector

Services for children before staring school are regulated by The Childcare Act (1991) and The Childcare (Pre-school Services) Regulations (1996) and the Amendment Regulations (1997). Pre-schools for children from the travelling community, although funded by the DES, also come under these regulations. Inspections are organised through the relevant health authority and are usually carried out on an annual basis. Most of the inspectors come from a nursing or environmental health background and the criteria for inspection are largely based on health and safety, with little mention of curriculum or pedagogy. Inspectors assess the physical surroundings of the childcare facilities, health regulations, child/adult ratios, child/space ratios, insurance and fees charged. Materials, equipment and activities are included in the regulations but are more a matter of health and safety than educational awareness.

Those caring for fewer than three children and those providing after-school care for children do not have to register with a health authority, nor are they covered by the regulations mentioned above. In reality this means the majority of childminders remain outside the registered and inspected system. The Childcare and Pre-School Services Regulations are under review in 2006 by a cross-sector review group.

Regulation of primary schools

Implementing the primary curriculum is overseen by inspectors from the DES. Schools are subject to whole-school evaluations and for the first time these evaluations will be published on the DES website.

PROFESSIONAL DEVELOPMENT AND TRAINING

Qualifications and training in the childcare sector

Ireland is committed to meeting the targets of the EU's Barcelona Agreement by having a 90 per cent participation rate of three to six year olds in education by 2010. Ireland has by far the lowest rate of three year olds participating in state-funded Early Years facilities in Western Europe. There are about 16,400 three to five year olds and about 6,000 younger children attending childcare services supported by EOCP (Equality Opportunities Childcare Programme) funding. In European terms early childhood education in Ireland is grossly under-funded.

One of the main issues, as well as funding, is the qualifications of those delivering what services there are. There has been a wide variety of qualifications within the childcare/pre-school sector in Ireland with many of those involved in the care of children having no relevant qualifications whatsoever. Estimates suggest that 30 per cent of staff have no qualification at all. The report of the Partnership 2000 Expert Working Group on Childcare (Department of Justice, Equality and Law Reform, 1999) recommends, among other things, that the childcare sector should aim to achieve the European Commission Network on Childcare target of a minimum of 60 per cent of staff working directly with children in collective services having at least three years training. However at present, there are no minimum standards concerning the educational component of services or the training and qualifications of staff.

The separation of responsibility for education and training across a range of government departments has been reflected in the separation of qualifications systems with linked but separate arrangements for schools, Further Education, Institutes of Technology, universities and a variety of training organisations. A variety of childcare courses has been featured within this diversity of systems, from privately-run short courses to three-year BA programmes such as those offered by the Dublin Institute of Technology. In order to regulate qualifications the Education (Qualifications and Training) Act (1999) became law and the National Qualifications Authority of Ireland (NQAI) was established to develop a National Framework of Qualifications (NFQ).

The NFQ was launched in October 2003 with the aim of being fully implemented by 2006. There are ten levels within the framework, from Level 1 Certificate to Doctoral degree. It is designed to incorporate awards and training awards and relate Irish education to each other. There is also a European dimension with the Bologna and Copenhagen Declarations (see www.europe.eu) seeking greater compatibility and comparability of qualifications within the European Union.

Each level is based on specific standards of knowledge, skill and competence. The award types are all major qualifications. It is envisaged that in time there will also be minor, supplemental, and special purpose awards, all of which have yet to be developed. The awarding bodies, the Further Education and Training Awards Council (FETAC) and the Higher Education and Training Council (HETAC), are currently devising the structures for these award types. As this happens, the range and type of awards available at each level will expand. So too will the routes through which learners can progress. A key feature of the new awards is that they will be made on the basis of 'learning outcomes', that is, what a learner knows and can do. The universities remain awarding bodies in their own right and the Department of Education and Science is the awarding authority for the Junior Certificate (a state examination taken after three years in secondary school) and the

Leaving Certificate (examination taken in the final year of second-level education).

Teacher education

There are five colleges of education within the Republic of Ireland, four of which are based in Dublin. They all have affiliation to churches or religious orders but have an open enrolment policy. The majority of students apply through the CAO (Central Applicants Office) during their final year of secondary school. They are awarded points according to their Leaving Certificate results and are allocated third-level places accordingly. The CAO's points for primary teaching have remained consistently high and result in successful applicants coming from the top quarter of students sitting the Leaving Certificate Examination in any year. A small percentage of places are held for mature students in the colleges. A BEd is the standard qualification and each of the colleges is affiliated to or is a college of a different university. The two largest colleges are St Patrick's College, Drumcondra, in Dublin – a college of Dublin City University – and Mary Immaculate College in Limerick – a college of the University of Limerick. Students take three years to complete their degree with the majority qualifying with an honours grade. There are about 400 students in each year group in each of the colleges. Both of these colleges also offer Graduate Diploma Courses in Special Needs and Masters and Doctorate programmes in Education. Early childhood education is one of the specialisms offered in the Masters programme. Mary Immaculate College in Limerick also offers a BA in Early Childhood Care and Education.

The other three colleges have a smaller intake and they are affiliated to Trinity College in Dublin. The smallest college, the Church of Ireland College in Dublin with about 30 students in each of the three years, caters for students who will work in Church of Ireland primary schools. *Coláiste Mhuire* in Dublin is an Irish-medium college and the majority of its students go to teach in *Gaelscoileanna* (Irish medium primary schools). *Coláiste Mhuire* has an intake of about 100 undergraduates per annum. The Froebel College, also in Dublin, has an intake of about 100 undergraduates per annum. The three colleges affiliated to Trinity offer a three-year degree but students have to take a fourth year of part-time study to qualify for an honours BEd.

All of the colleges also offer an 18 month full-time Postgraduate Diploma in Primary Teaching. Places on this course are restricted by government policy and candidates are assessed by interview. Some graduates opt to take a postgraduate teaching qualification in Scotland, England or Wales, but must sit an examination in written and oral Irish to be recognised to teach in Ireland. This is also the case for students taking their BEd in Northern Ireland or in England, Scotland or Wales. In 2004 a private for-profit company, Hibernia College, established an on-line Postgraduate Diploma course in Primary Teaching.

A Teaching Council (*An Chomhairle Mhúinteoireachta*) was established in 2006 and all teachers must register with it. The aims of the council are to promote teaching as a profession and the continuing professional development of teachers, to establish and maintain a register of teachers and to develop codes of professional conduct and practice which include teaching knowledge, skill and competence. During their first year in a school, a teacher is on probation and is inspected by the DES inspectors.

As mentioned in the introduction to this chapter, primary teaching is still seen as an attractive career in Ireland, although attracting young men into the profession is proving problematic with the average ratio in the colleges being one male for every eight females. Interestingly the Postgraduate Diploma in Primary Teaching attracts a greater ratio of male to females than the undergraduate degree.

Student teachers in Ireland become general primary school teachers which means they are qualified to teach any class within the primary system (children aged four to twelve). There are no specialisms. Students study the curriculum, teaching methodologies, and the foundation areas of psychology, philosophy, sociology and the history of education. All students have modules in early childhood education; however, the *OECD Thematic Review of Early Childhood Education* (Government of Ireland, 2004) is critical of the fact that only in some programmes is there a significant core subject in early childhood education. The OECD report *Starting Strong II* (2006) sees no significant improvement in this situation. Each year students also spend time in schools on teaching practice. Early childhood education is offered as a specialism as part of postgraduate degrees.

> What are the advantages and disadvantages of teachers being qualified to teach any class of children from four to twelve years of age?

FUTURE AND IMMINENT CHANGES

Ireland still has a comparatively high birth rate compared with many of its European neighbours. It is also rapidly changing into a much more multicultural society than previously. The Ireland that Owney and Aoife are growing up in is significantly different from that of children born in the previous decade. There have been significant numbers of immigrants from East European countries and some also from African countries like Nigeria. Such changes can be perceived as a rich resource for the future.

Irish society, however, needs to adjust to accommodate these new residents and the education system needs to resource the support systems necessary for the particular requirements of immigrant children. But as is often the case, action seems to follow the needs and demands of a society rather than leading it. There are major philosophical questions and practical issues facing Irish society in regard to the role and recognition of children as citizens and their care and education. It is significant that Owney's first encounter with the settled community will be when he starts primary school.

> In what ways were the early experiences of Owney and Aoife different and how would you predict that their later childhood experiences might differ?

Ireland has a National Children's Office, an Ombudsman for Children, and a *Dáil na nÓg* (a children's parliament). These are all to be welcomed as a recognition of children with their own rights, needs and voices. There is much more to be done in this area but the work is ongoing. One of the biggest problems for Ireland, despite its recent healthy economy, is the high number of children still living in poverty. Many, such as Barnardos, claim the divide between rich and poor in Irish society has widened, with 100,000 Irish children living in constant poverty and 1,000 children every year failing to transfer to second-level education. The infant mortality rate among the traveller community is three times the national average.

These concerns are highly relevant to education and in particular for early childhood education and care. The predicted life experiences and life expectancy of Oweny and Aoife are very different. Has Ireland's new wealth provided an increase in equality of opportunity for all of its children or is it becoming a more divided society? There are, however, many imminent changes in Early Years education and care for children from birth to six. There is growing awareness in Ireland of the need for and importance of quality Early Years provision for young children. Significantly, Early Years provision is now more regulated and accountable than had previously been the case.

Conor, born in Galway in August 2006, will experience a significantly different early childhood sector from either Owney or Aoife. There are more financial supports for his parents and if his mother opts to return to work as a nurse Conor will be placed in a regulated and inspected childcare facility. There are growing indications that by 2009 Conor will be entitled to a year of state-funded education before his entry into primary school. There is even the possibility that when Conor does enrol in primary school he may be in a class of fewer than 20 children, with a trained classroom assistant working full-time with the class teacher. These would indeed be significant changes.

> As you read this final section make a list of the imminent changes in early education and care in the Republic of Ireland. Also study the recommendations concerning the Republic in the second OECD report *Starting Strong II* (2006). In what ways might Conor's early education and care from birth to eight be affected as a consequence of these developments?

TOPICS FOR DISCUSSION

The role of the State in Early Childhood Education and Care

One of the key questions for early childhood education both before and as part of primary school is the role of the state. Should the state, through the Department of Education and Science and the Department of Children, become more directly involved in the funding and managing of facilities for children? Should primary schools become one of the providers for three to four year olds?

The role of the Churches in primary education

Is the role of the churches in the control of the primary school system becoming untenable in a multicultural Ireland?

The future training of the workforce for ECEC

Is it time for student teachers to specialise and become Early Years teachers rather than general primary teachers? These are all very real and immediate questions for the future planning of the education of Ireland's youngest citizens and residents.

The Irish government has allocated money to encourage growth in child-care places but there is still a need for increased funding to provide quality provision. A new Partnership Agreement (2006–2016) between the government, the trade unions, employers and community groups proposes among other recommendations that 50,000 new childcare places, including 10,000 pre-school places and 5,000 after-school places, be established as part of the 2.65 billion euro National Childcare Strategy. As has been shown there is now a system by which people can become qualified to work with young children. However, there are still many who do not have an adequate qualification to remain in a professional childcare system. Possibly a date should be set in two or three years time by which all of those working with young children must be qualified to do so in order to remain working in the sector.

Related to this is one of the most important and critical matters which needs to be addressed, that is, the proper remuneration of those working in the childcare sector. No matter how many quality criteria lists are drawn up, the system will not function well until childcare workers and Early Years educators are offered quality wages. This could well be the deciding factor in Ireland developing a comprehensive, quality early childhood care and education system.

The rights of the child

There have been significant, positive changes in the attention to early childhood in the Republic of Ireland in the past decade. However, as if reflecting the previous chaos surrounding the Early Years sector, the system where it exists is still somewhat haphazard. Some fundamental questions on the role and status of Irish children need to be asked and how we conceptualise childhood requires discussion at a national level.

Should the rights of children be enshrined in the Irish constitution? Would such a decision have any effect on the daily lives of children and their families? What would the implications be for the broader society? While continuing to work on particular aspects of structure and legislative change it is vital that there is a context and shared understanding of why and how these changes are being implemented.

Consider the implications of the OECD report *Starting Strong II*

The recommendations of the OECD report *Starting Strong II* (2006) for the Republic of Ireland address fundamental and necessary changes, particularly regarding the training and education for providers at all levels and access to quality care for all children. The provision for children from birth to six is still somewhat unco-ordinated and a coherent continuum of care and education which is visible and accessible should be the aim. Access and availability are crucial factors in future development and planning. Where does the responsibility for this lie? Is it the responsibility of the state or of private providers?

Recognised training and qualifications for all those working in the sector are essential and must be given priority. Equally, the wisdom of having four year olds being taught an 11-subject curriculum within the primary school system needs to be addressed. The OECD (2006) recommends the restructuring of the first two years of primary school to favour autonomy of early childhood education within the primary system. Their report is equally vociferous on the need for changes within the BEd degree to favour significant components in early childhood education.

Most importantly, the discussion on early childhood care and education has begun in the Republic of Ireland largely because of the economic demand for childcare places. It is essential that the debate is both broadened and moved forward so that its application in the daily lives of children exists in the context of a shared understanding of childhood.

KEY MILESTONES IN GOVERNMENT STRATEGY FOR EARLY CHILDHOOD EDUCATION AND CARE IN THE REPUBLIC OF IRELAND

* **1991** – Childcare Act
* **1992** – Irish government ratifies the UN Convention on the Rights of the Child
* **1996** – Childcare (Pre-school Services) Regulations
* **1997** – Childcare Amendment Regulations
* **1999** – The White Paper on Early Childhood Education - *Ready to Learn*
* **1999** – National Childcare Strategy
* **2000** – National Children's Strategy - *Our Children: Their Lives*
* **2000** – National Children's Office established
* **2003** – Children's Ombudsman created
* **2004** – NCCA: *Towards a Framework for Early Learning*
* **2004** – The Education of Children with Special Needs Act
* **2004** – OECD *Review of ECCE Policy in Ireland*
* **2004** – CECDE *Insights on Quality and Making Connections*
* **2006** – CECDE *Síolta: A Quality Framework* (CECDE, 2006)

REFERENCES

Central Statistics Office (2002) *Census of Population of Ireland* (2002). Cork: CSO.
Central Statistics Office (2006) *Census of Population of Ireland* (2006). Cork: CSO.
Centre for Early Childhood Development and Education (CECDE) (2006) *Síolta*. Dublin: CECDE.
Cohen, B., Moss, P., Petrie, P. and Wallace, J. (2004) *A New Deal for Children*. Bristol: The Policy Press.
Coolahan, J. (2004) *Irish Education: History and Structure*. Dublin: Institute of Public Administration.
Department of Health and Children (1997) *Child Care (Pre-School Services) Regulations 1996 and (Amendment) Regulations 1997*. Dublin: The Stationery Office.
Department of Justice, Equality and Law Reform (1999) *Partnership 2000 Expert Working Group on Childcare*. Dublin: The Stationery Office.
Dunne, J. and Hogan, P. (eds) (2004) *Education and Practice Upholding the Integrity of Teaching and Learning*. Oxford: Blackwell.
Dunne, J. and Kelly, J. (eds) (2002) *Childhood and its Discounts – The First Seamus Heaney Lectures*. Dublin: The Liffey Press.
Ferriter, D. (2004) *The Transformation of Ireland 1900–2000*. London: Profile Books.
Garvin, T. (2004) *Preventing the Future: Why was Ireland so Poor for so Long?* Dublin: Gill and MacMillan.

Government of Ireland (1937) *Bunreacht na hÉireann – Constitution of Ireland*. Dublin: The Stationery Office.

Government of Ireland (1999a) *Ready to Learn: White paper on early childhood education*. Dublin: The Stationery Office.

Government of Ireland (1999b) *Primary School Curriculum*. Dublin: The Stationery Office.

Government of Ireland (2000) *National Children's Strategy, 'Our Children: Their Lives'*. Dublin: The Stationery Office.

Government of Ireland (2003–2005) *Sustaining Progress*. Dublin: The Stationery Office.

Government of Ireland (2004) *OECD Thematic Review of Early Childhood Education and Care Policy in Ireland*. Dublin: The Stationery Office.

Kennedy, F. (2001) *Cottage to Creche. Family change in Ireland*. Dublin: Institute of Public Administration.

National Council for Curriculum and Assessment (NCCA) (forthcoming) *Framework for Early Learning*. Dublin: NCCA.

National Economic and Social Forum (2005) *Report 31 Early Childhood Care and Education*. Dublin: NESF.

OECD (2006) *Starting Strong II: Early childhood education and care*. Paris: OECD.

Quin, S., Kennedy, P., Matthews, A. and Kiely, G. (2005) *Contemporary Irish Social Policy*. Dublin: UCD Press.

Sugrue, S. (ed.) (2004) *Curriculum and Ideology: Irish experiences, international perspectives*. Dublin: The Liffey Press.

United Nations (1989) *United Nations Convention on the Rights of the Child*. Geneva: United Nations.

USEFUL WEBSITES

www.info.education.gov.ie

www.nco.ie   National Children's Office

www.cecde.ie   Centre for Early Childhood Development and Education

www.ncca.ie   National Council for Curriculum and Assessment

www.teachingcouncil.ie   The Teaching Council

www.spd.dcu.ie   St Patrick's College, Drumcondra

www.mic.ul.ie   Mary Immaculate College, Limerick

www.ippa.ie   Irish Pre-School Association, the Early Years Organisation

www.dit.ie   Dublin Institute of Technology

www.barnardos.ie   Barnardos

www.npc.ie   National Parents Council

www.into.ie   Irish National Teachers Organisation

www.esai.ie   Education Studies Association of Ireland

www.nfq.ie   National Framework of Qualifications

www.educatetogether.ie   Educate Together

www.paveepoint.ie   Pavee Point – The Travellers' Centre

www.cso.ie   Central Statistics Office

www.irishrefugeecouncil.ie   The IRC is committed to interculturalism

SCOTLAND

Eileen Carmichael and Juliet Hancock

A CHILD BORN IN SCOTLAND IN 2000: KIRSTEN'S STORY

Kirsten was born in May 2000, a hospital delivery by Caesarean section without undue complications. She was breast-fed until she was nine months old. Kirsten's family is made up of her father, Malcolm, and her older brother, Jamie, who was two years old when Kirsten was born.

The family owned a detached, three-bedroom house on the outskirts of Aberdeen and Malcolm worked offshore in the oil business, whilst Kirsten's mother, Helen cared for the children and the home. The family had been financially very secure since before Helen and Malcolm's marriage, due to Malcolm's lengthy offshore career. However, Helen was tragically killed in a road accident in 2003, leaving Malcolm to bring up the children on his own, with some support from his parents who lived close-by, but who work full-time.

When Helen died, Malcolm requested a transfer to onshore employment in the training department of his company, to which the company agreed. Malcolm's parents often looked after the children at the weekend, as well as regularly having the whole family over for meals during the week.

Malcolm arranged for a local childminder to care for Kirsten and to drop off and pick up Jamie from school each day. The childminder was very experienced although unqualified, and regularly attended the Childminding Association's network meetings. She brought Kirsten to the local playgroup three mornings a week and took both children to the park, the library, the soft playroom in the town and to the house of her sister who was also a childminder. She had a garden with a playhouse for the children to use and also a patch of ground where the children could dig, plant and play.

The playgroup Kirsten attended had two playleaders and a range of parent helpers. Both playleaders were in the process of studying for the Scottish Vocational Qualification in Childcare and Education, one at Level 2 and the other at Level 3. The playgroup was in partnership with their local education authority that annually monitored it; the playleaders' qualifications were funded through their local authority's workforce training and expansion programme. Both playleaders attended local authority in-service training as well as training provided by the Scottish Pre-school Play Association.

However, the company Malcolm worked for relocated to the south of England in late 2004. Malcolm made the decision that he could not relocate the whole family to an area where there was no family support and where the children would have to form new friendships and be introduced to a new system of education. This left him unemployed and in a position where he needed to re-think his career. Malcolm was successful in applying for a lecturing post at the local College of Further and Higher Education, which had a workplace nursery that Kirsten could attend in her pre-school year, as well as an out-of-school care facility which would pick Jamie up at the end of the school day.

Kirsten has always been a very active child. As soon as she had learned to walk, Kirsten ran everywhere and her parents used to joke that the next step in Kirsten's mind would be learning to fly. The childminder's provision allowed Kirsten to be physically active by playing in the garden, going to the park and visiting the soft playroom, and this was complemented by the college nursery which had a large, well-equipped outdoor area and access to the college gym once every fortnight. The nursery also made good use of its local forest area and coastal areas, taking groups of children on forest walks and trips to the beach.

Kirsten started Primary 1 (the first class in primary school in Scotland) in August 2005 as a five-year-old. Both children now attend their local primary school and Malcolm drops off and collects both children from the school's out-of-school care club at the start and end of the day. The school also operates a summer holiday club which both children attend for two weeks each year, and Malcolm and his parents take it in turns to care for the children for the rest of the school summer holiday.

Kirsten's school day in Primary 1 begins with the whole class congregating on the carpet in the book area for registration and 'sharing', where children take it in turns to talk about things they have brought from home. The class has 29 children in it: 11 girls and 18 boys. The children are divided into groups and banded, and the teaching of reading includes synthetic phonics as a whole-class group. Twice a week the whole school gathers together for Assembly and Kirsten's class has access to the gym two mornings a week for half an hour.

Concern has been expressed by staff at the children's school that Jamie is now not coping well in the aftermath of his mother's death. He is exhibiting challenging behaviour, finding it difficult to concentrate in class and has started to steal things from other children's drawers and lunch boxes. Malcolm is concerned that Jamie is also difficult to manage at home, is teasing Kirsten, having nightmares regularly and has started to wet the bed. Malcolm's mother is finding it difficult to look after Jamie at weekends and the last time she took the children shopping in the town centre, Jamie ran away and caught the bus home, leaving Kirsten and her grandma upset and frightened. The educational psychologist has begun to work with Jamie, and Malcolm is due to attend a meeting with the head-teacher and class teacher to discuss ways of supporting his son.

Kirsten continues to be an active and energetic child at home, but her class teacher has suggested that she is a little withdrawn and still not cop-ing with the large and very full playground at school. She regularly seeks out the playground helper to tell her she isn't feeling well. Kirsten's teacher has also observed that Kirsten frequently gravitates towards the sand-tray at 'Golden Time' on Friday afternoons, and is reluctant to engage with other activities and experiences. The structure of the Primary 1 school day has been difficult for Kirsten to adapt to and the formality of the classroom has made it difficult for her to be active and move around as she likes to do at home. Malcolm has noticed that when he collects Kirsten at the end of the school day and they arrive home, she has started to do a circuit of the living room furniture, leaping from chairs to settee to table, without touching the floor.

A CHILD BORN IN SCOTLAND IN 2000: FRASER'S STORY

Fraser was born in a maternity hospital in central Edinburgh on 3 February 2000. He was breast-fed for five months and then bottle-fed during the day as his mother, Shona, returned to her work in a bank after six months maternity leave, while his father, Don, continued working as a civil ser-vant. Both Shona and Don worked in Edinburgh and, after visiting a num-ber of nurseries, they decided to place Fraser in a private nursery close to his father's workplace. Don dropped him off on the way to work and picked him up at the end of the day. Both sets of grandparents lived in Edinburgh and, despite all four working full-time, they managed to see the children often.

In October 2001 Fraser's sister, Fiona, was born. Fraser had stopped attending the nursery when Shona was at home with the new baby and both children attended a local parent and toddler group as Shona felt Fraser had missed the company of other children since he had left nursery. Shona also welcomed the opportunity to meet other mothers and make new friends. Like Fraser, Kirsty was breast-fed for five months until Shona returned to work full-time after six months maternity leave and Fraser and Fiona attended the same private nursery close to Don's workplace. The nursery had excellent inspection reports, a stable staff team and a large outdoor area in daily use. The children were very happy and settled there.

However, Don and Shona found it increasingly difficult to pay the nurs-ery fees. Don's parents both retired in June 2002 and, aware of the finan-cial difficulties, offered to collect the children from nursery after lunch and look after them in the afternoons. Don and Shona accepted the offer and the children moved to part-time attendance at the nursery. Don's mother died suddenly in September and his father found it difficult coping by himself with Fraser and Fiona, who were now two and a half years and 11 months old and very active.

Fraser and Fiona returned to full-time nursery attendance just as Shona found she was pregnant again. Her first two pregnancies had been trouble free but the third pregnancy was difficult and Shona had to spend several spells in hospital. By working flexibly, enlisting the help of the grandparents and being offered help from parents at the parent and toddler group, Don was able to look after the children and visit Shona in hospital. However, both children were upset at their mother's absence and the changes in their routine, and Don found looking after them very difficult.

Their second daughter, Kirsty, was born in March 2003; perfectly healthy but a baby who cried a lot, was difficult to settle and seemed to need very little sleep. As the nursery was a local authority partner provider, Fraser now qualified for a free part-time nursery place from the summer term following his third birthday and continued attending the nursery five mornings a week, being dropped off by Don and collected by Shona. Fiona was at home with her mother and Kirsty, and they returned to the parent and toddler group they had attended before. Following her maternity leave, Shona intended to start working, mornings only and planned to have all three children attend the nursery and be collected after lunch, only to find there were no places available for Fiona and Kirsty. The couple had started to explore the availability of other childcare when, in September 2003, Don was offered a promotion which meant relocation to a rural area of Scotland. After much discussion the family moved away from Edinburgh in November 2003, taking the family 300 miles away from the grandparents.

Shona began to look for work near her new home but found that, while Fraser could have a half day place in the local nursery class during the school year, there was no nursery available to take children under three years old and no local registered childminders. Shona was unable to find employment that would fit her available hours. Fraser's nursery class was several miles from their new home and he travelled to and from the school on the local school bus. The nursery class provided Gaelic-medium education and Shona and Don found a website with information about the Gaelic language and about online classes. Shona, Don and Fraser began learning Gaelic together but the parents found it a difficult language to master. Don used the family car to go to work and Shona found herself increasingly isolated. Her health visitor told Shona about a parent and toddler group which met in a nearby village and here she met three local parents with four children aged under three. Two of the parents spoke Gaelic and helped Shona with her pronunciation, making it easier for both Shona and Fraser to help Don learn.

Fraser was due to start primary school in August 2004 (aged four years six months) but Shona and Don were concerned he would be the youngest in the class and perhaps not emotionally ready to begin his primary schooling. They spoke to the nursery class teacher, who also expressed concerns about his ability to cope with the primary school's more formal approach to education, and told them that with a February birthday he could delay until August 2005, when he would be five and a half years old. This meant both Fraser and Fiona would be together in the same nursery class following Fiona's third birthday.

They decided to delay primary entry until 2005 and Fraser is now enjoying school. His recent report has said that he has settled well and is working with enthusiasm. At home he enjoys reading to his two younger sisters. Fiona and Kirsty attended the nursery class together and Fiona is looking forward to starting primary school in August 2006. She is already able to read simple text and enjoys playing schools at home where she is 'teaching Kirsty to read'.

Late in 2004 Shona began to make enquiries about becoming a childminder. She contacted the Highland Pre-school Services who provided information and support and began her training and now holds a Scottish Vocational Qualification in Childcare and Education.

BACKGROUND

Scotland, the northern part of the island of Britain, covers 78,722 square kilometres of land, including 1,577 square kilometres of freshwater lochs. Few parts of the country are more than 64 kilometres from the sea. Scotland has some 790 islands, only about 10 per cent of which are inhabited. The largest groups are Shetland and Orkney to the north, and the Hebrides to the west.

Scotland's population in mid-2005 was estimated at about 5 million. Scotland's birth rate, (10.7 per thousand population in 2005), is lower than some European countries such as France (12.7 in 2002) and the Republic of Ireland (15.5 in 2003). The majority of the population is concentrated in the central area around Glasgow and Edinburgh while rural Scotland, covering 98 per cent of the land area, houses 20 per cent of the population. (A useful source for further detail on the information in this section is www.scotland.gov.uk)

In the 16+ age group in Scotland at the time of the last census in 2001, 30.6 per cent had never married; for 43.2 per cent it was their first marriage; 20 per cent were separated, divorced or widowed; 5 per cent had remarried. Many children were in single parent homes, a matter of concern in Glasgow households in particular where there was still some of the worst overcrowding, poorest heating and highest number of one-parent families in the UK; almost half the families in the city were headed by a single parent. Information such as this has important implications for the provision of early education and care.

You can find information on family patterns in Scotland and marital status in the last census (in 2001). See Clark, 2003, for the implications for education, or you can obtain further details about Scotland from www.scrol.gov.uk Scotland's census online; a website created to encourage use of and to widen access to the results of the 2001 census.

The Scottish Executive is the devolved government in Scotland. Responsibility for all devolved matters, including education and health, was passed to the Scottish Executive from the Scottish Office and other UK government departments in 1999. It is important to note that, although the English and Scottish Parliaments had united in 1707, the Secretary of State for Scotland had always had responsibility for education in Scotland. This responsibility was exercised through the Scottish Office with totally separate education legislation from England; this was, however, enacted by the parliament in Westminster. In Scotland there has been no National Curriculum, no SATs, no requirement for literacy and numeracy hours and no Ofsted involvement, such as in England. It is argued that parliamentary devolution makes for more transparency in the formation of educational policy, greater opportunities for civic participation in forums in which education is discussed and greater involvement in post-legislative scrutiny processes (Pickard and Dobie, 2003). This broadening of the consultation process has recently been highlighted during the development of the new Curriculum for Excellence which will cover the age range 3–18 (see www.acurriculumforexcellencescotland.gov.uk).

The Scottish Executive is a separate organisation from the Scottish parliament. The Scottish parliament passes laws on devolved issues and also scrutinises the work of the Scottish Executive. A significant and relevant example is that in January 2005 the Education Committee of the Scottish Parliament agreed to undertake an enquiry into the provision of pre-school education and care across Scotland and in June 2006 published its report (www. scottish.parliament.uk). The report exhorts the Scottish Executive to ensure that the highest priority is assigned to children's interests, particularly in supporting children under three, upskilling the Early Years workforce, establishing integrated structures and simplifying systems for delivering funding and reporting progress. The Scottish Executive response in August 2006 stated that, while sharing many of the committee's objectives, there were areas where it saw the route to achieving those objectives slightly differently.

The Scottish Executive Education Department (SEED) is responsible for administering policy on pre-school and school education, children and young people, and tourism, culture and sport (a similar role to the Department for Education and Skills (DfES) in England).

All of the main statutory agencies with responsibility for services for children have been involved in major organisational change since 1996. During this period, there have been major changes in early education and childcare services in Scotland. These changes have affected growth, delivery, type of provision and expectations of service providers in terms of their knowledge, skills and understandings.

Scotland has not formally followed the Early Excellence Centre approach of England, but an increasing number of Early Years Centres provides a range of services similar to those offered in centres south of the border. Such centres are more likely to be called Family Centre, Community Nursery, Child and Family Centre and so on. A plethora of names exists, just as there is a plethora of names for staff working in these centres, including nursery nurse, Early Years officer, Early Years educator, to name just a few.

A new parliament for Scotland was reconvened in 1999 with 129 members of the Scottish parliament. In 2004, the appointment of a Children's Commissioner, to listen to children and give weight to the issues they raise, illustrated in Scotland the new aspirations for children. Early childhood services are high on the agenda of the Scottish Executive, and there has been a whole raft of legislation and initiatives in this area. Policy developments in Scotland in some ways mirror those in England, such as the establishment of SureStart programmes, for children 0–3 years.

The manner in which children are protected and their rights set out is made clear in legislation, most importantly the Children (Scotland) Act 1995. The UN Convention on the Rights of the Child (see www.unhchh.ch) and other United Nations declarations on human rights have influenced the formulation of law in Scotland related to children and families; Scotland's *National Care Standards: early education and childcare up to the age of 16* (Scottish Executive, 2002c) is founded on the UN Convention and includes principles that reflect the rights of children, and influences how services for children and young people are run.

The 32 local authorities have made different responses to legislation and the expectations placed upon them, resulting in responsibility for children under five lying in a range of places, including education departments or children's services departments or children and family services, amongst other terminology. These changes reflect the beginnings of a move towards greater integration of services.

Scotland may be a small nation of five million people but it has a rich linguistic and cultural heritage. Historically there has been a wide range of spoken languages in Scotland, with Gaelic the longest established of Scotland's languages. Up until the seventeenth century, Gaelic was commonly known as Irish, which it still closely resembles.

Of the five million people living in Scotland, it is estimated that 69 per cent speak English only. There is in addition a Gaelic-speaking population of approximately 58,000, all of whom are bilingual in Gaelic and English. Today only 1.2 per cent of the population speaks Gaelic, mainly concentrated in the Western Isles. In Scotland, nearly 70,000 people are daily users of a number of other languages, the most common of which are Urdu, Punjabi, Hindi, Cantonese, Bengali, Polish, Arabic and Italian, with a small community of Japanese speakers. There are possibly even more speakers of different varieties of Scots, but there are no reliable statistics (Landon, 2001).

There is also a sizeable gypsy/traveller community in Scotland with their own oral tradition, called Cant, based on Romany, Scots and Gaelic.

There are differing policies at a local level over issues such as the creation of Gaelic immersion units, employment of bilingual staff, support for complementary language schools and classes and accessing translating and interpreting services. Presently the Scottish Executive translates its documents into Gaelic, Urdu, Punjabi, Bengali, Hindi, Chinese and Arabic, but this type of practice varies enormously across councils (Hancock, forthcoming).

Fraser's story is an example of a family for whom relocation, still within Scotland, meant a move from Edinburgh, a large city, to a Gaelic-speaking rural area where the children and their parents had to cope with the additional stress of learning a new language. You will see that learning Gaelic presented more problems for the parents than the children, a difficulty faced by many families in the modern world who move to another country where the medium of education is different from their mother tongue. What difficulties, and also interesting interaction between the parents and the young children, might such a situation stimulate?

Scotland has a formal legal relationship with Europe as part of the United Kingdom government's membership of the European Union. As such, the UK government's ratification of the European Charter for Regional and Minority Languages in 2001 has seen Gaelic secure legal status under the Charter, whilst Scots has been recognised as a regional language. In the school session 2005–6 there were 61 primary schools offering Gaelic-medium education.

POLICY AND PRACTICE IN EARLY CHILDHOOD EDUCATION AND CARE

In relation to Early Years education in particular, a great deal of activity has taken place in the field of policy that has impacted on practice and continues to do so. Some key factors in helping to create the current context for early childhood education in Scotland include:

- 1995   publication of *Performance Indicators for Pre-School Centres* (Scottish Office, 1995)
- 1997   publication of *A Curriculum Framework for Children in their Pre-School Year* (Scottish Office Education and Industry Department, 1997)
- 1999   publication of national guidance *A Curriculum Framework for Children 3–5* (Scottish Consultative Committee on the Curriculum/ Scottish Executive, 1999)

- 2000   publication of *The Child at the Centre*, self-evaluation tool for Early Years settings (Scottish Executive, 2000b)
- 2002   publication of *National Care Standards: Early education and childcare up to the age of 16* (Scottish Executive, 2002c)
- 2005   publication of *Birth to Three: Supporting our youngest children* (Scottish Executive/Learning and Teaching Scotland, 2005)
- 2005   publication of *A Curriculum for Excellence* (Scottish Executive, 2005a)
- 2006   *National Review of the Early Years and Childcare Workforce: Report and consultation* (Scottish Executive, 2006b)
- 2006   publication of *Response to the Report of the Education Committee on the Early Years Inquiry* (Scottish Executive, 2006d)

In May 1998, the government published *Meeting the Childcare Challenge: A childcare strategy for Scotland* (available at www.archive.official-documents.co.uk/document/cm39/3958/contents.htm), one of a number of measures aimed at supporting families and in particular raising children out of poverty. The strategy recognised that good quality childcare has benefits for children by promoting their development and learning, and also benefits for parents, by enabling them to work. The overall aim of the Childcare Strategy was to make high quality, accessible and affordable childcare available throughout Scotland. As part of the strategy, the Scottish Executive Education Department asked each of the 32 local authorities to convene a local 'Childcare Partnership' in their area. By 2006 the Childcare Partnerships were becoming increasingly accountable, more strategic and more effective. Through the integration of the Early Education and Childcare Plans into the new joint Children's Services Plans, they are working to forge strong, universal early education and childcare services that meet the individual needs of children and their families.

In Scotland, all three and four year olds have been entitled to a free, part-time, pre-school education place since 2002, with local authorities working in partnership with the private and voluntary sector.

The funded 412.5 hours are usually delivered over five sessions per week, each of around 2.5 hours, over the school year, although some authorities do have slightly different arrangements and a few providers, mainly in the voluntary sector, cannot always offer the full five sessions a week.

In 2006 there were 2,761 local authority or partnership pre-school education providers in Scotland, of which 50 reported providing education in Gaelic.

The number of full-time working women with dependent children increased by 1.9 per cent between 2003 and 2004; the increase was higher for single women with dependent children (3.9 per cent).

In September 2005, approximately 82 per cent of staff who worked directly with children in pre-school and childcare centres had a relevant qualification at some level, and 71 per cent had a childcare qualification at Scottish Vocational Qualification (SVQ) Level 2 or above.

There are approximately 263,000 children aged 0–4 years old in Scotland. This number is expected to decrease to 248,000 by 2010.

TABLE 5.1   Number of local authority or partnership pre-school education centres by type of centre and local authority in Scotland in January 2006

	Nursery class			Nursery school			
	Number of centres providing pre-school education	part of education authority school	part of Independent school	education authority	private	voluntary	management unknown
Total	2,761	1,144	41	440	549	568	19

Source: Scotland.gov.uk (Pre-School and Childcare Statistics, 2006)

In 2004, in the 15 per cent of most deprived areas, 52 per cent of childcare places were in local authority-provided centres compared with 38 per cent in the rest of Scotland. There was also a higher percentage of places in voluntary childcare in the 15 per cent of most deprived areas. The percentage of private childcare places (21 per cent) was significantly lower in the most deprived areas than in the rest of Scotland (see *Social Focus on Deprived Areas*, Scottish Executive, 2005b).

In July 2006, the Scottish Executive announced a £2 million pilot project aimed at giving two year old children in Dundee, Glasgow and North Ayrshire free access to nursery places, making over 900 extra nursery places available to families who need additional support and help.

Out-of-School Care (OSC) provision has also been an area of significant activity and development in Scotland, offering childcare for children between the ages of approximately 5–12 years and operating out-of-school hours during term times and holidays. A 'mixed economy' of OSC services has developed over recent years. The majority of clubs are run by voluntary organisations using parent management or advisory groups, but a growing number of clubs is now setting up as community businesses. Some out-of-school care services are run by local authorities and health authorities. Out-of-school care clubs are based in a variety of premises including schools, community centres, church halls and nurseries and all Out of School Care service must be registered with the Care Commission (see www.soscn.org). While there has been encouragement to meet local demand for out-of-school care, there has been no move in Scotland to mirror the extended schools developments that exist in some other parts of the United Kingdom.

Curriculum Guidance

A Curriculum Framework for Children in their Pre-school Year (Scottish Office Education and Industry Department, 1997) and *A Curriculum Framework for Children 3 to 5* (Scottish Consultative Committee on the Curriculum/ Scottish Executive, 1999), which extended the earlier advice, were based on a recognition of the fundamental importance of the adult role in supporting children's development and learning. They stemmed from the growing awareness of the importance of the quality of Early Years experiences and a commitment to building a 'coherent, continuous and progressive educational experience for all young people in Scotland' (1999: v).

Providers of local authority-funded education are required to observe these guidelines. However, each centre will have its own distinctive approach to the implementation of the curriculum framework so that it is implemented in a way appropriate to the needs of the children who attend. Her Majesty's Inspectorate of Education (HMIE) inspection reports assess the quality of Early Years provision against the framework. Further support in exemplifying *A Curriculum Framework for children 3 to 5* has been developed by Learning and Teaching Scotland (LTS), through its Early Education Support series. LTS is funded by the Scottish Executive to provide advice and guidance to both government and practitioners on matters relating to learning and teaching from birth to 18. Its website has an Early Years section and it also publishes the *Early Years Matters Newsletter* providing information about Scottish initiatives and practice (a useful website for further detail on the curricular information in this chapter is www.ltsscotland.org.uk/earlyyears).

This awareness continues in later guidance developed to support those working with very young children: *Birth to Three: Supporting our youngest children* (Scottish Executive/Learning and Teaching Scotland 2005) gives guidance for all those involved in caring for babies and very young children. It recognises the different and complementary ways in which very young children are cared for in different settings. It sets out the three key features of effective practice – relationships, responsive care and respect – and suggests sensitive and respectful approaches through examples from practice. In 2005 a pack containing video clips from a variety of settings and a booklet of staff development activities aimed at exemplifying these three key features, was produced by LTS. It is intended that practitioners will, within their own contexts, interpret and adapt the *Birth to 3* guidance as a framework for their own practice and the Care Commission (Scottish Commission for the Regulation of Care) has included questions regarding the *Birth to 3* guidance in their 2006–7 round of inspections.

Early Years Information and Communications Technology (ICT) has also been a rapid area of development for Early Years education in Scotland. In 2001 Learning and Teaching Scotland was asked by the Scottish Executive to carry out a review of the role of ICT in the early years. *Early Learning Forward Thinking: The policy framework for ICT in early years* (Learning and Teaching Scotland, 2003), Scotland's national strategy for ICT in the early years, is now in place and a current focus of the HMIE inspection process is to ascertain the degree to which the national ICT strategy is influencing thinking and practice within Early Years establishments across Scotland.

There is no national equivalent to the Foundation Stage Profile in England, but individual local authorities have developed their own advice to support continuity of learning from pre-school to primary school. It is interesting to note that whilst consultation is currently taking place in

England with regard to a Foundation Stage from birth to five, there has been no similar discussion in Scotland; rather, the move is now towards a curriculum for three to eighteen years (see below).

TRANSITIONS

Transitions begin at birth for many children in Scotland, with the transition from hospital to home. New statistics released in early April 2006 by BirthChoiceUK (see www.birthchoiceuk.com) showed that although more women in Scotland are giving birth at home, the overall home birth rate remains low, at 1.12 per cent, leading the National Childbirth Trust to express concern that the low home birth rate across Scotland means that the choice of a home birth is not widely available, or even accessible, for women. East Lothian has the highest number of women giving birth at home with a rate of 3.2 per cent; women in East Renfrewshire are the least likely to give birth at home, given the home birth rate of 0.2 per cent.

> The child case studies at the beginning of this chapter indicate the range of transitions children may undergo during early childhood, and the experience of Kirsten and Fraser is by no means uncommon. Reread these case studies, counting the number of adults with whom these children had to interact and the number of changes in settings faced by these young children and their families in the six years covered by the study. To what extent do you think such experiences are likely to be encountered by children in the other countries discussed here?

Many children, once they are having experiences outside of the home, may encounter daily transitions; from parental to non-parental care, from home to a childminder, from a childminder's home to a playgroup, nursery or school, and from school to out-of-school care both at the start and end of the school day. Pre-school establishments may cater for children from birth to five, but many offer provision only for children from three to five, for example nursery classes attached to a school, leaving some families having to access a diverse range of provision to meet family needs.

> This diversity of provision described above contrasts with the problems faced by Fraser's mother, when the family moved from a large city to a more rural area of Scotland. Kirsten and Fraser's stories show the variation in availability of early care and education across the country. In some areas it may not meet the needs of the young children and the mothers, many of whom now, often on financial grounds, want to work full-time or part-time. These problems are not confined to Scotland as you will have seen from the other chapters.

The experience of children themselves, as they move from setting to setting and experience to experience, and the sense that children make of these experiences continue to raise questions, not least with regard to taking account of prior learning (Fabian and Dunlop, 2002). Clark cites Watt (from her research into transitions in the 1980s) who stressed 'the need for "compatibility" without "sameness", and "stimulation" without "shock" in the early learning experiences of young children' (Clark, 2005: 92).

> How would you measure whether a transition provided a child with 'compatibility' without 'sameness' and 'stimulation' without 'shock'? How can learning environments continue to develop and adapt to be familiar, developmentally appropriate and sensitive to the needs of the children and their families? The information in the case studies should help you to think about the experiences through the eyes of the children and their families. Note that what was suitable for one of the children might not have been for another (For example, contrast Fraser and his sister Fiona).

The transition to primary school and subsequent transition to secondary have been, and continue to be, under scrutiny in Scotland. In May 2006, HM Inspectorate of Education published a report, *Ensuring Effective Transition* (2006a), which highlights the conditions in which effective transition arrangements can be developed and evaluated. The aims behind the report are to encourage effective, high quality transition, not only from pre-school to primary, but also from stage to stage, including Primary 7 to secondary education (a useful source for further details on inspection can be found at www.hmie.gov.uk).

Current research in Scotland illustrates that although 'transition to primary school has been the focus of considerable international research activity and policy innovation, yet it remains a topic of concern' (Stephen, 2006: 6). Stephen concludes that there is no right age for launching into a formal school career and believes that there is international recognition for a distinct three to six year old phase of education, identifying widespread support for those features of early education regarded as crucial for children's learning, including:

- an holistic view of learning and the learner
- active, experiential learning
- a respect for children's ability to be self-motivating and self-directing
- a valuing of responsive interactions between children and adults.

The concept of school readiness and the need to match provision with the needs of learners rather than 'relying on general organisational changes' (Stephen, 2006: 6) continue to spark discussion and debate within Scotland, not least within the context of *A Curriculum for Excellence* (Scottish Executive, 2005a) (see the section on 'Schooling', below). The future may see pre-school pedagogical approaches moving into primary school, 'in order to introduce new curricular content in ways which are familiar, developmentally appropriate and sensitive in terms of support' (Stephen , 2006: 7). This view is further supported by the Closing the Gap action research carried out by Hayward and Hedge in 2004, which exemplified that learners learn most effectively when they have confidence in their own abilities, 'when they believe they can learn, know what, why and how to learn, when they have a sense of purpose and when learning is as close to real life as possible' (Hayward and Hedge, 2004).

SCHOOLING

Context

Approximately 96 per cent of children educated in Scotland attend schools where the responsibility for provision rests with the local authority; these schools do not charge fees. The percentage attending private (fee-paying schools) varies across the country (see www.scis.org.uk). In the larger population centres some children will attend denominational schools, which are mainly Roman Catholic.

Primary education

Children in Scotland must start primary school in the August term after their fifth birthday and the intake is once per year. However, education authorities can make arrangements for children to start in the August when they are four, if they will turn five by the end of the following February. This generally means that children in Scotland start school when they are aged between four-and-a-half and five-and-a-half. However, free pre-school education can be extended where parents of children with birthdays in January or February choose to defer their child's entry to primary school and in these cases local authorities are required to provide an additional free year. Children with September to December birthdays are only able to access an extra year at the discretion of their local authorities. In 2006 there were 4,380 children with deferred entry to primary school.

> The month of birth has been given in all the case studies as this enables you to observe the effect that precise month of birth may have on the age at which a child enters primary school. Contrast the experience of Fraser, for whom deferred entry to primary school was permitted in Scotland, with what might happen say in England. Note that he was five and a half years of age when he entered school; had deferred entry not been permitted he would have been a year younger on entry to primary school.

TABLE 5.2   Structure of schooling in Scotland

Type of Setting	Age	Curriculum Guidelines
Nursery school, nursery class, nursery centre, playgroup, private nursery, childminder	3–5 years	A Curriculum Framework for Children 3–5
Primary school 5–12 years	5–7 years for most children	5–14 Curriculum Level A primaries 1–2/ 3
Primary school 5–12 years	7–9 years for most children	5–14 Curriculum Level B primaries 2/3–4
Primary school 5–12 years	9–10 years for most children	5–14 Curriculum Level C primaries 4–5/6
Primary school 5–12 years	10–12 years for most children	5–14 Curriculum Level D primaries 5/6–7
Secondary school 12–16/18 years	12–14 years for some children	5–14 Curriculum Level E/F sec 1/2
Secondary school 12–16/18 years	13/14–16/18 years	National Qualifications

Primary school classes are organised by age from Primary 1 (age approximately five) to Primary 7 (age approximately twelve). The term 'Reception class' is not used in Scotland. Generally, primary schools contain both boys and girls. In 2005 there were 2,194 primary schools in Scotland, of which 431 had fewer than 50 pupils. In some small schools, mostly those in rural areas, classes will be composite classes, containing children of several different ages. Each class normally has one teacher who teaches all or most of the curriculum. There were 8,097 teaching assistants, who undertake a range of administrative and support for learning tasks under the direction of classroom teachers in primary schools in Scotland. In 2006, the recommended class size in Scotland was 30 for a single-stage class P1–P3, and 25 for a composite-stage class. The Scottish School Census for 2005 shows that the average primary school class size was 23.6 pupils (compared with 23.9 in 2004). Composite classes had an average of 19.9 pupils (compared with 20.2 in 2004).

Teachers are required to hold a BEd degree or Postgraduate Certificate of Education in primary teaching, covering ages 3–12, and all teachers working in local authority primary schools are required to be registered with the General Teaching Council for Scotland, responsible since 1965 for the independent regulation of the teaching profession in Scotland (see www.gtcs.org.uk).

The 5–14 Curriculum Guidelines (General Teaching Council for Scotland, 1992) for Scottish local authorities and schools cover the structure, content and assessment of the curriculum in primary schools and in the first two years of secondary education. Unlike in England, schools are

TABLE 5.3   Curricular continuity and learning in Scotland, 3–14

Curriculum Framework 3–5	5–14 Curriculum Guidelines
Emotional, Personal and Social Development	Personal and Social Development
	Religious and Moral Education
Knowledge and Understanding of the World	Environmental Studies
	Mathematics
Communication and Language	Language (including a modern language)
Expressive and Aesthetic Development	Expressive Arts
Physical Development and Movement	

Source: A Curriculum Framework for Children 3–5 Scottish Consultative Council on the Curriculum.

not legally required to follow the guidelines. Table 5.2 indicates the organisation of types of setting, ages and curricular guidance in Scotland.

Table 5.3 shows some of the important areas of continuity and progression between *A Curriculum Framework for Children 3–5* and the *5–14 Curriculum Guidelines*. (Scottish Consultative Council on the Curriculum/ Scottish Executive 1999).

For each curricular area there are broad attainment outcomes, each with a number of strands or aspects of learning that pupils experience. Most strands have attainment targets at five or six levels: A–E or A–F and assessment are organised by the individual school. Teachers will judge a child's progress through the levels on the basis of a range of evidence, such as coursework and homework assignments, supported by local moderation and national assessments.

These processes help schools make sure their standards are the same as those of other schools throughout Scotland. If teachers choose, they can use national assessments in reading, writing and mathematics when they judge that a pupil has completed the work at one level and is ready to move on to the next. This may be at any time during a school session, unlike SATs tests in England.

The current curricular review is likely to become a strong influencing factor with the 'Great Education Debate' in Scotland in 2001–2 leading to the publication of a working party report entitled *A Curriculum for Excellence* (Scottish Executive, 2005a). Welcomed by the Scottish Executive, the report states that 'our aspiration for all children and for every young person is that they should be successful learners, confident individuals, responsible citizens and effective contributors to society and at work' (2005a: 3).

Among the many aims for the Curriculum for Excellence that specifically affect Early Years practitioners are the following:

• Guidelines should create a single, coherent, Scottish curriculum 3–18 to ensure a smooth transition (nursery to primary and primary to secondary) in what children have learned and also how they can learn.

- The approaches which are used in pre-school should be extended into the early years of primary schooling.
- That all children should experience a smooth change as they move from their pre-school experience into Primary 1.
- The importance of opportunities for children to learn through purposeful, well planned play should be emphasised.

Guidance is currently being developed and it is anticipated that the new curriculum approach is to be implemented from the start of the session in 2008–9.

How might the implementation of A *Curriculum for Excellence*, with one framework of 3–18, impact on the experience of children and young people? What are the dangers in such a development for the early education and care of young children? What safeguards would you hope to be built into this development for young children, and children with special needs? Consult the curricular documents to check if these are being introduced.

Further developments include The Scottish Schools (Parental Involvement) Act 2006 (see www.parentzonescotland.gov.uk/index.asp). It aims to support parents' involvement in schools and in their own children's education and it introduces a more flexible statutory system for parental representation in schools.

SPECIAL EDUCATIONAL NEEDS

At the time of the reconvening of the Scottish parliament, the Education (Scotland) Act 1980 was still in place, which has been heavily amended over the years and has guided provision for children with additional support needs. In November 2005 a new law, the Additional Support for Learning (Scotland) Act 2004 came into place (both of these Acts can be accessed at www.scottish.parliament.uk/business/research/pdfsubj maps/smda-10.pdf). Any child or young person with a Record of Needs when the Act came into place will automatically have additional support needs. The Act also legislates for increased parental involvement and a requirement that schools and educational establishments recognise the principles of involvement and act accordingly.

The focus on 'getting it right' at the earliest stages, working collaboratively and strengthening the duty placed upon local authorities to take regard of children's views underpins this legislation. Whilst the overall aim is for full integration and inclusion of all children, it is recognised that some children may have particular needs which are better met in establishments offering more specialised and individual care and education and that educational establishments do not and should not work in isolation from the rest of society, parents and other professionals.

SAFEGUARDING CHILDREN

Duties to protect children are enshrined in Scottish law, particularly in relation to the police and social work. In Scotland it is understood that everyone involved in working with children has a fundamental duty of care towards them and that the welfare of the child is paramount, putting the responsibility on all to help ensure that this is the case (see *It's Everyone's Job to Make Sure I'm Alright: Report of the Child Protection Audit and Review*, Scottish Executive, 2002e).

Protecting Children and Young People: Framework for Standards (Scottish Executive, 2004) was developed for children and families as well as for staff and agencies involved directly and indirectly in the protection of children, including volunteers. It sets out what each child in Scotland can expect from professionals and agencies to ensure that they are protected and that their needs are met, taking into account the views of children and young people as expressed in the Children's Charter (see www.scotland.gov.uk).

> How difficult will it be to take into account the views of young children and their families in framing policy? How might this be done and are there dangers in such an approach?

A number of high profile child protection cases have meant that services for children have remained in the spotlight to ensure cases such as those of Caleb Ness – who was born in July 2001, who died in October the same year aged just 11 weeks, and whose father was convicted of culpable homicide on the grounds of diminished responsibility – do not recur. There is an increased emphasis on early intervention, efficient integrated working and improved clarity regarding roles and responsibilities. Joint inspection of child protection services across Scotland involves a dedicated team whose remit is to inspect child protection procedures, including those of local authorities. Comprising HMIE, the Social Work Inspection Agency, the Care Commission, Her Majesty's Chief Inspector of Constabulary and NHS Quality Improvement Scotland, the aim of the inspection team is to ensure that vulnerable children receive a high quality of support.

Scotland's Children's Hearings System represents a radical change initiated by the Social Work (Scotland) Act 1968, now a part of the Children (Scotland) Act 1995 (see www.scotland.gov.uk). The Children's Panel is unique to Scotland, offering support to children who are referred to the panel in need of care and protection.

As the Children's Hearings System is unique to Scotland you might like to explore further how it developed and how it operates, taking into account the views of the children concerned and their families (see www.childrenshearingsscotland.gov.uk).

In 2006 concern is being expressed that 'looked-after children' do less well in school, gain fewer educational qualifications than their peers and face major difficulties as young adults. A great deal of publicity is being given to the many changes of foster home or other provision, and therefore of school, faced by many 'looked-after children' (see www.everychildmatters. gov.uk/socialcare/lookedafterchildren).

QUALITY ASSURANCE

Primary schools are inspected by HMIE which became an Executive Agency of the Scottish ministers in 2001 under the terms of the Scotland Act 1998. As an agency, it operates independently and impartially whilst remaining directly accountable to ministers for the standards of its work. The core business of HMIE, as it has been since 1840, is the inspection and review of schools and other educational establishments, to help support the process of continuous improvement in education and in raising standards of attainment; this emphasis on the relationship between inspection and improvement has not changed over the years. HMIE is committed to inspecting each primary school (either as an initial inspection or a follow-up) every seven years. Inspection reports are published in print and online and HMIE also publishes a range of self-evaluation materials to assist educational establishments to assess their provision as a whole, or in particular areas, and to report about current practice in Scotland.

In addition, Section 9 of the Standards in Scotland's Schools Etc. Act 2000 (see www.opsi.gov.uk) charges HMIE, on behalf of Scottish ministers, to provide an external evaluation of the effectiveness of the education functions of local authorities. These inspections are conducted within a published framework of quality indicators, *Quality Management in Education* (Learning and Teaching Scotland, 2000), which embody the Scottish government's policy on best value.

In both *The Child at the Centre* (Scottish Executive, 2000) (self-evaluation materials for pre-school centres published by HMIE) and the *National Care Standards: Early education and childcare up to the age of 16* (2002) (published by the Scottish Executive), education and care are further emphasised as an indivisible whole, with a clear emphasis on safeguarding children. Regulation and inspection play an important role in both influencing provision and creating expectations of educators in terms of skills, knowledge and understanding (see www.carecommission.com).

The *Report on the Integrated Inspection of Early Education and Childcare Services in Scotland* (HMIE, 2006) highlighted that inspections in pre-schools across Scotland have helped to raise standards and increase consistency in the sector.

Following concerns about over-inspection, consideration is being given to the frequency of HMIE inspections and whether high-quality provision needs to be inspected as often.

PROFESSIONAL DEVELOPMENT AND TRAINING

Within Scotland in 2006 there are approximately 28,000 childcare and education staff. There exists a vast audience, with diverse needs and requiring flexible and creative delivery, including childminders, playleaders, classroom assistants, out-of-school care staff, Early Years educators, primary and nursery teachers.

The Scottish Social Services Council's (SSSC) requirements for a trained workforce by 2009 will put pressure on staff to be qualified at a variety of levels, depending on position, role and responsibility. The SSSC also clearly highlights the growing need for evidence of ongoing professional development activity (see www.sssc.gov.uk).

Following the publication of the McCrone Report, *A Teaching Profession for the 21st century* (Scottish Executive, 2000a), teachers now have a 22.5 hour weekly teaching maximum over 195 days per year, a commitment to 35 hours continuing professional development annually and the opportunity to remain as classroom teachers while being recognised as knowledgeable professionals with enhanced salary. By contrast, the conditions for non-teaching staff remain poor.

Through the *National Review of the Early Years and Childcare Workforce* (2006a) the Scottish Executive is committed to ensuring that the employment opportunities for workers in the sector are improved and that the status of the sector is raised. The review identified three main themes that will guide all of the changes that will affect the Early Years and childcare sector in the future. Those themes are leadership, worker development and flexibility to allow the delivery of services that meet the needs of children and families in local communities. A flexible workforce that is able to work in different settings and with different professionals is seen as essential to deliver integrated and changing services.

The Scottish Executive's response *Investing in Children's Futures* (2006c) stated the key actions ministers intend to take. Childminders will be encouraged and supported to undertake qualifications and professional development that will be designed to accommodate the specific circumstances of sole workers. However, they will not be required to hold qualifications. Ministers are confident that taken together these actions will improve the status and recognition of the workforce and support improved recruitment, retention and progression within the sector.

Nursery teachers, a group who are not included in the above review, are required to hold a primary teaching qualification, either a BEd degree or a Postgraduate Diploma in Education (PGDE) and many have undertaken additional qualifications specific to teaching young children. Those working in local authority nursery schools and classes are required to be registered with the General Teaching Council for Scotland. In 2006 there were 1,648 full-time equivalent General Teaching Council for Scotland registered teachers working in local authority or partnership pre-school education centres.

The BA Childhood Studies degree has been in existence for several years and can be taken as full- or part-time study. Many holding nursery nurse qualifications have taken this additional higher level of study route and then gone on to take a postgraduate primary teaching qualification.

Significantly, a new BA degree for integrated services has been developed in partnership by James Watt College and the Faculty of Education, University of Strathclyde, which will focus on collaborative working and integrated service delivery. This full-time degree programme has been introduced at a time when the Scottish Executive is emphasising the need for different sectors to work together to provide integrated service delivery and the optimum response to service-user needs.

> The implementation of the Early Years Workforce Review will result in many changes for those involved in early education and care; what are its implications? How might its implementation support movement between and across sectors and encourage the development of leadership in Early Years education and care? Will Early Years staff come to be called pedagogues (as in some countries)?

FUTURE AND IMMINENT CHANGES

Much has happened in the last ten years in early education in Scotland, and the pace of change is set to continue. *A Curriculum Framework for Children 3 to 5* (Scottish Consultative Committee on the Curriculum/Scottish Executive, 1999) marked an important stage in the development of early childhood education in Scotland.

As a result of the national debate on the future of education in Scotland (Scottish Executive, 2004), A Curriculum for Excellence is now being developed. This will have implications for Early Years education. Early Years was strongly represented on the expert working party which resulted in recommendations including the requirement to extend the approaches used in pre-school into the early years of primary: 'Early indications are that an easier ride in the first year at school will not result in a longer educational journey and could mean more children stay on the bus' (Blane, 2004). This could mean that for children born in 2006, unlike Kirsten in our case study, a different and more harmonious experience is to be had in terms of transitions throughout her school life and the pedagogical approaches she experiences.

It is to be hoped that the impending educational reform and development will lead to change and an increased focus on and commitment to experiential and active learning for young children.

Scotland's parliamentary inquiry into the state of Early Years education reported the tensions which exist between meeting the needs of children and the needs of working parents, reminding all of the differing agendas of early care and education for the common good, and government imperatives regarding women returning to work.

> What are these tensions between meeting the needs of young children, and those of working parents? These conflicting needs can be seen in the experiences during their first six years of Kirsten and Fraser and their families. *Birth to 3: Supporting our youngest children* (Scottish Executive/Learning and Teaching Scotland, 2005) sets out three key features of effective practice: Relationships, Responsive Care and Respect. Should children under three, or at least those under one year of age, be in a setting other than their home environment for long periods of the day? What are the dangers of extending provision for children from birth?

For the child born in 2006, it may be that increasingly flexible levels of parental support and parental leave exist, including financial support to stay at home to raise a child in the early stages of its life. This would in part begin to answer some of the concerns surrounding the institutionalised nature of many children's experience in their early years.

Imagine a child born in 2006: she is called Mhaire and she lives in Dundee in the east of Scotland. The pilot of provision for two year olds has now become fully established, but not necessarily in the form of Children's Centres. The national guidance on birth to three is influencing thinking and becoming embedded in practice and the curriculum for ages 3–18 years extends and supports the key features of relationships, responsive care and respect through its emphasis on successful learners, confident individuals, responsible citizens and effective contributors.

The Workforce Review is effecting change and by the age of four, Mhaire is cared for by fully qualified Early Years educators in a setting where all staff are qualified.

In 2010, when Mhaire starts primary school, her parents may be able to access full service provision but this is not a certainty. Mhaire may be happy to start school at the age of four in a classroom environment that both mirrors and builds upon her Early Years experience. There will probably be no National Curriculum in place, but curricular guidance as previously in Scotland. Mhaire should have healthy meals and drinks at school, with the implementation of *Hungry for Success* (Scottish Executive, 2002d) and a minimum of two hours of quality PE experience per week. The guidance that Mhaire's class teacher is likely to follow when Mhaire starts primary schooling is likely to be less prescriptive than the previous 5–14 guidance and her teachers may have the freedom to teach creatively and reflectively in developing the four capacities of successful, confident, responsible and effective learners.

TOPICS FOR DISCUSSION

The place of children's views

What are the implications of listening to children and allowing their views to inform decision-making at policy and practice level, as is increasingly becoming a feature in developments in Early Years education and care in Scotland as elsewhere, and how can this be achieved?

The importance of a single framework for the curriculum from 3–18

What might be the implications of a Curriculum for Excellence with one framework for children from 3–18 in Scotland?

The effects of the Workforce Review

Will the Workforce Review result in Early Years practitioners becoming a more unified group of professionals? Is there a danger that this will isolate Early Years teachers from the rest of the teaching force in Scotland?

Achieving continuity between children's learning experiences in the home and in school

How can learning environments outside the home develop and adapt to become more developmentally appropriate, yet provide continuity in the learning experiences of young children in Scotland throughout their schooling?

KEY MILESTONES IN GOVERNMENT STRATEGY FOR EARLY CHILDHOOD EDUCATION AND CARE IN SCOTLAND

- **1995** Children (Scotland) Act
- **1996** publication of *Performance Indicators for Pre-school Centres*

- **1997** publication of *A Curriculum Framework for Children in their Pre-School Year* (Scottish Office Education and Industry Department, 1997)
- **1998** publication of *Meeting the Childcare Challenge: A childcare strategy for Scotland* (available at www.archive.official-documents. co.uk)
- **1999** publication of national guidance *A Curriculum Framework for Children 3 to 5* (Scottish Consultative Committee on the Curriculum/ Scottish Executive, 1999)
- **1997** Early Intervention Programme created
- **2000** publication of *The Child at the Centre* (HMIE, 2000), self-evaluation tool for Early Years settings
- **2001** publication of *For Scotland's Children* (see www.scotland.gov.uk)
- **2002** publication of *National Care Standards: Early education and childcare up to the age of 16* (Scottish Executive, 2002c)
- **2004** appointment of first Children's Commissioner for Scotland, Professor Kathleen Marshall
- **2005** publication of *Birth to Three: Supporting our youngest children* (Scottish Executive/Learning and Teaching Scotland, 2005)
- **2005** publication of *A Curriculum for Excellence* (Scottish Executive, 2005a)
- **2006** publication of *Nutritional Guidance for Early Years* (Scottish Executive, 2006a)
- **2006** Publication of *Education Committee 7th Report*, (Session 2 Early Years)
- **2006** Scottish Executive Response to the Report of the Education Committee on the Early Years Inquiry
- **2006** National Review of the Early Years and Childcare Workforce: Report and Consultation
- **2006** National Review of the Early Years and Childcare Workforce: *Scottish Executive Response: Investing in Children's Futures.*
- **2006** The Scottish Schools (Parental Involvement) Act

REFERENCES

Blane, D. (2004) 'Put the play back into learning', *TES Scotland Plus*, 16 January.
Clark, M. M. (2003) 'Education in Scotland: what can we learn from the census?', *Primary Practice*, 35: 31–3.
Clark, M. M. (2005) *Understanding Research in Early Education: The relevance for the future of lessons from the past* (2nd edition). Oxford: Routledge.
Fabian, H. and Dunlop, A.W. (eds) (2002) *Transitions in the Early Years: Debating continuity and progression for Young Children*. London: RoutledgeFalmer.
Fraser, H. (2004) 'The Time of Their Lives', in *Early Years Matters*, 6: 6.
General Teaching Council for Scotland (1992) *The 5–14 Curriculum Guidelines 1991*. Edinburgh: Scottish Office.
Hancock, A. (forthcoming) *Language Policy in Education in Scotland*.

Hayward, L. and Hedge, N. (2004) 'Early intervention for all: back to basics', *Early Years Matters*, 6: 8–9.

HM Inspectorate of Education (HMIE) (2000) *The Child at the Centre: Self-evaluation in the early years*. Edinburgh: HMIE.

HM Inspectorate of Education (HMIE) (2006a) *Ensuring Effective Transition*. Edinburgh: HMIE.

HM Inspectorate of Education (HMIE) (2006b) *Report on the Integrated Inspection of Early Education and Childcare Services in Scotland*. Edinburgh: HMIE.

Landon, J. (2001) 'Community Languages', *Multicultural Teaching*, 20 (1): 34–8.

Learning and Teaching Scotland (2000) *Quality Management in Education*. Glasgow: Learning and Teaching Scotland.

Learning and Teaching Scotland (2003) *Early Learning Forward Thinking: The policy framework for ICT in Early Years*. Glasgow: Learning and Teaching Scotland.

Pickard, W. and Dobie, J. (2003) *The Political Context of Education after Devolution*. Edinburgh: Dunedin Academic Press.

Scottish Consultative Committee on the Curriculum/Scottish Executive (1999) *A Curriculum Framework for Children 3 to 5*. Edinburgh: Scottish Executive.

Scottish Executive (2000a) *A Teaching Profession for the 21st century*. Edinburgh: Scottish Executive.

Scottish Executive (2000b) *The Child at the Centre*. Edinburgh: Scottish Executive.

Scottish Executive (2002c) *National Care Standards: Early education and childcare up to the age of 16*. Edinburgh: Scottish Executive.

Scottish Executive (2002d) *Hungry for Success: A whole school approach to school meals in Scotland*. Edinburgh: Scottish Executive.

Scottish Executive (2002e) *It's Everyone's Job to Make Sure I'm Alright: Report of the Child Protection Audit and Review*. Edinburgh: Scottish Executive.

Scottish Executive (2002f) *The National Debate on the Future of Education in Scotland: The best for All our Children*. Edinburgh: Scottish Executive.

Scottish Executive (2004) *Protecting Children and Young People: Framework for Standards*. Edinburgh: Scottish Executive.

Scottish Executive (2005a) *A Curriculum for Excellence*. Edinburgh: Scottish Executive.

Scottish Executive (2005b) *Social Focus on Deprived Areas*. Edinburgh: Scottish Executive.

Scottish Executive (2006a) *Nutritional Guidance for Early Years: Food choices for children aged 1–5 in early education and childcare settings*. Edinburgh: Scottish Executive.

Scottish Executive (2006b) *National Review of the Early Years and Childcare Workforce*. Edinburgh: Scottish Executive.

Scottish Executive (2006c) *National Review of the Early Years and Childcare Workforce: Scottish Executive Response: Investing in children's futures*. Edinburgh: Scottish Executive.

Scottish Office (1995) *Using Performance Indicators in Nursery School/Class/Pre-Five Unit: Self-Evaluation*. Edinburgh: Scottish Office.

Scottish Executive/Learning and Teaching Scotland (2005) *Birth to Three: Supporting our youngest children*. Edinburgh: Learning and Teaching Scotland.

Scottish Office Education and Industry Department (1997) *A Curriculum Framework for Children in their Pre-school Year*. Edinburgh: Scottish Office Education and Industry Department.

Scottish Parliament (2006) *Education Committee 7th Report*. (Session 2 Early Years). Edinburgh: Scottish Parliament.

Stephen, C. (2006) *Early Years Education: Perspectives from a review of the international literature*, Summary Report, Insight 28. Edinburgh: Scottish Executive.

UN (1989) *United Nations Convention on the Rights of the Child*. Geneva: Office of the High Commisioner for Human Rights.

USEFUL WEBSITES

---

www.archive.official-documents.co.uk   Contains 'Meeting the Childcare Challenge: A Childcare Strategy for Scotland'

www.acurriculumforexcellencescotland.gov.uk   Information about the development of *A Curriculum for Excellence* (Scottish Executive, 2005)

www.carecommission.com   The Scottish Commission for the Regulation of Care is the body responsible for inspecting early education and childcare provision

www.hmie.gov.uk   Her Majesty's Inspectorate of Education (HMIE) in Scotland is the body responsible for inspecting and reporting on the quality of education in Scotland

www.ltscotland.org.uk/earlyyears   Learning and Teaching Scotland's Early Years web pages with information about national guidance, Early Education Support Series publications and Early Years education and care in Scotland

www.scotland.gov.uk   for further information on the initiatives mentioned in this chapter including:

The Child at the Centre   Self-assessment materials for centres providing publicly-funded pre-school education

For Scotland's Children   A report setting out the Scottish Executive vision for children

Hungry for Success   A report giving advice to schools about healthy eating

Scottish Executive   Scottish Executive Response to the Report of the Education Committee on the Early Years Inquiry, August 2006

Scottish Executive   National Review of the Early Years and Childcare Workforce: Report and Consultation, August 2006

Scottish Executive   National Review of the Early Years and Childcare Workforce: Scottish Executive Response: Investing in Children's Futures, August 2006

National Care Standards   Early education and childcare up to the age of 16 – the minimum standards for the provision of registered childcare

The Early Education and Childcare Division of the Scottish Executive Education Department   responsible for children under five years of age

Surestart Scotland   a programme aimed at supporting children under three years of age and their families

www.scottish.parliament.uk   The Scottish Parliament, with information about Acts of the Scottish parliament and the work of its members (MSPs)

www.sssc.uk.com   The Scottish Social Services Council is the body responsible for setting the qualification standards and maintaining a register of those fit to work in childcare provision

WALES[1]

Siân Wyn Siencyn and Sally Thomas

A CHILD BORN IN WALES IN 2000: SIONED NIAMH'S STORY

Sioned Niamh lives in a south-east valley town some ten miles north of Cardiff. She was six years old in June and is in Year 1 in the local Welsh-medium immersion primary school. This is a large school with over 400 children, aged three to eleven years. Over 97 per cent of the children in the school come from non-Welsh speaking homes. Sioned Niamh started part-time in the school's nursery class the September after her third birthday.

Her mother, Eleri, comes from Welsh-speaking west Wales and Welsh is her first language. She met Donal, who comes from Cork, whilst backpacking, two years before Sioned Niamh was born. Donal and Eleri initially intended to settle in Ireland but when Eleri found that she was pregnant, they decided to stay in Wales. Donal, who is a graduate professional, found work in Wales though not at the level he had hoped. They had been renting a tiny flat in Cardiff but decided, with financial help from their families, to buy a small terraced house in the valleys. Donal and Eleri agreed that, when choosing a name, both her Welsh and Irish cultural heritage would be acknowledged. Eleri has spoken nothing but Welsh with Sioned Niamh and although Donal speaks English with her, he is using the Welsh he has picked up with his daughter.

When Sioned Niamh was a baby, Eleri did not work outside the home. Although this was financially difficult as Eleri had no paid maternity leave from employment, she did receive the basic state benefits for a few months. Eleri joined her nearest *Cylch Ti a Fi* and did some voluntary work with *Twf*. When Sioned Niamh was 15 months old, Eleri decided to return to higher education. She contacted the local Early Years Development and Childcare Partnership (EYDCP) for information on childcare, who in turn referred her to the Genesis project. Eleri discovered that there was a Welsh-medium integrated centre three miles away and, furthermore, that Genesis would contribute towards the cost of Sioned Niamh's childcare.

---

1 See page 161 for information on acronyms and Welsh terminology

For the last year or so, the primary school has been keen to develop its Early Years provision. Sioned Niamh's Reception class teacher had attended three days of in-service training on understanding play, as part of the school's preparation for the Foundation Phase. As part of the school's development of its multicultural awareness programme, Donal went into Sioned Niamh's class on St Patrick's Day to play his *bodhrán* (a hand-held drum).

The whole school is now keen on developing outdoor learning. Donal is an enthusiastic mountain walker and Sioned Niamh has been joining her father on the hills since she was a tiny baby in a backpack. Both Donal and Eleri enjoy a bit of gardening. Donal is leading a group of volunteers who are helping the school to landscape their outdoor learning spaces so that they are really exciting places for young children. Some parents are worried that Donal's ideas are a little too risky.

After graduating, Eleri decided to set up her own business selling used children's clothes, toys, and equipment through the internet. She was able to do this from the spare bedroom. She and another mother whom she met at the *Cylch Ti a Fi* have now opened a small shop in the centre of town. Sioned Niamh stays in the after-school club three days a week when Donal picks her up at 5.30 pm. Childcare during the school holidays is a bit of problem for the family. Local full-time playschemes are expensive and are few and far between. Eleri's mother is a full-time professional who lives over two hours away in the west. Sioned Niamh stayed with her grandparents outside Cork for two weeks last summer.

A CHILD BORN IN WALES IN 2000: LEWIS'S STORY

Lewis was born in May 2000. He lives with his mother Melanie and younger brother Morgan who was born in January 2002 in a very small rural village in north-west Wales, 12 miles from the nearest seaside town. Their house, which is situated on the edge of the village, has three bedrooms and a large garden. It is rented from the local housing association.

Melanie has no close family living in the area. She was born and raised in a large town in north-east Wales (where her parents still live) and moved to the area with Lewis and Morgan's father before the boys were born. When Lewis was born, his father was working as a security guard at the local caravan park a short walk from their town flat by the sea. However, when Melanie became pregnant with Morgan the relationship with her partner broke down and he left the town. Melanie could not afford to rent the flat alone and was re-housed by the local housing association at her current home 12 miles away.

During the last six months of her pregnancy with Morgan, the midwife visited her regularly at her home. Melanie doesn't drive and therefore could not make the appointments at the local surgery 12 miles away. There were four families with children in the village but none with children under five years of age. The health visitor had some concerns over Lewis's lack of contact with other children and suggested that Melanie and he attend the nearest *Cylch Ti a Fi*, three miles away in the next village. The *Cylch* holds sessions twice a week on a Monday and a Wednesday. The village is on a bus route but public transport only passes through the village on Wednesday and Friday. Melanie and Lewis were able to attend the Wednesday session by catching the bus in the morning and being collected by a neighbouring farmer returning from market in the early afternoon. Melanie and Lewis missed several sessions due to poor weather.

The nearest maternity unit is over 40 miles away. Both Melanie's parents took leave from their work and came to stay in order to care for Lewis. After Morgan's birth, it became very difficult for Melanie and Lewis to attend the *Cylch Ti a Fi*. She mentioned this to her health visitor who contacted the pre-school referral team. When Lewis was two and half, he was able to attend the *cylch meithrin* with funded transport. After much lobbying in this area, the criteria for special needs had been extended to include children in need due to social and rural isolation. The health visitor has also ensured that the toy library calls on Melanie when visiting the next village, therefore giving the boys access to a wider range of activities at home. Both boys started in the two-teacher school (in the same village as the *cylchoedd*, Welsh medium playgroups) the term after their third birthdays. As the school is three miles away, the local authority provides transport.

The school is now developing its community links and sees itself as an unofficial integrated centre. Two days a week Melanie goes with the boys in their taxi to school. On these days she attends Information Technology sessions (provided free through European Social Funding) and Welsh for Adults classes. As she is not able to return home before the end of school, she stays and acts as a volunteer in class. As the school is a Welsh-medium school and the infant children are taught entirely through the medium of Welsh, she works with the teacher and children in the class for seven to eleven year olds.

Through contact with other parents at the school, Melanie and the boys now have a wider social circle. Although Melanie does not have a car, she has persuaded another parent to teach her to drive. With her new IT skills, the head-teacher has asked her to do some paid secretarial work in the school. Although this will impact on her benefits, she is pleased to be in employment. Lewis and Morgan are very proud of their mother's involvement with their school.

BACKGROUND

Wales has, for the last decade and more, quietly established its own priorities in early education, health and care, and is becoming increasingly more confident in its autonomous status. The implementation of the Government of Wales Act 1999 (HMSO, 1998) has resulted in what is in many respects a self-governing Wales, particularly when it comes to education and other services for young children and families. Indeed by 2003, Wales was advancing its own radical proposals for an Early Years curriculum, a play-centred approach to promote the learning of children up to seven years of age. The drive toward further devolution will be significantly further advanced by the Government of Wales Act 2006 (HMSO, 2006) that gives the Welsh Assembly primary jurisdiction over its own domestic affairs, including education and health services.

The population of Wales is mainly located around the urban centres of *Caerdydd*/Cardiff and *Casnewydd*/Newport in the south-east, *Abertawe*/Swansea more to the south-west, and *Wrecsam*/Wrexham in the north-east. The area of greatest population growth is *Ceredigion* on the mid-central coast of Cardigan Bay – an increase of 27.6 per cent since 1981, due, in the main, to inward-migration from England.

Wales is a small country with a population of just under three million in 2004, almost 5 per cent more than the population in 1981. There are some 33,500 children aged three years and around 75,000 children under five years of age. Of the total population, some 19 per cent are under 16. The number of children under five years old has fallen over the last ten years and the number of children aged one to fifteen years old is projected to be lower in 2010 as the number of births is now lower than it has been in almost 30 years. Infant mortality rates are substantially lower than thirty years ago (Office of National Statistics, 2004).

The Welsh language

The Welsh language, generally agreed to be the oldest living language in Europe, is still very much alive with its own vibrant culture. Results of the 2001 census show a significant increase in the numbers of people speaking Welsh: more than 20 per cent of people in Wales now speak Welsh compared with 18.5 per cent in the 1991 census. In addition, more than 28 per cent are able to understand Welsh. Of all the population aged three years and over, 582,400 (20.8 per cent) said they were able to speak Welsh. This compares with 18.7 per cent who in 1991 said they spoke Welsh, and 19.0 per cent in 1981. The highest percentages of Welsh speakers are found amongst children: 40.8 per cent in children aged five to fifteen years old. The main change in the position of the language over the past decade has been the increase in south-east Wales. The percentage of Welsh speakers in the younger five to nine and ten to fourteen year old age groups has been higher than the percentage in the fifteen to twenty four year old age group since 1971, and the difference between the percentages of those groups has been increasing every decade since 1971. There was a large increase in 2001, perhaps reflecting the effect of the Education Reform Act 1988 (DfES, 1988).

Most Welsh speakers are bilingual, the exceptions being some very young children and some older people. A visitor to Wales cannot but see and hear the language. Road signs are bilingual, as are public notices and place names. The status of Welsh is safeguarded in statute; the Welsh Language Act 1993 (HMSO, 1993) and the Government of Wales Act 1999 (HMSO, 1998) ensured that the Welsh and English languages are treated on 'the basis of equality'. Following the Education Reform Act 1988 (DfES, 1988), which introduced the National Curriculum, Wales had its own version and Welsh became compulsory in schools up to the age of sixteen, either as a core or a foundation subject. Indeed, it is the bilingual experience that gives Wales its particular uniqueness.

> Reflect on the advantages of early bilingualism and the value of bilingualism generally for children such as Lewis and Sioned Niamh. Note the recent significant increase of children and young people who speak Welsh.

Mudiad Ysgolion Meithrin (MYM) has played a key role in normalising the Welsh language and bilingualism. Approximately 35 per cent of three year olds in Wales are in Welsh-immersion nursery settings (in some areas of course it is more like 90 per cent), much of this is due to the contribution of MYM. In the last few years, MYM has been developing its interests to include Welsh-medium day nurseries and has three operational at present and others at the planning stage.

Iaith Pawb: A National Action Plan for a Bilingual Wales (Welsh Assembly Government (WAG), 2003a) is the Welsh Assembly government's proposal for both normalising and extending bilingualism in Wales. Although it has a broad sweep, from economic and community regeneration to cultural activities, there is particular emphasis on the critical importance of children in the early years:

> The Assembly attaches great importance to developing Welsh language provision for the early years (0–5 years). It is a tremendous advantage if young children can learn to speak Welsh naturally within the family. For children whose parents do not speak Welsh, Welsh medium nursery education is a particularly effective means of enabling them to become bilingual. (WAG, 2003a: 39)

Twf (literally translated as growth), funded under *Iaith Pawb* by the Welsh Language Board, is a long-term project which aims to share information with parents and prospective parents about the advantages of raising children bilingually. *Twf* field staff work closely with health visitors and midwives and with a range of Early Years organisations and initiatives, including WPPA groups, Basic Skills Agency Language and Play workers, and MYM in order to promote early bilingualism within the family. Sioned Niamh's mother Eleri enjoyed a period of voluntary work experience with *Twf* and as a result was encouraged to return to higher education.

Minority Ethnic groups in Wales

According to the 2001 census figures (see www.statistics.gov.uk/census/default.asp), 2.1 per cent of the population of Wales are from a minority ethnic background, which accounts for almost 62,000 people. As with other countries of the UK (in England, for example, 45 per cent of all minority ethnic groups live in London), the main concentrations of minorities in Wales live in the urban areas of south Wales. Cardiff has the highest number and percentage of population (25,7000 and 8.4 per cent) followed by Newport (6,600 and 4.8 per cent). *Ynys Môn* (Anglesey) has the lowest number with 500 people (0.7 per cent of the population) from minorities. There has been some recent debate about ethnic-rural living. This has been in response to comments made by Trevor Phillips, chair of the Commission for Racial Equality, regarding rural areas being seen as 'no-go areas' for people from minority ethnic groups (see bbc.co.uk/wales).

Child poverty in Wales

In a conference entitled 'Child Poverty in Wales – Much Work to be Done' in January 2005, Lucy Akhtar of the End Child Poverty Network Cymru, a coalition of key statutory and charity organisations in Wales, put it baldly when she stated:

> Children in Wales have the worst well-being in the UK. (Akhtar, 2005)

However, research by the Joseph Rowntree Foundation into social exclusion in Wales (Kenway et al., 2005) suggests that Welsh poverty rates have fallen faster than those in England or Scotland in the past decade and are now no worse than the average for the UK as a whole. But one in four children continues to live in poor families and there are significant levels of poverty throughout the country: roughly a third of the 170,000 children in homes below the poverty threshold live in the Valleys, a third in Cardiff and the rest of the south, and a third in north, west and mid-Wales. Furthermore, the research found that:

> although the conventional measure of poverty (households with less than 60 per cent of UK median income) has improved over ten years, the number in Wales who live in 'deep poverty' (40 per cent of median household income) has remained the same at around 250,000. (Kenway et al., 2005: 23)

Homelessness in Wales has risen sharply, doubling from 8,000 in 2000 to 16,000 in 2004. One third of homeless households are families with children. Another of the key problems facing families in poverty is transport and accessing adequate public transport. One of the groups most likely to be without a car is lone parents who reported significant difficulties in reaching shops and local hospitals.

> Although poverty and disadvantage are at their deepest in the Valleys, our report shows that people in all parts of Wales face these problems. (Kenway et al., 2005: 10)

Child Poverty Action Group Cymru provides the following disturbing picture of the life chances of poor children in Wales. These children are:

- more likely to be born prematurely and have a lower birth rate
- 15 times more likely to die in a fire at home
- 5 times more likely to die in an accident
- 3 times more likely to be hit by a car
- 10 times more likely to be become a teenage mother
- more likely to suffer from high obesity levels
- less likely to stay on at school or enter higher education
- more likely to leave school with no or few qualifications.
  (Child Poverty Action Group Cymru, 2006: 6)

In addition to the above, consider the impact of poverty on children who live in rural areas of Wales, such as Lewis and Morgan. How might their childhood experiences be affected by a lack of private and public transport?

National Assembly of Wales 1999

The establishment of the National Assembly of Wales in 1999 signalled a number of significant differences from England in the way children's services are developed – and also key differences in approaches to children.

Wales, long convinced of the need and certainly in touch with European thinking, had seen many years of consistent and passionate lobbying for its own Children's Commissioner. Children in Wales, the Welsh equivalent of the National Children's Bureau, had been a key player in mobilising this lobby. A persistent problem was the lack of legislative powers and the intransigence of Westminster governments to respond to this lobby. Neither the Thatcher nor Major Conservative governments would concede on this issue and, to much disappointment, neither did the New Labour government after its election in 1997. But members of the newly-established National Assembly of Wales were much more committed to the idea of someone independent who would stand up for children's and young people's rights.

The Whitehouse Report *Lost in Care* (Department of Health, 2000), published following a long inquiry into the abuse of children in local authority-run homes in north Wales during the 1970s, was a seminal publication. There was a degree of public outrage not only at the treatment of these children but also at the inaction of the authorities to respond to the children's complaints. Waterhouse's first recommendation was that Wales have a Children's Commissioner, and the Care Standards Act 2000 (HMSO, 2000) provided the legislative opportunity to create the post. Peter Clarke started work as Wales's first Children's Commissioner on March 1 (St David's Day) 2001. He was appointed following a series of interviews, including one with a panel of children and young people.

Although (at the time of writing) still restricted by Westminster's legislative frameworks on the matter, Wales has its own values relating to issues such as smacking. *Sdim Curo Plant! Cymru* (Children are Unbeatable! Cymru) was launched in September 2000, as the Welsh co-ordinating body for the lobby to change the law on smacking. The WAG, from its establishment, has been strongly committed to both the UN Convention on the Rights of the Child and the aims of *Sdim Curo Plant! Cymru*. In a plenary debate on 14 January 2004 about the Green Paper *Every Child Matters* (DfES, 2003), National Assembly members voted in favour of a ban on smacking children by 41 votes to nine. The motion carried was:

> regretting that the UK Government continues to retain the defence of reasonable chastisement and has taken no significant action towards prohibiting the physical punishment of children in the family. (Children in Wales, 2006)

Attempts by *Sdim Curo Plant! Cymru* to ensure equal protection for children in a Children Bill have up until now failed. Instead, the Westminster government supported a new clause, Section 58 of the Children Act 2004 (DfES, 2004), that allows the 'reasonable punishment or reasonable chastisement' defence to continue. The Government of Wales Act 2006 (HMSO, 2006) might well allow Wales to enact its own vision and values by rejecting, once and for all, this official condonement of the smacking of children.

POLICY AND PRACTICE IN EARLY CHILDHOOD EDUCATION AND CARE

Childcare outside the family appears to be a relatively new practice in Wales. In 1986, for example, Wales had only one known setting registered for full daycare. Working parents would traditionally make informal childcare arrangements with family members, or, more likely, mothers would give up work to care for their young babies and infants. Sessional care was more common, for example MYM had some 70 *cylchoedd meithrin* when it was established in 1971, this figure rising to about 800 in the late 1980s. Lewis and his mother benefited from his attendance at a *cylchoedd meithrin* when he was two and a half, as a result of funded transport.

There has been a sea-change over the past twenty years. The Care Standards Inspectorate for Wales provides the information on registrations for 2006 as shown in Table 6.1.

Both Lewis and Sioned Niamh attended *Cylch Ti a Fi* (provision which was not available to their parents when they were infants). However, childcare provision remains patchy. *A Childcare Revolution in Wales*, a report by the Bevan Foundation (2006), found that across the whole of Wales there is just one childcare place for every seven children under the age of eight. Furthermore, the more disadvantaged communities have far fewer childcare places: in Blaenau Gwent, for example, there is only one place for every 20 children. The report highlights the barriers to childcare:

- **Poor Availability** – For example, in Merthyr Tydfil there are 5,800 children under eight but only 497 childcare places and 14 childminders.
- **Poverty and Disadvantage** – The areas where children are most likely to live in poverty and where parents are less likely to work offer the least help to tackle family poverty and get parents into jobs.
- **High Costs** – Average cost of formal childcare is £134 a week for each child, putting it out of reach for those families who most need it.
- **Lack of Flexibility** – Childcare provision of the 'nine-to-five' type doesn't match the demands of the local job market for shift working. (Bevan, 2005: 5).

TABLE 6.1   Types of provision and numbers of childcare settings in Wales in 2006

Type of provision	Number of settings
Full daycare	471
Crèches	78
Sessional daycare	809
Childminders	2332
Open-access play provision	93
Out-of-school provision	577

One particular project, established and part-funded by the WAG and the European Social Fund, is the Genesis project. It was initially piloted in Rhondda Cynon Taf in 2002 but is now operating throughout Wales. Genesis Cymru's aims are clear: to reduce barriers faced by parents who wish to either return to learning or return to work. The support available may include free or subsidised childcare, a mobile crèche and in some areas the project runs its own community day nurseries. The benefits of the Genesis project are illustrated by the case of Sioned Niamh who was assisted by the scheme to find Welsh-medium childcare and additionally Genesis contributed towards the cost.

Statutory education in Wales begins in the term after a child's fifth birthday, although the vast majority of children start school earlier than this. Obtaining reliable information on numbers of three year old children in maintained and non-maintained provision poses a problem. Children may be part-time users of two or more services. A child may, for example, be registered with a childminder who will take the child to the *cylch meithrin* in the mornings and to part-time nursery provision in a primary school in the afternoons. Lewis's story demonstrates how he and his mother Melanie benefited from this provision.

Wales had the lowest proportion (just over 5 per cent) of maintained primary school classes with more than 30 pupils in 2004/05, compared with a UK average of 12 per cent.

TABLE 6.2   Children under five and maintained provision in Wales in 2004

Provision	Quantity
Nursery schools	40
Children in nursery schools	2,225
Full-time teachers in nursery schools	91
Qualified nursery assistants in nursery schools	103 (full-time equivalent)
Unqualified nursery assistants	14
Primary schools	1,624
Pupils	282,576
Full-time teachers in primary schools	12,904
Maintained primary schools with nursery pupils	1,238
Children aged 3 and 4 years in maintained education provision (either full-time or part-time)	70,300
Registered places for children of five years in daycare facilities	35,914
Maintained Welsh-medium primary schools	442 (27.2% of all schools)

Source: Key Education Statistics in Wales, 2004

Beware of taking statistics at face value. A factor contributing to the statistic on p.143 is the number of small schools in rural Wales, such as the one attended by Lewis and his brother Morgan. Their school is similar to many in rural Wales, in that there are only two classes; one class for four to six year olds and another class for seven to eleven year olds. Consider the benefits and drawbacks of small schools like the one above for children's education and social development.

The last Conservative government of the UK conceded the argument in favour of the public funding commitment to nursery education in 1995. This was a radical move forward for England but not so for Wales. Almost all local authorities in Wales had traditionally provided places for four year old children in schools. Indeed, some LEAs (in particular, West Glamorgan in the south and Clwyd in the north) had funded nursery education for children from three years for most of the 1970s and 1980s.

The Welsh Office's consultation document *Guidance for local Early Years Development and Childcare Partnerships in Wales* (1999b) outlined a government intention to establish Early Years partnerships under local authority remit and was circulated widely. It became increasingly evident that the expectations of extensive government funding for educational provision for young children would mean the professionalisation of the voluntary sector if it were to survive these sweeping changes.

The voucher system of parental choice of either maintained (local authority schools) or non-maintained (voluntary sector or private provision) education was introduced early in 1996. One of the first actions of the New Labour Government following the general election in 1997 was to abolish vouchers – to almost universal approval in Wales.

In order to receive the status of approved setting, both maintained (which were de facto approved through their status as statutory provision) and non-maintained provision had to comply with the 1996 *Awdurdod Cwricwlwm, Cymwysterau ac Asesu Cymru* (Wales Curriculum, Qualifications and Assessment Authority) framework, *Desirable Learning Outcomes for Children's Learning before Compulsory School Age* (ACAC, 1996). The introduction in the same year of this curriculum for children under compulsory school age also saw Wales and England doing things differently. *Desirable Learning Outcomes* is still in use in Wales. With its focus on the learning child, its robust celebration of the value of play in children's learning, *Desirable Learning Outcomes* in Wales was published to universal acclaim. The same was not true of the document for England, *Desirable Outcomes For Children's Learning On Entering Compulsory Education* (SCAA, 1996). Indeed David (1998), when comparing the *Desirable Learning Outcomes* document for children in England (SCAA, 1996) and the *Desirable Learning Outcomes* for Children in Wales (ACAC, 1996), stated:

> What are we to make of the stark contrast in the approach reflected in the two sets of documentation? Is it that national expectations, in other words the constructions of childhood are different ... It would seem that being under five in England is to be less joyful, less celebrated, less imaginative, less romantic, more pressurised, more rigid ... than in Wales. (David, 1998: 61)

So great was the critiquing of the SCAA document that it was soon replaced by *Early Learning Goals* (DfEE/QCA, 1999), since transformed into *Guidance for the Foundation Stage* (DfEE/QCA, 2000).

The *Desirable Learning Outcomes* document in Wales made reference to Welsh language provision and the expectation that all children would have some experience of Welsh during their time in provision for the under-fives:

> Experiencing Welsh at an early age, when language acquisition skills are at their most effective, can be a valuable preparation for the child's learning of Welsh at school.

> All under fives can be given opportunities to hear about Wales, about their locality, about customs, about names, about stories and legends, about people and events. These experiences form part of rewarding and lively learning experiences for children of nursery age in Wales and allow children to have their experiences of life in Wales enhanced. (ACAC, 1996: 4)

In order to be eligible for approved setting status, provision had to comply with OHMCI (Office of Her Majesty's Chief Inspector, which later became Estyn) education Early Years inspection guidelines. These included a section on Welsh language and *Curriculum Cymreig* – the latter refers to that area of learning which uniquely relates to Wales and the Welsh identity – experiences provided for children within the setting. This policy enabled both Lewis and Sioned Niamh to start to engage with the Welsh language before formal schooling despite their differing pre-school experiences (see both Lewis's and Sioned Niamh's stories).

When all these requirements were met (qualified staff, adult: child ratio, range of experiences offered, buildings and environment, equipment and so on), provision would be eligible to receive the £1100 per child under four years which parents would have to 'spend', as it were, in that particular approved setting. However, as over 90 per cent of four year old children were already in maintained provision in Wales (that is, they were in schools), the exercise was relatively meaningless in Wales.

Flying Start

In October 2005, the Minister for Education and Lifelong Learning, Jane Davidson, launched Flying Start, her programme for birth to three year olds in Wales. It is an ambitious programme which will target £46 million over the period 2006/08 towards children and families in deprived areas. There has been some critiquing of the indicator of deprivation used: those areas where over 45 per cent of children in local primary schools are entitled to free school meals is seen as being a crude tool to measure complex issues relating to social exclusion.

Flying Start services in these targeted areas will include centre-based child-care for all two and three year olds on a part-time basis, health visitor support, parenting programmes, early literacy and 'books-for-babies' initiatives. The intention is to develop new integrated centres or use local primary schools. It is the government's intention that Flying Start targets the language, cognitive, social and emotional development of the children involved, as well as their physical health. The minister stated at its launch that:

> Flying Start and the Foundation Phase are very closely linked. Together they provide a unique, made-in-Wales offer to our youngest children and their families. In time, I am confident that the impact of these programmes will transform the landscape of learning in Wales.

> (Jane Davidson, 4 November 2005, 6th Annual Congress of National Primary Centre Cymru)

This programme sees the integration of childcare, early learning, parenting, and health services as one vision for promoting the well-being of children in Wales. Although there are concerns about its implementation Flying Start has, in the main, been welcomed as a cornerstone in the WAG's drive to combating child poverty.

Flying Start is clearly a well-intentioned and significant initiative. The programme is targeted on areas where there are high numbers of children claiming free school meals. What are the limitations of using measures such as this when targeting poverty and social exclusion (see Kenway et al., 2005)? What other measures of poverty could be used to target services for families with young children?

TRANSITIONS

'Currently transition arrangements between the maintained and non-maintained sectors (in Wales) are inconsistent and arbitrary' (Siraj-Blatchford et al., 2006: 6). The issue of transitions in Wales has, over the last few years, focused mainly on children's transition from primary to secondary education. Very little work has been undertaken, either in terms of policy development or research, on the crucial topic of the transition of young children moving between settings or from one age-group provision to the next. A young child of two to three years in Wales, as in Sioned Niamh's case, may well be moving between care settings: *cylch meithrin* on three mornings a week, day nursery for two afternoons, with grandparents for one day and job-share working parents for another day.

The evidence in favour of robust systems and practices for ensuring that young children are carefully supported during transitions is well established (Brooker, 2002; Elfer et al., 2003). The WAG formed a Childcare Working Group in 2004 (chaired by the Minister for Economic Development and Transport – reinforcing the perception that childcare is seen primarily as an employment issue) which acknowledged that childcare would be delivered by a range of diverse services and noted that 'government must ensure that all these sectors complement each other so as to create a joined up childcare service' (WAG, 2005: 3). This is proving more challenging to implement than first envisaged here.

CSIW's national minimum standards (NMS) for full daycare require settings to implement a key worker system. The key worker will be responsible for the child's well-being on a daily basis and will ensure clear exchange of information with parents. The NMS also refers to settling-in processes, partnerships with parents, and transitions to other settings.

The establishment of integrated centres in all local authorities will make a significant contribution towards easing the transition pressures for very young children. These integrated centres provide Early Years education, childcare, community/parent training and open access play to communities in disadvantaged areas, and are part of local regeneration strategies. The Institute of Welsh Affairs (IWA) undertook research on these integrated centres (see Seaton, 2006) providing details of the key features and making recommendations for future policy developments. The IWA report concluded that 'these centres offer a uniquely Welsh approach to the delivery of integrated services for families and children and are likely to put Wales at the forefront of Early Years provision' (IWA, 2006: Conference, 13 March, available at www.iwa.org.uk/debate/debatepresentations2006.htm).

Other than parental choice of for example Welsh-medium education or faith schools, there are no specific admissions policies for children entering the statutory primary sector. Wales does not have a centralised admissions policy and local authorities have responsibility for admissions.

Schools will have their own procedures and policies for internal transition of children from nursery to Reception and further on through the school system. More and more schools are already planning for the transition from the Foundation Phase to Key Stage 2 (Siraj-Blatchford et al., 2006: 6). It is anticipated that the roll-out of the Foundation Phase will, in itself, make transition easier. Children will move gradually within the phase.

Many schools are extending links with parents by providing care as well as education for young children aged three to seven. This integrated, wrap-around care (a range of childcare services based around part-time education that enable children and families to take part in learning and play opportunities) enhances the experiences provided for children. These additional services rely on a range of funding sources and accessing this funding is often complex and bureaucratic (Estyn, 2003: 11).

> What benefits will integrated centres and wrap-around care bring to families such as Lewis's and Sioned Niamh's?

SCHOOLING

In education the last few years have seen changes that have led, in some instances, to dramatic differences between Wales and England. As previously discussed, control over the education system was devolved to Wales when the Welsh Assembly came into being in 1999. The Welsh Assembly's Department for Training and Education is ultimately responsible for education in Wales. This includes:

- providing and funding state education
- training teachers
- maintaining educational standards
- overseeing the curriculum and examinations.

Education in Wales is therefore now significantly different from England in terms of curriculum and assessment and in the public scrutiny of schools.

In particular, *The Learning Country: Foundation Phase 3–7 years* (WAG, 2003b) signals a further distinction for Wales, not only in the organisation of the curriculum, but also in the ethos and principles that underpin that curriculum. There are, therefore, fundamental differences between the Foundation Phase in Wales and the Foundation Stage in England.

The Learning Country: Foundation Phase 3–7 years

The proposed curriculum for children from three to seven years of age emerged in the form of a consultative document, *The Learning Country:*

Foundation Phase 3–7 years, in February 2003 (WAG, 2003b). This was preceded 18 months earlier by *The Learning Country: A paving document* (WAG, 2001b). Jane Davidson, Minister for Education and Lifelong Learning in the Welsh Assembly Government, wrote in the foreword to this document:

> We share strategic goals with our colleagues in England – but we often need to take a different route to achieve them. We shall take our own policy direction where necessary, to get the best for Wales. It's right that we put local authorities, local communities and locally determined needs and priorities at the centre of the agenda for schools. (WAG, 2001b: 2)

The Foundation Phase is based very firmly on the tradition of learning through play and in understanding the holistic nature of young children's learning. Its implementation will lead to the abolition of Key Stage 1 and will, in all probability, mean the undermining of Key Stage 2. Wales has, of course, already abolished statutory national testing for seven to fourteen year olds and has never subscribed to primary school league tables.

The Foundation Phase advocates a carefully planned play-based curriculum that aims to 'help children learn how to learn; develop thinking skills; and acquire positive attitudes to lifelong learning' (WAG, 2003b: 12). The main focus of the Foundation Phase in Wales is the child's *personal, social development and well-being* which are placed at the centre of the curriculum and are viewed as fundamental to young children's learning. The original *Desirable Learning Outcomes* document (ACAC, 1996) had six areas of learning:

- language, literacy, and communication
- mathematical development
- personal and social development
- knowledge and understanding of the world
- creative development
- physical development.

The proposed Foundation Phase curriculum adds another area of learning: *Bilingualism* . This underlines the importance that the WAG gives to Wales as a bilingual nation and reflects the changes in population. Following the implementation of the pilot phase, the *Foundation Phase Action Plan* (WAG, 2006b) expanded the area of learning *personal and social development* to include *well-being and cultural diversity*.

The Foundation Phase document acknowledges that good early learning does 'not depend exclusively on the use of one particular curriculum model' (WAG, 2003b: 10). It does, however, state that 'there is evidence that a curriculum in which children are involved in planning and reviewing their work … has a positive long-term effect on their social and intellectual development' (WAG, 2003b: 10).

The document positions the new Welsh early learning approach firmly in the tradition of other countries, practitioners and systems: 'Practice in Denmark, Germany, Reggio Emilia in Italy and New Zealand shows how children can be encouraged to make decisions about their learning, to be independent and physically active in doing so' (WAG, 2003b: 10).

The thinking behind the Foundation Phase comes also from concerns about the kinds of early learning experiences of young children in Wales. These key critiques of the traditional or more formal way have been identified as children spending too much time doing tasks at tables and having insufficient opportunities to develop language skills by talking about their activities. Furthermore, the document goes on to highlight Estyn's evidence that 'too little emphasis is placed on developing children's creative expression and cultural understanding' and its damning concern that children are introduced to formal reading and writing 'before they are ready' (WAG, 2003b: 5).

The Foundation Phase is currently being piloted in 41 settings throughout Wales, representing both maintained and non-maintained provision, and is being closely scrutinised by a team of experienced researchers led by Iram Siraj-Blatchford and Kathy Sylva. The first report of the Monitoring and Evaluation of the Effective Implementation of the Foundation Phase Project (MEEIFP) in February 2006 makes encouraging reading. Practitioners, for example, in the first year of the Foundation Phase pilot identified the following strengths:

- Curriculum based on play, active and experiential learning.
- Child-centred curriculum.
- Broader, holistic, more relevant curriculum. (Siraj-Blatchford et al., 2006: 5)

There are, however, some key areas identified as requiring considerable improvement, for example the need for 'clear guidance materials on the areas of learning and associated pedagogy, and better planned and funded training … ' (2006: 5). Although there has been an unqualified welcome for the proposal to enhance staffing ratios – eventually to 1:8 for under-fives and 1: 15 for five to seven year olds – the authors of the Monitoring and Evaluation Report make an interesting point:

> Care should be taken to ensure that improving ratios does not take precedence over high quality training for staff working in schools and settings. Staff qualifications show a stronger relationship to quality of provision than ratios. (Siraj-Blatchford et al., 2006: 10)

Consult the research evidence on the relationship between adult/child ratios and quality of training of staff.

Despite promising reports from the pilot settings and indeed more widely, as Thomas's research into perceptions and expectations of the Foundation Phase indicated (Thomas, 2005), excitement about the Foundation Phase was dampened by the announcement in November 2005 of some delay in the rolling-out of the programme. The Foundation Phase is ambitious and this was not entirely unexpected. (See Table 6.3)

There is a number of interesting challenges that will face providers in Wales as a result of the implementation of the Foundation Phase: for example, documented and narrative assessment will replace the traditional checklist type of

TABLE 6.3   The Foundation Phase timetable in Wales

School year	Cohort
2005–2006	3 to 6 year olds and some 7 year olds in the schools with mixed age classes in pilot schools and settings only
2006–2007	3 to 7 year olds in pilot schools and settings only
2007–2008	3 to 7 year olds in pilot schools and settings only
2008–2009 2009–2010	3 to 5 year olds in all schools, voluntary and private settings and childminders funded by the local education authority through the Early Years Development and Childcare Partnership (EYDCP), and 5 to 7 year olds in the pilot schools
2010–2011	3 to 7 year olds in all schools, voluntary and private settings and childminders funded by the local education authority through the EYDCP.

assessments, and retrospective planning may well be the norm as opposed to the rigid forward planning that has dominated the past ten years and more.

Primary Education

In Wales children start statutory education in the term after their fifth birthday. In Key Stage 1 and Key Stage 2 the main differences from England currently are that the National Literacy Strategy and The National Numeracy Strategy are both recommended as guidance in schools but are not statutory documents in Wales.

Since 1990, Welsh has been a compulsory subject for all students in mainstream state schools in Wales. Children study Welsh either as a first or second language. Welsh is taught as a first language in Welsh-medium schools, and as a second language in English-medium schools. Typically, in Welsh speaking schools English is introduced at age seven for children from Welsh language homes. There is no statutory requirement to teach English at Key Stage 1 in Welsh-medium schools. Support for Welsh language teaching is provided by a national team of mobile teachers called *Athrawon Bro*. They travel from school to school to support teachers and pupils in learning Welsh, and learning through Welsh.

In 2001, over 16 per cent of primary school children were considered fluent in Welsh, compared with 13 per cent in 1986/87 (National Assembly for Wales Statistical Directorate, 2001). Throughout the population in Wales the highest percentages of Welsh speakers were found amongst children (40.8 per cent for children aged five to fifteen years). There was a large increase in 2001, perhaps reflecting the effect of the prominence given to Welsh in the National Curriculum, especially as a foundation subject in English-medium schools. An overall curriculum review is due in 2008.

The assessment of children in schools also differs significantly from England. Wales has abolished the publication of league tables and has scrapped compulsory tests for seven year olds. Tests for eleven and fourteen year olds will also be phased out by 2007–2008. In November 2004, the Minister for Education and Lifelong Learning announced the outcome of the consultation on her proposals for future assessment arrangements. These followed a two-year review of school curriculum and assessment arrangements, which drew on developments taking place in other countries and also aimed to take account of a range of relevant international research.

As a result, from 2005 onward, teacher assessment is the only means of statutory assessment of primary school children in Wales. For 2006 all schools will have received optional task and test material. There will be no external marking service. All testing will be replaced by teacher assessments and a new skills test for ten year olds focusing on numeracy, literacy and problem-solving. By 2008, although England and Wales will follow the National Curriculum, they will have quite different testing regimes. Wales also has a separate inspections agency called Estyn (see below), which means 'extend', and a General Teaching Council was established on 1 September 2000 to give an independent voice for teachers in Wales.

The General Teaching Council for Wales (GTCW) is the statutory self-regulating professional body for the teaching profession in Wales. The GTCW has three main roles: regulatory (all qualified teachers teaching in state schools in Wales must be registered with the GTCW); advisory (the GTCW advises the WAG and other organisations on teaching issues) and operational (the body administers funding programmes for teachers' professional development needs). (For further information see www.gtcw.org.uk/).

Creativity is also given a prominent role in education in Wales. A *Cwricwlwm Cymreig* has been established to ensure a Welsh context and ethos to each subject in the National Curriculum for Wales. One of the main features of *Cwricwlwm Cymreig* is to develop an understanding of the creative and expressive arts in Wales. According to Estyn schools in Wales have shown:

> marked improvements in the quality of the education they provide and in the standards that pupils achieve over the last ten years. Teachers and other staff play a key role in the personal and social development of their pupils. They will also play an important part in realising the National Assembly's vision of a Wales in which young people are confident, active citizens who show creativity, entrepreneurial skills, and an informed concern for other people and the environment. (Estyn, 2002: 1)

SPECIAL EDUCATIONAL NEEDS

The Special Educational Needs and Disability Act 2001 makes provision relating to special educational needs in England and Wales only (see www.opsi.gov.uk/acts). Wales is, therefore, only marginally different from England in the legislation relating to Special Educational Needs (SEN).

The SEN Code of Practice for Wales (NAFW, 2002) provides the guidance and procedures for Wales. The code describes the following areas of SEN:

- communication and interaction difficulties
- cognition and learning difficulties
- behaviour, emotional and social development
- sensory, physical and medical need.

It also outlines how children with SEN – the term Additional Learning Needs (ALN) is becoming more commonly used in Wales than SEN – will be supported in Early Years settings and schools through a graduated approach. For example, the code states that:

> once practitioners have identified that a child has special educational needs, the setting should intervene through *Early Years Action*. If this intervention does not enable the child to make satisfactory progress the SENCO may need to seek advice and support from external agencies. These forms of intervention are referred to ... as *Early Years Action Plus*. (NAfW, 2002: 32)

In October 2003, the Welsh Assembly published a consultation document setting out draft guidance on inclusive education. This document provided guidance on the practical operation of the statutory framework of the *Education Act 1996* and the *Special Educational Needs and Disability Act 2001* (NAfW, 2003: 14).

This document outlines the WAG's commitment to inclusive education and identifies the key principles which include a strong commitment to mainstream provision:

> With the right training, strategies and support, nearly all children and young people with SEN can be successfully included in mainstream education. (NAfW, 2003: 14)

Numbers of children with Statements of SEN have remained fairly constant since 1991 although there has been a significant reduction in special schools, reflecting of course the commitment to inclusion. Some 25 per cent of new statements in 2004 were for children under five.

In 2003, the Welsh Assembly began a comprehensive policy review of special educational needs in Wales. The first report, on early identification and early inclusion, was published in 2004. The review found some disturbing perceptions and experiences; for example, many parents found that seeking specialist advice and support for their children with SEN was 'often a frustrating and distressing process' (WAG, 2004: 11). Furthermore, of parents whose first language was not English only about a third felt that available support was easily accessible, and when asked to consider barriers to the early identification of SEN:

... the vast majority of parents identified the shortage of specialist staff as the key issue: in particular, the shortage of speech and language therapists. The situation was regarded as chronic with regard to Welsh language specialist provision and also for children and parents whose first language is neither Welsh nor English. (NAfW, 2003: 14)

Voluntary sector services however were seen as providing a valuable service, often giving parents 'opportunities to discuss their concerns with experts and other parents'. The voluntary sector, particularly the partnership of MYM and the WPPA, has long-established referral schemes operating at county level which enable the early inclusion of young children with special needs into their community provision. This might involve funding additional staff, specialist equipment, or transport.

From 1993, parents had the right to appeal against decisions made by local education authorities regarding their children's SEN to the Special Educational Needs Tribunal. This independent body had jurisdiction in England and Wales. However, with the publication of the SEN *Code of Practice* for Wales in 2002, it became increasingly obvious that Wales needed its own Tribunal. The Special Educational Needs Tribunal Wales (SENTW) was established on 1 April 2003.

Welsh-medium services for children with special needs have been the subject of consistent concern over the years. Language appropriateness of, for example, speech and language therapy delivery remains a contentious issue. Parental pressure for appropriate services, with the support of voluntary organisations such as MYM, is ongoing. The WAG, through the Welsh Language Board, commissioned a comprehensive review of Welsh-medium and bilingual provision and services for pupils with special educational needs (HMSO, 2002). The WAG has now published *Acknowledging Need: An Action Plan* (WAG, 2006b) setting out its proposals to ensure equity of provision for Welsh speaking and bilingual children.

By 2008, the WAG also intends to implement arrangements for joint commissioning of all services across health, education and social services through a pooled budget. This Children and Young People's plan will, it is hoped, make inter-agency working easier which will in turn make the lives of young children with Additional Learning Needs (ALN) and disabilities, and their families' lives also, a little less fraught.

> How will the commitment to 'inclusion for all' impact on all young children in Early Years settings and in school? Consider the problems for children whose home language is other than Welsh or English.

SAFEGUARDING CHILDREN

The term 'safeguarding children' has come to replace the term 'child protection'. Safeguarding is a wide concept which means promoting children's welfare and putting measures in place to improve children's safety and prevent abuse. Child protection is that part of the safeguarding process where it is necessary to intervene when there is a reasonable belief that a child is at risk of significant harm. However, the wider concept of safeguarding includes children who are, for a range of reasons, vulnerable. This will include gypsy and traveller children who have high rates of exclusions from school, asylum-seeking children, young carers, and disabled children (Preston, 2005).

Statistics relating to children and domestic abuse create a disturbing picture of vulnerability; for example 33 per cent of children try and intervene during attacks on their mother and 90 per cent of children are in the same room or the next room during attacks on their mother (South Wales Police, 2005 – see www.south-wales.police.uk). The WAG has a number of initiatives promoting collaborative working to safeguard this group of vulnerable children, for example *Good Practice on Domestic Abuse: Safeguarding children and young people in Wales* (WAG, 2004) is a resource to help schools identify and meet the needs of children who may be experiencing domestic abuse at home.

Historically in Wales, as elsewhere in the UK, the child protection system has developed through a series of reactive acts of parliament, policies and procedures arising from inquiries into the deaths of children from abuse and the systemic failings attributed to key professionals responsible for protecting children.

The first inquiry report (Curtis Committee Report: HMSO, 1946), into the death of Denis O'Neil, fostered out by Newport County Council, led to the introduction of the Children Act 1948 (HMSO, 1948) and the appointment of children's officers with specific responsibility for children's welfare. Social workers and medical practitioners were alerted to possible signs and symptoms of child abuse by Henry Kempe's work in the 1960s but it was not until 1973, following the death of Maria Colwell, that the first multidisciplinary child protection frameworks were established including Area Child Protection Committees and child protection case conferences.

The publication of the Waterhouse report *Lost in Care* (DoH, 2000) on the Bryn Estyn Inquiry into sexual abuse of boys at a residential home in north Wales led to the introduction of the Children's Commissioner for Wales.

The Goldfinch police investigation (Select Committee in Home Affairs, 2002) into abuse in residential homes and approved schools in south Wales led to enhanced criminal record checks for residential workers. The Children's Commissioner's Office undertook the Clywch Inquiry into the sexual abuse of pupils at a Welsh-medium secondary school in south Wales (Children's Commisioner for Wales, 2004).

The Welsh Assembly government's Children First programme (see www.childrenfirst.wales.gov.uk) has been funded since April 1999. Children First aims to transform the management and delivery of social services for children in Wales impacting upon all children in need, including protecting children in care from abuse or neglect. The programme sets out a number of key objectives for children's services related to clear outcomes for children, including an annual evaluation of local authority Children First Management Action Plans.

The National Framework for Assessment began to be rolled out in Wales from 2000, taking forward the assembly's modernising social services agenda. The assessment framework sought to shift the balance away from a heavy emphasis on child protection investigation and to focus on all children in need (as the Children Act had intended) with Children First monies being invested in preventive and Early Years support to families.

In 2002 Wales led the UK in establishing consistent national child protection procedures through the introduction of the All Wales Child Protection Procedures (replacing individual authorities' procedures). These are currently being revised. In 2003, *Every Child Matters* (DfES, 2003) introduced the development of a common assessment framework across services for children and the creation of Local Safeguarding Children Boards as the statutory successors to Area Child Protection Committees. The subsequent Children Act (DfES, 2004) strengthens the responsibility of all agencies to address the issue of safeguarding vulnerable children.

QUALITY ASSURANCE

The Care Standards Inspectorate for Wales (CSIW) and Estyn are the statutory bodies with responsibility for inspection and registration of Early Years provision and in Wales Estyn is also the statutory body with responsibility for inspection of schools. Voluntary sector provision such as *cylchoedd meithrin* and playgroups are all inspected by CSIW and some, that is those listed as approved providers, are also inspected by Estyn. These are the non-maintained settings that are approved and publicly funded for three year old children. However, the WAG has indicated its intention to develop one comprehensive quality assurance scheme for all non-maintained settings in Wales. This means that Estyn will also introduce the Common Inspection Framework to all non-maintained settings in September 2008.

The anomaly of non-maintained settings avoiding statutory registration processes by opening fewer than two hours a day will be eliminated and all providers will register irrespective of the number of contact hours that they provide each day.

PROFESSIONAL DEVELOPMENT AND TRAINING

Initial Teacher Education and Training (ITET)

The curriculum for teacher training in Wales is, at present, governed by what is known as Circular 13/98 (Welsh Office, 1998b), the government guidance on the content of teacher training courses. It is a curriculum weighted heavily in the direction of National Curriculum subject knowledge with little or no focus on child development, children's learning, or on the social and emotional development of young children. This is now, of course, at odds with the WAG's The Learning Country (NAFW, 2001) programme. Circular 13/98 (Welsh Office, 1998b) is, at present, being reviewed and there is general expectation that teacher education and training will be more consistent with current thinking on the role of the teacher/educator in the twenty-first century. The Furlong Report, commissioned by the WAG in 2005 to consider the future of ITET in Wales, states: 'the teachers of tomorrow in Wales will need to accept and embrace change; they will need a new form of professionalism that is appropriate for the schools of tomorrow in Wales' (Furlong et al., 2006: 1).

Wales trains some 1070 primary teachers every year with 57 per cent entering the profession with BA (Education with QTS) degrees. Almost all these degree programmes are three year courses. The Higher Education Statistics Agency (HESA) monitors first destinations of graduates and HESA data indicate that up to 24 per cent of teacher graduates go into teaching posts outside Wales. Wales is, therefore, still a significant exporter of teachers. Furlong's recommendations include a 50 per cent decrease in the numbers of teacher training places and teacher training programmes to be centred in three main regional institutions.

> With the growing divergence of the educational service in Wales from that in England, this position (that is, training for both Wales and England) is neither sustainable nor desirable ... (Furlong et al., 2006: 3)

The key question and cause of much debate is why should Wales and Welsh taxpayers pay to train teachers to work elsewhere! Another significant challenge will be training teachers in the new philosophy and pedagogy of the Foundation Phase. The next few years will be interesting in the field of ITET in Wales.

What challenges might ensue for teachers trained in Wales who wish to teach in another part of the UK and vice versa?

Early Years professionals

Although there are seven Higher Education Institutions (HEIs) offering teacher training courses, specialist Early Years programmes are scarce. However, there is an increase in numbers of programmes offered in HEIs that focus on young children, including BA or BSc Early Childhood Studies or Childhood Studies in five HEIs, and BA Early Years Education in one. There has, as elsewhere, been a trend towards Foundation degrees, although there are no plans, as yet, to consider Level 5 a necessary level of qualification for employment purposes. *The Analysis of the Current Training and Professional Development Available*

Within the Early Years and Foundation Phase Sectors of Education and Care (Egan and James, 2003) recommended to the WAG that it should consider Level 4 to be a level at which it should target additional staff for implementation of the Foundation Phase. Higher Education Certificates (Level 4) are being developed in specialist areas of study such as Nursery Management.

At present, the Care Standards Inspectorate for Wales (CSIW) regulations require that full daycare has a registered person with at least a Level 3 qualification. These qualifications are listed in ACCAC's *National Qualifications Framework for Early Years Education* (ACCAC, 2005). A minimum of 80 per cent of the non-supervisory staff must have at least Level 2. Those in charge of sessional care will, by 1 April 2008, need to have attained at least a Level 3 qualification. During the interim period until then, the registered person in sessional care must provide an action plan for meeting this new requirement.

Promoting bilingualism in training and qualifications

The demand for Welsh-medium and bilingual services both from parents and from public policy has resulted in increasing numbers of students wanting training through the medium of Welsh. By 2006 almost all qualifications were available, from Level 2 to an MA *Addysg Blynyddoedd Cynnar*/Early Years Education, through the medium of Welsh.

Iaith Pawb acknowledges this with targeted funding to MYM to train an additional 300 Welsh-medium Early Years workers to Level 3 under its *Cam wrth Gam* (National Training Scheme) programme.

Geiriau Bach (a Welsh-speaking Early Years course) is a project also funded under *Iaith Pawb* and based at Trinity College Carmarthen, Wales. It enables those working in English-medium Early Years provision to extend their use of Welsh and so develop bilingual experiences for young children. The project also offers students the opportunity to work towards an HE Certificate in Welsh and Bilingual Practice in the Early Years.

FUTURE AND IMMINENT CHANGES

Provision for young children is at the forefront of the political landscape in Wales. The Welsh Assembly government has made a clear commitment to investing substantially in this area. The discourse relating to services for young children reflects this focus on children's well-being and that the child is at the centre of the debate. There is, for example, an expectation that planning for learning will be a more dynamic process with documented learning and narrative assessments being more widely used. Teachers will become more active observers and also skilled narrative assessors, listening to young children carefully. Tick boxes will fade away and worksheets may well become documents of historic interest.

The aim is to provide high quality provision through educated, professional and reflective practitioners who continue to update their knowledge and training in line with research. This, together with the need to provide high quality Welsh-medium provision, has implications for training of practitioners in a variety of roles and at a range of levels. Indeed, training will be one of the major challenges facing Wales in the next few years if it is to attain the staffing ratios and qualification levels indicated in the Foundation Phase vision.

The children of Wales will, in the early twenty-first century, become adults who are socially and emotionally competent, intellectually engaged with the challenges of life-long learning, politically active and socially responsible, bilingual, and economically active. Wales is a small country with a very ambitious vision.

Megan was born in Neath in September 2006. From birth she will benefit from a range of services that have been improved and developed, as a result of devolved government to Wales, since Lewis and Sioned Niamh were born in the year 2000. These include Cymorth, Children First, Genesis and Integrated Children's Centres. As in England, SureStart has begun to make an impact on the provision and services for families with young children in areas of socio-economic deprivation. However, the SureStart programme has not been completely successful in meeting all its aims (see National Evaluation of SureStart, 2005) and, as the Bevan Report (2005) showed, childcare remains patchy in Wales. The implication for Megan, as it was for Lewis and Sioned Niamh, is that her pre-school education and care may well depend on her postcode.

For Megan though, the introduction of Flying Start may enable her to benefit from a range of initiatives focused on her language, cognitive, social and emotional development as well as her physical health. These include parenting programmes, early literacy and 'books-for-babies' initiatives. The transition to school may well be eased by the availability of Integrated Centre provision. Megan will also benefit from free swimming and free school breakfasts for primary school children, to be introduced by WAG in 2007.

Of particular significance for Megan and other children born in Wales in 2006, is The Government of Wales Act (HMSO, 2006). This Act represents the biggest transfer of power from Westminster to Wales since the Welsh Assembly was set up in 1999. It gives powers to the Assembly to make laws in Cardiff. However, when the WAG wants to take on responsibility for creating laws in a particular area of devolved powers, for example health or education, it will be dependent on votes in both houses of parliament in London to obtain permission to make those laws. As a result of this increase in the powers of the WAG, there is therefore a distinct possibility that Wales will ban smacking whilst Megan is still an infant.

When Megan starts primary school in 2011 she will benefit from wrap-around care in an Integrated Centre. The curriculum will be child-led and based on play within the Foundation Phase and it is very likely that Megan will be taught in a smaller class than in England. She will have the opportunity to attend a Welsh or an English speaking pre-school and school, and will join the growing number of children and young people speaking Welsh. She is also likely to be taught by teachers trained in Wales through the Welsh teacher training curriculum.

TOPICS FOR DISCUSSION

Bilingualism in Wales

What are the advantages of establishing in young children fluency in the national language from the earliest years, as in Wales? Note that Welsh is the medium of instruction in many schools and that a knowledge of the culture of Wales also forms part of the curriculum for young children. How does that contrast with the curriculum in England for example? Consider the advantages and linguistic capabilities of children who speak other languages at home and in the community and Welsh and English at school. What difficulties might there be for children at Welsh-medium schools with Additional Learning Needs, if support is not available from Welsh language speakers?

Poverty

Recent statistical evidence (Kenway et al., 2005) shows that one in four children in Wales lives in poverty. How might poverty impact on children's lives outside school (for example holidays, opportunities for play, recreation, sport and leisure)? Also, how will the 'hidden' costs of schooling such as uniforms, outings and after-school clubs affect a family?

Integrated Centres

Why do you think Integrated Centres and those providing wrap-around care tend to be physically located around existing schools? Do you envisage any problems with this arrangement and what might be the possible alternatives?

The Foundation Phase Curriculum

Compare the Foundation Phase Curriculum in Wales with the Foundation Stage Curriculum in England. Reflect on the benefits of a curriculum that is play-based and child-centred for children in the early stages of primary school with one that is more focused on academic learning.

Small Schools

Discuss the advantages and disadvantages of small schools. In many rural parts of Wales, and in Scotland also, many primary schools have a very small roll (total number of children) and many have composite classes (made up of children from different year groups and ages).

Professional Training

In what ways will the presence of many Welsh-medium schools and the encouragement of the Welsh language and culture impact on the content and balance of the training of Early Years practitioners?

ACRONYMS

ACCAC   *Awdurdod Cwricwlwm, Cymwysterau ac Asesu Cymru* (Wales Curriculum, Qualifications and Assessment Authority) ACCAC became part of the WAG's Department of Education Lifelong Learning and Skills (DELLS) on 1 April 2006 (previously ACAC)

ALN   Additional Learning Needs

CSIW   Care Standards Inspectorate for Wales

EYDCP   Early Years Development and Childcare Partnerships

GTCW   General Teaching Council for Wales

HEI   Higher Education Institution

HESA   Higher Education Statistics Agency

ITET   Initial Teacher Education and Training

IWA   Institute of Welsh Affairs

MYM   *Mudiad Ysgolion Meirthrin.* (The Association of Welsh-medium playgroups)

NMS   National Minimum Standards

OHMCI   Office of Her Majesty's Chief Inspector (Now *ESTYN)*

QCA   Qualifications and Curriculum Authority (England)

QTS   Qualified Teacher Status

SCAA   The School Curriculum and Assessment Authority (England)

SEN   Special Education Needs

SENCO   Special Educational Needs Co-ordinator

SENTW   Special Educational Needs Tribunal Wales

WAG   Welsh Assembly Government

WO   The Welsh Office

WPPA   Wales Pre-school Playgroup Association

WELSH TERMINOLOGY

Cwricwlwm Cymreig	The Welsh Dimension to the Curriculum
Cylch Meithrin	Welsh-medium immersion playgroup. 2.5 years to admission to school (580 groups – 2003/4)
Cylch Ti a Fi	Welsh-medium parent and toddler groups. Infancy to 2.5 years (442 groups – 2003/4)
ESTYN	Her Majesty's Inspectorate in Wales
Iaith Pawb	A National Action Plan for Bilingual Wales
Sdim Curo Plant! Cymru	Children are Unbeatable! Cymru (Wales)
TWF	Initiative to promote the use of Welsh in families with young children

REFERENCES

ACAC (1996) *Desirable Outcomes for Children's Learning before Compulsory School Age*. Cardiff: ACAC.

ACCAC (Curriculum and Assessment Authority for Wales) (2000a) *Desirable Outcomes for Children's Learning before Compulsory School Age*. Cardiff: ACCAC.

ACCAC (Curriculum and Assessment Authority for Wales) (2000b) *Key Stages 1 and 2 of the National Curriculum in Wales*. Cardiff: ACCAC.

ACCAC (Curriculum and Assessment Authority for Wales) (2004) *The Foundation Phase in Wales: A draft framework for children's learning*. Cardiff: ACCAC.

Akhtar, L. (2005) *Child Poverty In Wales–Much Work to be Done*. Cardiff: Child Poverty Action Group.

Baker, C. (2000) *The Care and Education of Young Bilinguals*. Clevedon: Multilingual Matters.

Bevan Foundation (2005) *A Childcare Revolution in Wales*. Tredegar: Bevan Foundation.

Brooker, E. (2002) *Starting School: Young children learning cultures*. Buckingham: Open University Press.

Child Poverty Action Group Cymru (2006) *Tackling Child Poverty in Wales: A good practice guide for schools*. Cardiff: End Child Poverty Network Cymru and Children in Wales.

Children in Wales (2006) Available at: www.childreninwales.org.uk/areasof work/ endingphysicalpunishment/childrenareunbeatable/index.html

David, T. (1998). 'Learning properly? Young children and the desirable outcomes', *Early Years*, 18 (2): 61–6.

DfEE (Department for Education and Employment)/QCA (2000) *Curriculum Guidance for the Foundation Stage*. London: Qualifications and Curriculum Authority (QCA).

DfES (1988) *Education Reform Act*. London: HMSO.

DfES (2003) *Every Child Matters*. London. HMSO.

DfES (2004) *Children Act*. London: HMSO.

DoH (Department of Health) (2000) *Lost in Care: Report of the tribunal of inquiry into the abuse of children in the care of the former county council areas of Gwynedd and Clwyd since 1974*. London: HMSO.

Egan, D. and James, R. (2003) *Analysis of the Current Training and Professional Development Available Within the Early Years and Foundation Phase Sectors of Education and Care*. Bristol: Tribal PPI.

Elfer, P., Goldschmied, E. and Selleck, D. (2003) *Key Persons in the Nursery: Building relationships for quality provision*. London: David Fulton.

Estyn (2002) *Excellent Schools: A vision for schools in Wales in 21st century*. Cardiff: Estyn.

Estyn (2003) *Advice on School Partnership: A report on good practice in primary schools*. Cardiff: Estyn.

Furlong, J., Hagger, H. and Butcher, C. (2006) *Review of Initial Teacher Training Provision in Wales*. Oxford: Oxford University, Department of Educational Studies.

Hanney, M. (2000) *Early Years Provision for Three Year Olds*. Cardiff: NAW.

HMSO (Her Majesty's Stationery Office) (1946) *Report on the Care of Children Committee/Curtis Report* – CMD.6922. London: HMSO.

HMSO (Her Majesty's Stationery Office) (1993) *Welsh Language Act*. London: HMSO.

HMSO (Her Majesty's Stationery Office) (1998) *Government of Wales Act 1999*. London: HMSO.

HMSO (Her Majesty's Stationery Office) (2000) *Care Standards Act*. London: HMSO.

HMSO (Her Majesty's Stationery Office) (2001) *Special Educational Needs and Disability Act*. London: HMSO.

HMSO (Her Majesty's Stationery Office) (2002) *The Welsh Language Schemes (Public Bodies) Order*. London: HMSO.

HMSO (Her Majesty's Stationery Office) (2006) *Government of Wales Act 2006*. London: HMSO.

Kenway, P., Parsons, N., Carr, J. and Palmer, G. (2005) *Monitoring Poverty and Social Exclusion in Wales 2005*. York: Joseph Rowntree Foundation.

NAfW (National Assembly for Wales) (2000) *Better Wales*. Cardiff: NAfW.

NAfW (National Assembly for Wales) (2001) *The Learning Country*. Cardiff: NAfW. (Available online at: www.wales.gov.uk/subieducationtraining/content/learningcountry/tlc-contents-e.htm)

NAfW (National Assembly for Wales) (2002) *Special Educational Needs: Code of Practice for Wales*. Cardiff: NAfW.

NAfW (National Assembly for Wales) (2003) *Handbook of Good Practice for Children with Special Educational Needs*. (Available online at: www.wales.gov.uk/subieducationtraining/content/guidance/sen-handbook-e.pdf)

NAfW (National Assembly for Wales) (2004a) *Policy Review of Special Educational Needs: Part 1: Early Identification and Early Inclusion*. Cardiff: NAfW.

NAfW (National Assembly for Wales) (2004b) *Special Educational Needs Code of Practice for Wales*. (Available online at: www.learning.wales.gov.uk/scripts/fe/news_details.asp? Newsid=1206)

NAfW (National Assembly for Wales) (2006) *Policy Review of Special Educational Needs: Part 2: Statutory Assessment Framework (Statementing)*. Cardiff: NAfW.

National Assembly for Wales Statistical Directorate (2000) *Pupils with Statements of Special Educational Needs: January 2000* (Report SDB 113/2000). Cardiff: NAfW.

National Assembly for Wales Statistical Directorate (2001) *Digest of Welsh Statistics*. Cardiff: WAG.

NESS (National Evaluation of SureStart) (2005) *Implementing SureStart Programmes: An in-depth study*. London: DfES/SureStart.

National Literacy Trust (2005) *Education in Wales*. (Available online at: www.literacytrust.org.uk/Update/Wales/index.htm #background)

Office of National Statistics (2004) *Infant mortality rates, England and Wales, 1975–2000*. (Available online at: www.statistics.gov.uk/StatBase)

Preston, G. (ed.) (2005) *At Greatest Risk: The children most likely to be poor*. Cardiff: Child Poverty Action Group.

SCAA (School Curriculum and Assessment Authority) (1996) *Desirable Outcomes for Children's Learning on Entering Compulsory Education*. London: SCAA.

SCAA (School Curriculum and Assessment Authority) and ACAC (Curriculum And Assessment Authority For Wales) (1996). *A Guide to the National Curriculum*. London: SCAA and ACAC.

Seaton, N. (2006) *Development and Implementation of Integrated Centres in Wales*. Cardiff: Institute of Welsh Affairs.

Select Committee on Home Affairs (2002) Memorandum 58, May. (Available at: www.publications.parliament.uk/pa/cm200102/cmselect/cmhaff/836/836m59.htm.)

SENTW (Special Educational Needs Tribunal for Wales) (2004) *Annual Report 2003–04*. Llandrindod: SENTW.

Siraj-Blatchford, I., Sylva, K., Laugharne, J., Milton, E. and Charles, F. (2006) *Monitoring and Evaluation of the Effective Implementation of the Foundation Phase Across Wales* (February). Cardiff: Department for Training and Education, Welsh Assembly Government.

Thomas, S. A. (2005) 'The Foundation Phase: Perceptions, attitudes and expectations'. Unpublished MA thesis, University of Wales (Trinity College).

WAG (Welsh Assembly Government) (1999) *Children First*. Cardiff: WAG. (Available online at: www.childrenfirst.wales.gov.uk/index.htm)

WAG (Welsh Assembly Government) (2001a) *Laying the Foundations: the Early Years Provision for Three year Olds*. Cardiff: WAG.

WAG (Welsh Assembly Government) (2001b) *The Learning Country: A Paving Document*. Cardiff: WAG.

WAG (Welsh Assembly Government) (2003a) *Iaith Pawb: A National Action Plan for a Bilingual Wales*. Cardiff: WAG.

WAG (Welsh Assembly Government) (2003b) *The Learning Country: Foundation Phase 3–7 years*. Cardiff: WAG.

WAG (Welsh Assembly Government) (2004) *Good Practice on Domestic Abuse: Safeguarding Children and Young People in Wales*. Cardiff: WAG.

WAG (Welsh Assembly Government) (2005) *The Childcare Strategy for Wales*. Cardiff: WAG.

WAG (Welsh Assembly Government) (2006a). *Quality Standards in Education Services for Children and Young People with Sensory Impairment (Circular 34/2005)*. Cardiff: Department for Training and Education, WAG.

Welsh Assembly Government (WAG) (2006b) *Acknowledging Need: An action plan*. Cardiff: WAG.

Welsh Assembly Government (WAG) (2006c) *Foundation Phase Action Plan*. Cardiff: WAG.

WO (Welsh Office) (1998a) *Guidance on Early Years Education: Building Excellent Schools Together*. Cardiff: Welsh Office.

WO (Welsh Office) (1998b) *Requirements for Courses of Initial Teacher Training (Circular No. 13/98)*. Cardiff : WO.

WO (Welsh Office) (1999a) *Shaping the Future for Special Education: an Action Programme for Wales*. Cardiff: WO. (Available online at: www.wales.gov.uk/polinifo/education/special/spcled_e.htm)

WO (Welsh Office) (1999b) *Guidance for local Early Years Development and Childcare Partnerships in Wales*. Cardiff: WO.

USEFUL WEBSITES

http://old.accac.org.uk/redirect.html	ACCAC (Curriculum and Assessment Authority for Wales)
www.csiw.wales.gov.uk	Care Standards Inspectorate for Wales (CSIW)
www.childrenfirst.wales.gov.uk/	Children First
www.childreninwales.org.uk	Children in Wales
www.childcomwales.org.uk	Children's Commissioner for Wales
www.cpag.org.uk/	Child Poverty Action Group
http://new.wales.gov.uk/topics/educationandskills/	Education and Skills Department (WAG)

www.trinity-cm.ac.uk/geiriaubach/	*Geiriau Bach* (Welsh Early Years Professional Development) *Ysgol Addysg Blynyddoedd Cynnar*/The School of Early Years Education, *Colegey Drindod*/Trinity College, *Caerfyrddin*/Carmarthen.
www.mym.co.uk	*Mudiad Ysgolion Meithrin* (MYM)
www.playwales.org.uk	PlayWales – organisation promoting all aspects of children's play in Wales
www.swansea.ac.uk/childhood	Department of Childhood Studies, Swansea University
www.wales.gov.uk/	Welsh Assembly Government (WAG)
www.bwrdd-yr-iaith.org.uk	*Bwrdd yr Iaith Gymraeg*/Welsh Language Board
www.walesppa.org	Wales Preschool Playgroups Association (WPPA)

EARLY CHILDHOOD EDUCATION AND CARE ACROSS THE UNITED KINGDOM AND THE REPUBLIC OF IRELAND

Margaret M Clark and Tim Waller

INTRODUCTION

In this final chapter we will provide a summary and comparison of the developments reported in the five preceding chapters on the provision of Early Childhood Education and Care (ECEC) across the United Kingdom and in the Republic of Ireland. In September 2006, as we were completing this book, the second report of the OECD review of developments in policy and practice across twenty countries, *Starting Strong II*, was published (OECD, 2006). The first report, based on 12 countries, had also been available to us (OECD, 2001). As we indicated in Chapter 1, both reports have a section on Ireland (on the Republic of Ireland, as we have referred to it in this publication) and both are listed as having a section on the United Kingdom, though as we indicated in our Introduction, much of the information is on England and it is difficult for readers to identify what does apply to the whole UK. In *Starting Strong II* in the country notes it is stated underneath the title in brackets that 'most of the following profile applies to England only' (OECD, 2006: 415). You should now be in a better position to appreciate just how different the developments in policy and practice are across the UK.

Each of the five chapters (2–6) in the present book followed the same main headings to assist you in comparing policy. They are as follows:

- Background
- Policy and Practice in Early Childhood Education and Care
- Transitions
- Schooling
- Special Educational Needs
- Safeguarding Children
- Quality Assurance
- Professional Development and Training
- Future and Imminent Changes.

The four tables in this chapter will help you to make comparisons between the developments in the five countries (the four making up the United Kingdom plus the Republic of Ireland) in terms of the following:

- Early childhood education and care provision (see Table 7.1)
- Childcare costs (see Table 7.2)
- Early childhood education and care: curricula and assessment (see Table 7.3)
- Workforce strategies (see Table 7.4).

You are encouraged to undertake practical work using the ten case studies; two at the beginning of each chapter 2–6. The guidelines we have provided will enable you to gain greater insight into the lives of young children and their families and the extent to which the availability of early childhood education and care varied across the countries, even between areas within the countries. Take account of the information about a child born in 2006 at the end of each chapter to consider how different the situation might be for children in the future should proposed developments come to fruition. You should also consider what problems and transitions would be faced by young children and their families were they to move from one part of the United Kingdom to another, a situation not faced by any of the children whose first six years we tracked.

The scene will be set by a brief reminder of current issues in early childhood education and care and types of curricula/programmes offered to young children. The key issues and findings in the recent OECD report *Starting Strong II* will be identified. The importance of research evidence will be highlighted and you will be provided with references for further reading. Finally, we will alert you to controversies and issues, some of which do not yet seem to appear on the policy agenda.

CURRENT ISSUES IN EARLY CHILDHOOD EDUCATION AND CARE

To set the scene before summarising the developments in early education and care across the United Kingdom and the Republic of Ireland, brief reference will be made to a number of the issues identified by those involved in the OECD reviews (2001, 2006).

In an article entitled 'Starting Strong: the persistent division between care and education', John Bennett identifies a number of important issues and challenges faced by many governments in the twenty-first century, based in part on the first OECD review (Bennett, 2003). Among those identified was the persistent division between care and education in many countries, the negative consequences of this division and the need for strategies to co-ordinate these services. As regards this connection he considers the rationale for state involvement in ECEC. While, as he argues, there is a more positive attitude to state involvement in education as opposed to care at the pre-school and school level, many have regarded the provision of care as a more private matter where the state's involvement should be more limited, only involved in providing for those who do not have the means to pay. However, in recent years as you will see from *Starting Strong II* (OECD, 2006) and from the policies developing across the United Kingdom and in the Republic of Ireland, there are moves towards the co-ordination of these services and in some countries their unification under the same ministry.

> It is important to consider the disadvantages when provision is targeted, or when market forces determine where there is provision and the types of services offered. There are, of course, disadvantages when all services are provided and possibly dictated by the state.

Until recently in many countries few services have been available for children under three years of age and there has been limited maternity leave and seldom any paternity leave. In many countries increased provision of free pre-school education for children over three years of age (including the countries discussed in this book with the exception of the Republic of Ireland) is now available. This provision may become widely available, but with only part-time attendance offered this may not meet the needs of families. In many countries there appears to be a lack of care, and in particular out-of-school care, to meet the needs of lone parents or families where both parents are working.

Bennett notes that several countries visited during the OECD (2001) study were seen to adopt a broad definition of early childhood development where education and care were not perceived as separate entities. In such countries there were low child-staff ratios to insure adequate interaction for each child. Also, to quote:

> There was a trust in the child's own ability to develop and learn, but this trust was underpinned by the careful provision of learning environments run by professional staff, specifically trained to provide care and education in a manner appropriate for young children. Much emphasis was placed on the outdoor environment and on the child's freedom to explore and choose his or her own activities. (Bennett, 2003: 31–2)

In the countries involved in the first OECD review *Starting Strong* some were already found to provide strong state support both to parents in terms of maternity and possibly paternity leave and in terms of services for children under three; others provided as yet limited parental leave and little or no support for under-three services.

Can early childhood provision of education or care be left entirely to the market or do such services require a strong infrastructure that governments are best placed to provide? What are the dangers of either leaving the provision of such services to the market or their provision being controlled by the state?

ISSUES IN CURRICULUM DEVELOPMENT

A publication entitled *Starting Strong Curricula and Pedagogies in Early Childhood Education and Care: Five curriculum outlines* (OECD, 2004), based on a workshop attended by the national co-ordinators of early childhood policy held in Stockholm in 2003, gives details of innovative pre-school programmes from five countries. In Chapter 2 of that publication issues involved in developing a curriculum for young children are explored (see www.oecd/org/earlychildhood).

Pre-school curricular approaches

The following are the five curricula discussed:

*   *Experiential Education*   Effective learning through well-being and involvement (from Flanders and the Netherlands)
    It is claimed that this programme 'strives for the development of (future) adults who are self-confident and mentally healthy, curious and exploratory, expressive and communicative, imaginative and creative, well-organised and entrepreneurial, with well-developed intuitions about the social and physical world and with a feeling of belonging and connectedness to the universe and all its creatures' (OECD, 2004: 7).
*   *The High Scope Curriculum*   Active learning through key experiences (from the United States)
    The High Scope curriculum was developed more than forty years ago, to help children from disadvantaged areas to be successful in school and society. Its principles are intended as an 'open framework' based on the belief that 'children learn best through active experiences with people, materials, events and ideas, rather than through direct teaching or sequenced exercises ...' (OECD, 2004: 8).
*   *The Reggio Emilia Approach*   Truly listening to young children (from Italy)
    'The Reggio Emilia approach to early education is committed to the creation of conditions of learning that will enhance and facilitate children's construction of their powers of thinking ... with the conception of the child as a subject of rights and as a competent, active learner, continuously building and testing theories about herself and the world around her' (OECD, 2004: 12).

- *Te Whāriki*   A woven mat for all to stand on (from New Zealand)
  'Rather than employing a one-world view of human development emp-
  tied of context, or articulating a curriculum with the subject-based
  learning areas and essential skills of the school, Te Whāriki chooses a
  socio-cultural approach to curriculum based on a desire to nurture
  learning dispositions, promote bi-culturalism and to reflect the realities
  of the young children in the services' (OECD, 2004: 17).

- *The Swedish Curriculum*   Goals for a modern pre-school system (from
  Sweden)
  'A fundamental notion in the new approach of the Swedish pre-school
  is that the child's learning is grounded in play and meaning making.
  Knowledge is not to be found in the child or in the world (including
  adults) but in the relationship between them ...' (OECD, 2004: 21).

> Compare these curricula with developments in the United Kingdom and the
> Republic of Ireland (see the OECD website for further details at www.oecd.org/
> edu/earlychildhood).

The following quotation on 17 November 2006 in *Education*, an online
publication only available to subscribers to the *Education Journal*, draws
attention to a new government initiative in England:

> Children's Minister Beverley Hughes has vowed to train a new 'parenting work-
> force' to ensure parents who failed to read stories or sing nursery rhymes to their
> children could be 'found and supported'. She declared that children's well-being
> was at risk unless action was taken. The threat of action was unveiled by Mrs
> Hughes as she gave the first details of Mr Blair's 'national parenting academy',
> a body that would train teachers, psychologists and social workers to intervene
> in the lives of families (2006: 4).

> What is your view on initiatives such as the above? Curricular documents are now
> appearing covering not only children from three to five years of age, but also from
> birth to three. How might initiatives such as these affect the self-esteem of parents
> of young children (see Table 7.3)?

Key issues in the development of curricula for young children

In recent years there has been a move in many countries, including those discussed in the preceding chapters, towards formulating frameworks/curricula

for the education and care of young children. However, there may be tensions between the two aims; the first focuses on the individual child and his or her development, a feature of many of the curricula, and the second on having in the curriculum common goals to provide a direction for children's learning. The quality of ECEC depends on the skills of the staff, and their willingness to guide and challenge the children's experience and meaning making. To quote from OECD, 2004:

> Our commitment is that *all curricula should give centres, teachers and children the largest possible freedom*, but still retain the direction of overall common goals. (OECD, 2004: 26–emphasis in original)

Here the issue is raised as to whether the learning goals are the same in pre-school and in compulsory school, but operating at different levels of complexity.

Are there dangers that curricula developed for pre-school, rather than providing a foundation for children's learning in later years, may merely be a downward extension of any national curriculum? As noted in Chapter 1 this fear was expressed in the Nordic countries. One example of a curriculum planned to give continuity to children's learning is *A Curriculum for Excellence* (see website listed below) for children from 3–18 being developed in Scotland. Assess the extent to which that will build on foundations that may achieve continuity in children's learning (see Table 7.3 and www.acurriculumforexcellencescotland.gov.uk).

The OECD document on curricula and pedagogies (OECD, 2004) raises several important issues: namely the role of play in young children's learning, the extent to which play is an activity by itself or is a means to learning, and whether all curricula for ECEC should deal with play and learning and the relation between them.

It also questions whether there is currently a lack of, and need to develop, evaluations and assessments of curricular programmes for young children. Concern is expressed with regard to assessment in that if only small details are evaluated, the whole idea of fostering young children's thinking and creativity may be lost.

What kind of curricular documents might reflect a child-centred approach to early education and care? To what extent do current curricula and assessment procedures across the United Kingdom and the Republic of Ireland being developed for young children to the age of eight years take account of the role of play? Do the assessment procedures deal only with 'small details', thus falling into the trap noted above?

A SUMMARY OF INFORMATION ON EARLY CHILDHOOD EDUCATION AND CARE ACROSS THE UK AND IN THE REPUBLIC OF IRELAND

(based on Chapters 2–6)

> It is important that you consider the differences in developments across the UK and in the Republic of Ireland. To what do you attribute these differences? Do you believe in spite of the differences that they are still based on common beliefs about childhood and the role of the state?

Early childhood education and care

Table 7.1 presents an overview of ECEC provision showing that there are relatively comparable types of provision across services for children below three years of age in the UK. The Republic of Ireland does not have a tradition of this type of provision and there is still limited childcare in the public sector. However, since the recent expansion of the economy, by 2006 childcare was very much on the agenda in the Republic (see Chapter 4). The availability of ECEC for children under three years of age still varies according to location within the separate countries.

> What are the implications for young children and their families of the expansion of early childhood education and care and the encouragement of mothers of young children to return to work?

Nursery education has increasingly become available for three and four year old children across the UK and the Republic of Ireland over the last ten years leading up to 2006. However, there is far greater variation in provision for children once they reach their fourth birthday. Despite there being statutory ages for starting primary school, the reality is that most four year olds in England and Northern Ireland, four and a half to five and a half year olds in Scotland, four year olds in Wales and most four year olds and nearly all five year olds in the Republic of Ireland, are likely to be in primary school.

> For comparisons on policy and developments with regard to age of starting formal schooling in the 20 participating countries in the OECD (2006) study, see the OECD website (www.oecd.org/edu/earlychildhood).

TABLE 7.1 Early childhood education and care in the UK and the Republic of Ireland by country

Age/Country	England	Northern Ireland	Republic of Ireland	Scotland	Wales
Birth-Two	*Public* SureStart Children's Centre *Private* Childminder Private nursery Nanny Voluntary Crèche Parent–Toddler Group	*Public* SureStart Initiatives Day Nursery *Private* Childminder Private nursery Nanny Voluntary Crèche Parent-Toddler Group	*Public* Very limited public provision *Private* Crèche or Childminder	*Public* SureStart Day Nursery *Private* Childminder Private nursery Nanny Voluntary Crèche Parent-Toddler Group	*Public* SureStart Flying Start Integrated Centre Day Nursery *Private* Childminder (often family members such as grandparents) Private Nursery Nanny *Voluntary* Crèche
Two-Three	As above and Pre-school	As above and Nursery Education, particularly in areas of social need	As above and IPPA.	As above and Playgroup 2–3 years	As above and playgroup Welsh-medium playgroup Welsh-medium Parent – Toddler Group
Three-Four	Nursery education As above (Private)	As above (private) Nursery education Playgroup Reception class	IPPA Naíonraí – Irish-medium playschool Early Start (DES) Montessori-Pre-school Traveller Pre-school	Nursery education As above (Private) Playgroup 3–5 years	Nursery education Welsh-medium nursery education (All children in Wales have a nursery and Reception place available after their third birthday – normally nursery for half a day for three year olds and Reception is full-time for four year olds) As above (Private)

TABLE 7.1   (Continued)

Age/Country	England	Northern Ireland	Republic of Ireland	Scotland	Wales
Four-Five	Reception class (school) **Compulsory age for starting school: Five** (Most children start in September of the academic year in which they are five)	Primary1 (school) **Compulsory age for starting school: Four**	Pre-school	Pre-school	Reception class (school) **Compulsory age for starting school: Five** (Most children start in September of the academic year in which they are five) Welsh-medium Reception class
Five-Eight	Infant school Primary school Private schools	Primary school	**Compulsory age for starting school: Six** Primary school (Most children start school at four)	**Compulsory age for starting school:Five.** Children must start in the August term after their fifth birthday (if five between August and February then may start in August)	Infant school Primary school Welsh-medium primary school Private schools

Childcare costs

Research published on their website by the Daycare Trust (2004) in England showed that parents want SureStart provision to be universal rather than merely in areas of recognised poverty. The Daycare Trust (2006) consulted children's information services in England, Scotland and Wales for their annual survey of childcare costs. More than two thirds of these services reported that parents were concerned about a 'lack of affordable, quality childcare in their area' (2006: 1). (See Table 7.2 for recent figures on the estimated cost of daycare in England, Scotland and Wales, based on the survey by the Daycare Trust, 2006.)

According to the Daycare Trust, childcare costs vary a great deal across England, Scotland and Wales (unfortunately they provide no information for Northern Ireland). The report showed that the cost of a typical full-time nursery place in England had increased by 27 per cent in five years. This rise was nearly 20 per cent above inflation. The typical weekly cost of a full-time place with a childminder for a child under two in England is £132 (over £6,800 a year), in Scotland the typical cost is £132 and in Wales £124. According to the Daycare Trust 'Parents paying the highest costs revealed in the survey could be paying almost £21,000 a year for a full-time nursery place' (2006: 1).

The highest childcare costs in the survey were found in London and the south east of England with a nursery place for a child under two typically costing £197 a week in inner London at the time of the survey. However, this was the only region of the countries surveyed where there had been no increase in childcare costs in the previous 12 months (up to 2006). This is the Daycare Trust's fifth annual survey and the 2006 survey was the first time that the highest childcare costs in the survey were charged by childminders rather than nurseries (a full-time place with some childminders in London and south east England can cost up to £500 a week). The largest increases in the year 2005-2006 were in Wales with a 7 per cent rise and Scotland with an 8 per cent rise, compared with 2 per cent in England. This information is from www.daycaretrust.org.uk (the web site of the Daycare Trust).

ECEC curricula and assessment

Table 7.3 shows that in 2006 there is still considerable variation in policy regarding the curriculum for children under three. England produced *Birth to Three Matters* in 2003, and in Scotland *Birth to Three: supporting our youngest children* was published in 2005. In 2006 *Síolta - the National Framework for Early Childhood Education* was introduced in the Republic of Ireland. In Wales and Northern Ireland there had been no similar development by 2006.

A recent development across the UK has been the amendment of curriculum guidance for early education. The trend is to expand early education

TABLE 7.2   Childcare costs in England, Scotland and Wales, February 2006 (£)

	Nursery (under 2)	Nursery (2 and over)	Highest Nursery Cost	Childminder (under 2)	Childminder (2 and over)	Highest Childminder Cost	Out-of-school club	Highest out-of-school club
England average	144	134	400.00 *	132	129	500.00 *	41	250
Scotland	132	122	200.00			350.00	33.00	135.00
Wales	128	122	165.00	124.00	124.00	262.50	30.00	79.00
GB ** average	142	133		132	130		40	

*Figure given is the actual highest, not the average highest cost

* *No data are available for Northern Ireland

Source: Compiled from a survey of 150 out of 200 Children's & Childcare Information Services in Great Britain, based on 50 hours a weeek in a nursery or with a childminder and 15 hours a week at out-of-school club

TABLE 7.3 Early childhood education and care: curricula and assessment across the UK and the Republic of Ireland

Age/Country	England	Northern Ireland	Republic of Ireland	Scotland	Wales
Birth-3	Birth to Three Matters (2003)	No singular framework of guidance	Síolta – the National Quality Framework for Early Childhood Education	Birth to Three: Supporting our youngest children (2005)	No singular framework of guidance (some settings refer to Birth to Three Matters)
3–5	Foundation Stage 3–5 yrs (2000) In 2006 consultation was taking place regarding the proposed merging of Birth to Three Matters with the Curriculum Guidance for the Foundation Stage to become the Early Years Foundation Stage from 2008	Curricular Guidance for Pre-School Education (1997 and 2006) (From 3–4 years, due to the early and compulsory starting school age)	*(Framework for Early Learning 3–6 years being developed by NCCA)*	A Curriculum Framework for Children 3–5 (1999) *A Curriculum for Excellence 3–18 proposed from 2008–9*	Desirable Outcomes for Children's Learning Before Compulsory School Age (1996) *(Foundation Phase for ages 3–7 introduced from 2008)*
5–8	National Curriculum Key Stage 1 5–7 years Key Stage 2 7–11 years	Northern Ireland Curriculum *(Revised curriculum coming into effect Sept 2007 with a Foundation Stage for years 1+2)*	*Primary Curriculum (1999)* from four years of age	5–14 Curriculum Guidelines (1992) *(A Curriculum for Excellence 3–18 proposed from 2008–9)*	National Curriculum (Wales) Key Stage 1 5–7 years Key Stage 2 7–11 Years Includes compulsory Welsh
Assessment	Foundation Stage Profile (Formatively and at the end of first and second year of the Foundation Stage) Teacher assessment and SATs at 7 and SATS at 11	Transition form from pre-school to primary End of Key Stage 1 assessments *(Currently under review)*	Teacher assessment built into the curriculum	Teacher-based assessment No SATs	Teacher-based assessment No SATs

(Statements in italics are proposals yet to be implemented)

TABLE 7.4 Workforce strategies across the UK and the Republic of Ireland

	England	Northern Ireland	Republic of Ireland	Scotland	Wales
ECEC workforce strategy	Children's and Young People's Workforce Development Council (CWDC) launched in April 2005 *Integrated Qualifications Framework (IQF) (Pilot phases 1 and 2 for assessment of candidates to become Early Years Professionals carried out in 2006–7)* *'Ten Year Strategy' driving policy to raise qualification profile. (All settings to have a graduate in post by 2015)*	Under consultation (see Effective Pre-school Project in Northern Ireland [EPPNI] Melhuish et al., 2003)	National Framework of Qualifications launched in October 2003 with the aim of being fully implemented by 2006	National Review of the Early Years and Childcare Workforce: Report and Consultation (2006)	No clear plans as yet (Following the introduction of the Flying Start programme [2005] and the Furlong Report into Teacher Education [2006] there is likely to be a review of workforce strategy after the WAG elections in May 2007)

upwards, as may be seen in for example the Foundation Stage in England, the proposed Foundation Phase 3–7 in Wales and the Foundation Stage in Northern Ireland. Scotland has gone further in developing an integrated curriculum from 3–18 to be in place by 2008. In England, attention is now directed to the consolidation of the two frameworks for children under five (Birth to Three and the Foundation Stage).

With regard to formal schooling, the curriculum and assessment methods in England currently stand out from the rest of the UK and the Republic of Ireland, with an emphasis on teaching to the legal requirements of a prescribed curriculum and measurement against 'national standards' in Standard Assessment Tasks (SATs) at seven and eleven years old and still with limited reliance on teacher-based assessment (see Chapter 2).

> How important is the type of curriculum advocated? Do you think there is any truth in the statement that age of children on entry to primary school and the curriculum often offered are detrimental to the children's development, and if so, in what ways? Consider this with particular reference to what you now know about age of starting school and the curricula discussed in Chapters 2–6.

Workforce strategies

As Table 7.4 demonstrates, there is variation within the UK and the Republic of Ireland regarding the strategy for developing the Early Years workforce. In every country an increase in the services for ECEC appears to have come much sooner than the professional development of the practitioners, except in the Republic of Ireland where a national framework of qualifications was launched in 2003; this was followed by England in 2005. Scotland is, at the time of writing, consulting about its workforce strategy and there are no published plans as yet in Northern Ireland or Wales.

It should be noted that childcare is a female-dominated occupation. Not only in the UK and the Republic of Ireland, but also in most countries in the OECD 2006 survey, men were less than 1 per cent of the workforce in ECEC (see OECD, 2006: 159–60). Furthermore, according to the Daycare Trust, few men have so far been attracted into the new courses that are now being offered (see www.daycaretrust.org.uk).

> The quality of a programme and the competence of the staff are closely linked. In view if this what features should be included in their training? Why do you think there are so few men working with young children? What benefits do you think there might be from increasing the number of men in the workforce?

THE IMPORTANCE OF RESEARCH EVIDENCE

The relevance for the future of lessons
from the past

In the rapidly changing educational scene it is easy to be blinkered by the pace of change and the flood of documents – and to fail to heed earlier warnings and insights into the development of young children (see *Understanding Research in Early Education: The relevance for the future of lessons from the past*, Clark, 2005).

The final chapter of *Children Under Five: Educational research and evidence* (Clark, 1988) includes a critical evaluation of research into the education of children under five in the United Kingdom up to 1988. A number of points is made and warnings sounded, some of which are still disturbingly relevant in 2006. It is true, as you will have seen from the preceding five chapters, that there has been a massive expansion in the early education and care of young children and a move to provide more out-of-school care. In about twenty years the situation for young children and their families has been transformed, with many more mothers of young children working either full- or part-time and also many more lone parents. Already by the 1980s there were many more children under five in educational provision with, however, wide differences between areas in the amount and types of provision.

Younger children in England were in Reception class in the primary school who previously would still have been at home or in a pre-school. Much research in the United Kingdom was funded in the early 1980s, at a time when a massive expansion of pre-school education was planned. Most of the provision was still in areas of high priority when economic constraints led almost immediately to a reversal of national policy in this non-mandatory aspect of education, and before the researches were completed. It was noted that access to education had already become unequal for young children by the time they reached the statutory age for starting school. It appears that this may still be true today in spite of the recent expansion in pre-school services in many countries.

Although there was evidence of a growth in services for the over-threes in many of the countries involved in the first OECD review in 2007, Bennett has drawn attention to hidden weaknesses within any general statistics, quoting Leseman, 2002, as having found:

> The children who do not have access are often children with special educational needs, that is children with disabilities; children from disadvantaged backgrounds or children from ethnic or cultural minorities. (Bennett, 2003: 29)

> You should bear this point in mind when considering the uptake of any services for young children and their families, especially when the uptake is reported only in percentages.

The problems for children entering primary school with no or limited experience beyond their home and of 'strange adults' could be further exacerbated unless staffing in the primary school is sufficiently generous and the staff well-qualified enough to make effective communication with young children possible. It is still true that for some children entry to primary school is a transfer from one, or more than one, pre-school setting in which a foundation may have been laid, yet for other children entry to primary school may still be their first experience away from home with 'strange' adults. For some children, possibly a growing number in the United Kingdom, the language of instruction in the primary school may indeed not be the language used at home, or one in which they are competent.

Brooker (2002, 2005) has shown that the traditional 'child-centred' pedagogy of Early Years classrooms may not meet the needs of children from culturally diverse backgrounds. Her study investigated the experiences of children from minority ethnic communities as they started school in England. She examined how the home experiences of the children influence their adaptation to school and the shift the children make to being a 'learning' pupil. In particular, Brooker (2005) argues that the western 'play ethos' prevalent in much Early Years practice promotes the 'idealisation' of individual activity and learning through play and exploration. This is very different from some children's learning experiences at home, where the emphasis is placed on social participation. Brooker (2002) reveals the disadvantages faced by Bangladeshi children when their learning abilities are measured by reference to knowledge, behaviours and skills not valued at home.

As you will have seen from the previous chapters it is still true that a very different curriculum may be offered to children, even of the same age, depending on whether they happen still to be in a pre-school or to have entered primary school. Likewise the curriculum experienced by young children will differ even within the United Kingdom when they do enter primary school depending on where they live. Should their family move from one country to another the children are likely to have to make quite major adjustments.

Studies of transition have shown that for some children the primary school may provide a less stimulating and challenging experience than those same children had previously, and to which they were responding, making meaningful choices, concentrating for long periods, engaging in dialogue with adults, and sustained co-operation with peers (see Clark 1988, 2005). There is still only limited research evidence on continuity in children's experiences from birth to eight years old and from home to school. Many of the researches have been limited in duration with a focus on transition rather than continuity of learning experiences from home to school, from one type of service to another, or from pre-school to primary school. Few studies have considered continuity with regard to the curriculum and links between the expectations of the home and the school.

In this context the longitudinal EPPE (The Effective Provision of Pre-school Education) studies still ongoing in 2006, which so far have taken place in England, Northern Ireland and Wales, are providing valuable information not only on the effects of pre-school education and care, but also features of the provision in terms of the environment and the staffing that lead to high quality education and care. Related studies contain evidence on the effects of different curricular approaches on young children's learning. In addition, two related small-scale studies are of relevance; one where children in the large EPPE study who did attend pre-school are compared with a home sample who did not; the other involved home-educated children, that is children who did not attend school during the reception stage (see Clark, 2005, for a discussion of these) (as the EPPE studies are still continuing at the time of writing, the best source to consult for findings is www.ioe.ac.uk/projects).

At the time of the study of *Young Fluent Readers* by Clark in 1976, that is of young children who entered primary school at the age of five already reading with fluency and understanding, few of these children had attended a pre-school, though a few had attended a play group at least briefly (Clark, 1976, 2005). Their parents did not feel the need to obtain outside assistance with their young children's education at the pre-school stage. Admittedly there will be fewer children now who do not attend some form of pre-school education or care. However, bear in mind that up to the time of writing there is no suggestion of making pre-school education compulsory; thus there will be parents who for a variety of reasons may decide to keep their children at home until they enter primary school. Yet the fact that in the future most children will have attended some form of pre-school provision is likely to influence the expectations of teachers at the early stages in primary schools, possibly to the detriment of those children whose first experience of a large group situation is on entry to primary school.

> For what reasons may parents decide not to avail themselves of pre-school services for their family? What advantages and disadvantages might there be for children who enter primary school direct from home, especially at a time when more and more children have attended more than one pre-school setting prior to entry to school? In what ways could this affect teachers' early judgements of young children who have not attended any pre-school setting?

In the United Kingdom emphasis has been placed on the needs of children living in poverty, particularly those in inner cities, but so far there has been limited research into the needs of children living in rural areas. Yet in a country such as the United Kingdom, and in the Republic of Ireland, there are many families living in remote rural areas (as you would have seen from several of the case studies).

In spite of the massive expansion in early childhood education and care over the past ten years in particular, inequality in provision still remains, possibly as limited provision to meet the needs of some families, or only at a cost beyond the means of many families.

Pedagogy and the curriculum: children's services or children's spaces?

A clear division is apparent between England (and some other English-speaking countries), the Nordic countries and much of the rest of Europe concerning both the concept of Early Years pedagogy and policy and practice (Moss and Petrie, 2002; Alexander, 2004; OECD, 2006). Moss and Petrie (2002: 138) argue that the meaning of the word 'pedagogy' is problematic in England and in English-speaking countries in general – where it tends to be limited to a narrow and restricted definition concerning schooling and formal learning. Further, Alexander (2004: 11) argues that 'the prominence of curriculum in English educational discourses has meant that we have tended to make pedagogy subsidiary to curriculum'. Pedagogy has a much wider meaning in other European countries where it relates to theory, practice, policy and practitioner training. For Moss and Petrie (2002) it also refers to childcare, social and family support and welfare.

The recent OECD (2006) report argues that this division is also apparent in the trend towards integration of Early Years services:

> Research suggests that a more unified approach to learning should be adopted in both the early childhood education and primary school systems, and that attention should be given to transition challenges faced by young children as they enter school. The search for a more unified approach has generated different policy options. France and the English speaking world have adopted a "readiness for school" approach, which although defined broadly focuses in practice on cognitive development in the early years, and the acquisition of a range of knowledge, skills and dispositions. A disadvantage inherent in this approach is the use of programmes and approaches that are poorly suited to the psychology and natural learning strategies of young children. In countries inheriting a social pedagogy tradition (Nordic and Central European countries), the kindergarten years are seen as a broad preparation for life and the foundation of lifelong learning. (OECD, 2006: 13)

Moss and Petrie (2002: 40) have challenged Early Years practitioners and policy-makers to re-conceive service provision for young children. They argue that the notion of 'children's services' should be replaced by 'children's spaces'. Children's spaces are 'characterized by particular ethics, relationships and practices' (Moss and Petrie, 2002: 106).

Moss and Petrie also describe two inter-related features of children's spaces that are particularly relevant to Early Years pedagogy. First, children's spaces are cultural spaces where values and rights are created, and discursive spaces for expressing differing perspectives and forms of expression and dialogue: 'In this sense the concept of children's spaces implies possibilities for children and adults to contest understandings, values and practices, and knowledges' (Moss and Petrie, 2002: 9). Second, within these spaces there is the possibility of a dual role for children. While children should be social agents with the right to a voice and to contribute to decisions that affect them, their main role within these spaces is to meet each other, spend time together and form a social group. Within children's spaces there is, therefore, a need for privacy and to create opportunities for children to be 'adult-free' (Moss and Petrie 2002: 107).

The concept of children's spaces advocated by Moss and Petrie raises the possibility of enabling both children and adults to be 'governed less by power, to be critical thinkers and to do so in interaction with others' (Moss and Petrie, 2002: 111). What occurs in children's spaces is therefore defined by the ethos and style of interaction between adults and children. This has implications for children's participation in Early Years pedagogy as Waller (2006) suggests:

> '... rather than thinking about engaging children's views simply to influence planning and design (and the corresponding danger of instrumentalizing children's play), we need to rethink participation in terms of 'spaces for childhood' within which children can exercise their agency to participate in their own decisions, actions and meaning-making, which may or may not involve engagement with adults'. (Waller, 2006: 93)

Also, as Moss and Petrie contend, working in children's spaces involves 'a re-conceptualization of the role of workers with children and methods of working' (2002: 111). In this role, staff are reflective practitioners, thinkers, researchers and co-constructors of knowledge with children. Moss and Petrie's concept of children's spaces concurs with the OECD policy observations from 2006. To quote:

> The early childhood centre becomes a space where the intrinsic value of each person is recognized, where democratic participation is promoted, as well as respect for our shared environment. *Learning to be, learning to do, learning to learn and learning to live together* should be considered as critical elements in the journey of each child toward human and social development. (OECD, 2006: 18 – emphasis in original)

To what extent are the curriculum models and policies for children from birth to eight years old in the United Kingdom and the Republic of Ireland compatible with the approaches to pedagogy and policy trends as noted above from OECD, 2006?

ISSUES AND CONTROVERSIES

Discuss the evidence base for the following quotations from *Understanding Early Childhood: Issues and controversies* (2005) by Helen Penn:

A culture is taken for granted by those who belong to it. We think about what we ourselves do as (mostly) rational and self-chosen, but in fact we may be drawing on very traditional ideas. (Penn, 2005: 90)

The situation of most of the world's children is very different from those we conventionally study in North America and Europe. It is these Euro-American children who are taken as the norm in child development. (Penn, 2005: 97)

How can beliefs/theories about childhood be stretched to fit the exciting newer evidence about how thoughtful and social very young children can be? (Penn, 2005: 132)

We underrate the pleasure that children get from each other's company and overrate the contribution of adults. (Penn, 2005: 182)

... the government fanfares would have us believe that, somehow, a corner has been turned. A better knowledge of history would indicate how little has changed, and how much more change is necessary to break away from the policies of the past. (Penn, 2005: 124)

Key issues raised in Chapter 1 that you should now be better able to debate include the following:

Are there initiatives seen only in certain regions/areas? Are there policy issues that have scarcely found their way on to the agenda? If so what do you think they are?

Do policies appear to be taking into account the role of the range of professionals involved in the education and care of young children, including for example nursery nurses, childminders and teaching assistants?

What are the implications for young children and their families of the expansion in early education and care? Consider the advantages and disadvantages.

What effect might there be on family life from the encouragement in many countries for the mothers of young children to return to work?

To what extent do current developments show evidence of the participation of children and of 'listening to children' and not merely the payment of lip service to the importance of children's views?

Further issues include the following:

> To what extent do current developments take account of the cultural identity of individual communities?
>
> In the UK a very small percentage of staff in the education and care services are men. How serious an omission is this and can any steps be taken to rectify it?
>
> Is sufficient attention being directed to the role of fathers in their children's upbringing?
>
> Not all lone parents are mothers. According to the Daycare Trust, 11 per cent of lone parents are men. Are there additional problems faced by men as lone parents, and if so what are they?
>
> Is sufficient attention being directed to the needs of children in care, now referred to as 'looked-after children', many of whom have frequent changes of foster home or residential home and therefore of school which affect their life chances? Children who are in the care of local authorities are described as 'looked-after children'. They are one of the most vulnerable groups in society. (See *Working with Children in Care: European perspectives*, Petrie et al., 2006.)

A final warning:

> Policy documents often contain statements as facts, as though there can be no argument about them, when they may reflect personal beliefs, the cultural norms of that country, or the political leanings of those involved in drafting these documents. Be cautious about accepting statements in these documents as facts even where there appears to be a consensus! *(See Understanding Early Years Policy, Baldock et al., 2005.)*

REFERENCES

Alexander, R. (2004) 'Still no pedagogy? Principle, pragmatism and compliance in primary education', *Cambridge Journal of Education,* 34 (1): 7–33.

Baldock, P., Fitzgerald, D. and Kay, J. (2005) *Understanding Early Years Policy.* London: Paul Chapman.

Bennett, J. (2003) 'Starting Strong: the persistent division between care and education', *Journal of Early Childhood Research,* 1 (1): 21–48.

Brooker, L. (2002) *Starting School: Young children learning cultures.* Buckingham: Open University Press.

Brooker, L. (2005) 'Learning to be a child: Cultural diversity and early years ideology' in N. Yelland (ed.), *Critical Issues in Early Childhood Education.* pp. 114–30. Maidenhead: Open University Press.

Clark, M.M. (1976) *Young Fluent Readers: What can they teach us?* London: Heinemann.
Clark, M.M. (1988) *Children under Five: Educational research and evidence.* London: Gordon and Breach.
Clark, M.M. (2005) *Understanding Research in Early Education: The relevance for the future of lessons from the past. Abingdon:* Routledge.
Moss, P. and Petrie, P. (2002) *From Children's Services to Children's Spaces.* London and New York: RoutledgeFalmer.
OECD (2001) *Starting Strong: Early childhood education and care.* Paris: OECD.
OECD (2004) *Starting Strong: curricula and pedagogies in early childhood education and care: Five curriculum outlines.* (Available at www.oecd.org/edu/earlychildhood)
OECD (2006) *Starting Strong II: Early childhood education and care.* Paris: OECD. (Available at www.oecd.org/edu/earlychildhood)
Penn, H. (2005) *Understanding Early Childhood: Issues and controversies.* Maidenhead: Open University Press.
Petrie, P., Boddy, J., Cameron, C., Wigfall, V. and Simon, A. (2006) *Working with Children in Care: European perspectives.* Maidenhead: Open University Press.
Waller, T. (2006) ' "Don't Come Too Close To My Octopus Tree": recording and evaluating young children's perspectives on outdoor learning', *Children, Youth and Environments*, 16 (2): 75–104.

INDEX

Chapters 2–6 have the same main headings. These headings appear in the index preceded by an asterisk. For ease of access the pages for each country are listed.